AFTER ~~5 DAYS~~ RETURN ~~TO~~

. William Blume

~~Gene~~ral P.O. Box 137

~~New~~ York City U. S. A.

TRANS ATLANTIC AIR MAI~~L~~

Madame Lebrue

~~?~~ lot I Baraque

~~s/ Préfecture 6 . . .~~

~~Camp de Gurs~~

Basses- Pyrénées

Parvenu Olivar ...

timbre, PV dessi.

Hôtel du devant
Marseille

VIA
AIR MAI

ELPAS

Kahn

Unoccupied

REGISTER

No 383060

REGISTER

Austerity baby

Austerity baby

Janet Wolff

MANCHESTER
1824

Manchester University Press

The right of Janet Wolff to be identified as the author
of this work has been asserted by her in accordance
with the Copyright, Designs and Patents Act 1988.

Published by Manchester University Press
Altrincham Street, Manchester M1 7JA
www.manchesteruniversitypress.co.uk

British Library Cataloguing-in-Publication Data

A catalogue record for this book is available from
the British Library

Library of Congress Cataloging-in-Publication Data
applied for

ISBN   978 1 5261 2130 1   paperback

First published 2017

The publisher has no responsibility for the
persistence or accuracy of URLs for any external or
third-party internet websites referred to in this book,
and does not guarantee that any content on such
websites is, or will remain, accurate or appropriate.

Typeset and designed by axisgraphicdesign.co.uk
Printed in Great Britain by TJ International Ltd,
Padstow

Cover: Bertha Wolff with author as young child

Contents

Our Honeymoon Trip.

to

Europe.

July 3rd, 1909 ————— September

Cover of Henry Norr's diary

1: Atlantic moves

We have traveled quite a distance, but we never had so poor a day
of it as to-day. It was the only day of our trip that we didn't enjoy the
traveling. We got on a train at 4 p.m. and were supposed to reach
Manchester at 8. Twice we had to change trains and each time you
got to go and look up your train and see that it's taken out. It's a
nuisance. To make matters worse, we had nothing to eat all day but
a couple of ham sandwiches and some cold chicken which though
historic (for it was brought up probably in the time of Shakespeare),
was not very digestible. Of course the train was late and we got
into Manchester at 9.15. Luckily, Maurice, knowing how punctual
English trains are, did not get discouraged, and waited for us. It was
a relief to get settled down at last, and an indescribable pleasure to
come amongst friends after six weeks of hotel life. And here we saw
friends I hadn't seen for nineteen years and most of whom I couldn't
even recall. It was a reunion indeed and everyone was happy that we
were able to meet. We remained at the home of our cousin, Israel,
and he and his wife were very nice to us and went out of the way to
accom[m]odate us. It was a relief to feel among your own, with your
own flesh and blood and to know that people were nice to you not
because they hoped or worked for a tip, but because they loved you
and were a part of you. We staid up late to-night till 1 a.m. and some
of the other cousins came over, Ely and his wife and Dora and we
talked of old times and present times and future times and when we
retired, a sleep of rest and contentment enveloped us.
(Travel diary of Henry Norr, 1909)

Henry Norr, born in St Petersburg in 1880, moved to the United States
with his family (parents and two sisters) in about 1891. His father,
Jacob Norr, was a tailor, who also established himself in the real estate
business in New York. His mother, Dina, was a wig-maker for orthodox
Jewish women. Henry went to City College, became a secondary
school teacher, and, in 1926, took the post of principal of Evander
Childs High School in the Bronx. His obituary in *The New York Times*
in 1934, on his early death of a heart attack at the age of fifty-three,
quotes the new City Superintendent of Schools, Harold G. Campbell,
as saying that 'Mr. Norr was one of the best high school principals
in the City of New York. In spite of an innate modesty and a retiring
disposition, he was one of the most forceful characters in secondary
education ...

His going leaves a great void in our secondary schools which it will be difficult to fill.' (Mr Campbell also offers another compliment, which would today perhaps have been worded a little differently: 'He had a genius for handling boys and girls.')

In 1909, Henry married Minnie Gold. The travel diary is the detailed handwritten account of their honeymoon trip in Europe, in the course of which the couple visited the English branch of the Norr family (whose spelling of the name was 'Noar'). Jacob's oldest brother, Joseph, had emigrated to England in 1886, and worked as a tailor in Manchester. Israel, Eli, Dora and Maurice – mentioned in Henry's diary – were four of Joseph's seven children. Maurice Noar was my maternal grandfather. He came to England as an infant, and would have been about twenty-four when he met his American cousin at the railway station in 1909.

It was Henry's son, David Norr, who showed me the diary in December 2003, at his house in Scarsdale, New York. I took the train from New York on a very snowy day, and he met me at the station to take me for lunch at home with his wife, Carol. It snowed all afternoon, so much that we weren't sure if I would be able to get a taxi back to the station that day. I had never met David Norr before. In fact, I had never heard of him until a couple of months earlier, when a cousin of my mother's in Manchester, who had kept in touch with the American relatives, urged me to see him while I was still living in New York. He was eighty years old at the time of my visit – still active as a financial analyst, and keen to discuss family history with me. Later he sent me photocopies of the 'Manchester' pages of his father's diary.

August 17th
The day is a dull and threatening one and the atmosphere is murky. But here in Manchester it is considered a fair day indeed, for rain and fog is the average lot of Manchestrians. The city's main industry is cotton goods manufacturing and there are a great many mills here. The smoke of the chimneys together with the usual foggy atmosphere, casts a sort of mist about the city that blackens all the buildings, and the black and gray stone of London here become almost coal-black.

We are barely into the Manchester visit, and I am already getting defensive, and a bit irritated with the tone. Of course he is right, both about the weather and about the colour of Manchester buildings (though not about the inhabitants, who are of course Mancunians). Before the Clean Air Act of 1956, and the decline of industry, the pale stone was usually black with soot, and the air was often filthy. We sometimes had to walk home from school wearing smog masks. Still, the tone seems, to me, a bit condescending. It continues:

Page from Henry Norr's diary

Extract from Henry Norr's diary

Austerity baby

August 18th.

This is an ideal Manchester day — that is, pouring all day. There is no fog, but a light mist envelops the city all the time — rain or shine. We were unable to do very much because of the bad weather, but in the afternoon it cleared up and Maurice and Roger who came to see us this afternoon, took us for a walk in the outlying sections of the city, Salford, as it is called. Here you can see some fairly good homes and quiet streets. We also saw the Cricket Grounds and the Race track. The English, following the example of their illustrious Ruler, are lovers of horses in general and of betting in particular and the race-track is an institution of the town.

Living with folks who have become Anglicized, we can get a pretty good idea of the English workman's home life. We were surprised to find how many times a day the people eat here. Breakfast, Lunch at 12, Tea (a meal with it) at 6, Supper at 9 and a light meal before retiring. They tell us this is the regular custom here but perhaps in their attempts to treat us well, they try to overfeed us. Another thing that surprised us is the way the English drink — whiskey and beer. Everyonce in a while you take a drink. And the women and even the children drink too. It seems strange to us to hear one woman (the hostess) say to her guest, "Have a whisky?" But then the English have a reputation that way.

To-night we went to Ely's house and we were again well received and again we were up till midnight. We are not keeping the early hours we did on the Continent but then we are getting up late and we have nothing to do all day.

Supper at 9 and a light meal before retiring. They tell us this is the regular custom here but perhaps in their attempts to treat us well, they try to overfeed us. Another thing that surprised us is the way the English drink — whiskey and beer. Everyonce in a while you take a drink. And the women and even the children drink too. It seems strange to us to hear one woman (the hostess) say to her guest, "Have a whisky?" But then the English have a reputation that way.

August 18th
This is an ideal Manchester day – that is, pouring all day.

Then there are the English eating – and drinking – habits to comment on, only partly affectionately:

> Living with folks who have become Anglicized, we can get a pretty good idea of the English workman's home life. We were surprised to find how many times a day the people eat here. Breakfast, Lunch at 12, Tea (a meal with it) at 6, Supper at 9 and a light meal before retiring. They tell us this is the regular custom here but perhaps in their attempts to treat us well, they try to overfeed us. Another thing that surprised me is the way the English drink – whisky and beer. Every once in a while, you take a drink. And the women and even the children drink too. It seems strange to hear one woman (the hostess) say to her guest, 'Have a whisky?'. But then the English have a reputation that way.

There is a rather poignant counter to this expression of American puritanism. Here is the point of view of the English Noars, from a family history compiled in 1998, recalling Henry Norr's honeymoon trip: 'He got the English cousins quite wrong as a bunch of drunkards, because wherever he visited, out came the Whisky bottle: little did he realize that it took a visit such as theirs before strong drink was taken.' Still, apart from a few more such asides, this is a wonderful document, with descriptions of family members, accounts of walks round the city, a trip to the Manchester Hippodrome theatre, a visit to Bolton to see another cousin. The handwriting is beautiful, and the thoughts of a young visitor to Europe just over a hundred years ago never less than fascinating to read. In particular, it seemed important for once to be somehow in touch with my mother's family history. For a number of years it had been my father's life, in Germany in the 1930s and as a refugee in England, interned for a year in the Isle of Man, which had preoccupied me. On my mother's side, the dramas of persecution and flight were less immediate, a prehistory to her own life and experience. Even her parents were small children when antisemitic pogroms in Eastern Europe obliged the families to travel west. Now I began to see both how interesting these lives had been, and how the memory of forced exile persists through the generations. Although I have some resistance to the notion of 'second-generation' Holocaust survivors (that is their children, assumed to inherit their trauma at one remove), I am entirely persuaded by Marianne Hirsch's notion of 'postmemory'.

> Postmemory characterizes the experience of those who grow up dominated by narratives that preceded their birth, whose own belated stories are evacuated by the stories of the previous

generation shaped by traumatic events that can be neither
understood nor recreated.

I have come to understand that this inheritance can have a longer
trajectory, across more than one generation. Mary Cappello
has written movingly about the 'ways that we inherit the pain or
deformation caused by the material or laboring conditions of our
forbears', linking her own chest pains to those of both her father and
her grandfather. In her case, the inherited injury – actual and psychic
– related to the poverty and shame of earlier generations. As I read
about Ashkenazi Jews in north Manchester in the twentieth century,
and recalled visiting my own relatives as a child, I began to grasp the
idea of the transmission of fear, caution and suspicion, even decades
after the event. The children of those immigrants from Eastern Europe
retained, and in turn passed on to their own children, the unarticulated
but painful recollection of persecution. What Anne Karpf has referred
to as 'the war after' is one fought by Jews of Eastern European origins
as well as refugees from Nazism. My mother as well as my father.

It was also from David Norr that I learned that one of the American
cousins – Harris Norr, also known as Swifty Morgan – who made a
living as a professional card player on transatlantic liners, may have
been the model for Damon Runyon's character the 'Lemon Drop Kid'.
Also cause for reflection was the fact that, while I had been developing
my personal and academic interest in the English-Jewish artist Mark
Gertler, largely on the grounds that he may have been a distant relative
of my maternal grandmother – Rebecca Gertler, wife of Maurice Noar
– I now discovered I had a bona fide, rather famous artist cousin in the
United States. This was Leland Bell, nephew of Harris Norr and second
cousin of Henry Norr. All of this has been especially interesting to me
recently, since my return to England after eighteen years in the United
States, and as I continue to rethink (and rewrite) my own stories about
the two countries.

It seems to me now to be so transparent, the rewriting of narratives at
different stages of life. Today, I seem inclined to take England's side
against any criticism (especially, perhaps, by an American). But not so
long ago I put quite a bit of energy into my own demonising of England
– the other side of my idealising of 'America', perhaps. In 1976, my
father wrote a short memoir of his own, reflecting on his experiences
in Germany in the 1930s, recording the increasing problems that he

Lady Ottoline Morrell,
Mark Gertler, 1918

Leland Bell,
Standing Self-Portrait, 1979

confronted in his work as a chemist and the growing isolation in his everyday life. Towards the end, he expresses his gratitude to Britain:

> It is too often forgotten, how much we owe the British Government of the day, who, with the help of Jewish and other British organisations, in which people like Eleanor Rathbone played a leading part, saved tens of thousands of Nazi victims, when all the other countries refused to do anything.

> I was glad, therefore, when a few years ago some of those who managed to start a new and successful life here launched a 'Thank-You-Britain Fund', which soon raised about fifty thousand pounds for a scholarship now administered by the British Academy. Its income is used to finance University scholarships in the field of Human Studies, particularly the welfare of people of this country.

Ten years later, though I don't think I ever discussed this with him, I was immersing myself in another point of view, reading the growing literature on England's own history of antisemitism and following David Cesarani's account of Britain's rather more compromised activities in the mid-twentieth century (including the postwar acceptance of Nazi war criminals into the country). I learned that the internment of aliens in 1940 (about which my father, who spent nearly a year in an internment camp, had nothing critical to say) was in fact an outrage.

I read (and also wrote) about the earlier resistance to Jewish immigration to Britain, culminating in the 1905 Aliens Act. In relation to my work on Mark Gertler and other Jewish artists in Britain, I read the work of historians, literary critics and art historians who exposed the ideologies of 'Englishness' (rural, southern, class-bound) across a wide range of texts and discourses. I even read John Osborne's *Damn You England*, before realising that there were probably limits to the allies I should be rounding up in the case I seemed to need to make. Obviously a real personal, and psychic, investment here. It clearly wasn't as simple as a critique of Thatcherite Britain, or disappointment in the 1980s decline of higher education in England. Or even the weather.

The culmination of my narrative – the idea I had that, somehow, I needed to leave England to save my life – was an event that allowed me to conclude that this was literally true. England tried to kill me, and America saved me. In the spring of 1990, when I had been living in California for about eighteen months, a routine physical examination showed that I had thyroid cancer. Surgery (a thyroidectomy) further

Thank-You Britain Fund letter

'THANK-YOU BRITAIN' FUND

8, Fairfax Mansions, London, N.W.3

A. Wolff Esq.,   20th August 1964.
41, Pine Road,
Didsbury,
Manchester, 20.

Dear Friend,

Some months ago you were good enough to promise support for an act of collective gratitude by all the refugees from Central Europe who have made their home in this country.

This seems to be a good moment to count our blessings. Already a new generation is growing up among us to whom the word "Kristallnacht" is as unfamiliar as the terror it held.

Now, therefore, is the time to act.

The 'Thank-You Britain' Fund has been formed to give practical expression to the gratitude we owe. The money collected - we hope to raise between £40,000 and £60,000 - will be invested to create a perpetual income for the benefit of British scholarship and research. The British Academy, which is to the Humanities what the Royal Society is to the Sciences, has agreed to administer this income as the 'Thank-You Britain' Research Award and periodically to choose suitable candidates for one or more research posts to be attached to a British university. The research will concern itself with the broad field of Human Studies, preferably having a bearing on the welfare of the people of this country. There will also be an annual public lecture on a related subject.

Here is a permanent, direct and useful way in which we can respond to a genuine need in this country today, and do so in a way which befits the events we intend to commemorate.

THANK YOU BRITAIN.

revealed that the cancer was already in one lymph node. There was, and is, no such thing as a routine physical exam in England, and, since I had no symptoms, I could only conclude that it would likely have been too late by the time the cancer was discovered, had I still lived in England. Then I read Marilynne Robinson's 1989 book, *Mother Country*, and realised that England had *given* me the cancer in the first place. Robinson's book indicts the Sellafield nuclear processing plant, in the English Lake District, for the contamination of the environment and the British government for its criminal negligence with regard to safety laws and procedures. According to Robinson, 'Sellafield is the world's largest source of radioactive contamination'. She offers this startling contrast:

[8]

> The release of radiation from Three Mile Island is usually estimated at between fifteen and twenty-five curies of radioactive iodine. Many hundreds of thousands of curies of radioactivity have entered the environment each year through Sellafield's pipeline and its stacks, in the course of the plant's routine functioning. In other words, Three Mile Island was a modest event by the standards of Sellafield.

Robinson's well-documented study maintains that, through 'about three hundred accidents, including a core fire in 1957 which was, before Chernobyl, the most serious accident to occur in a nuclear reactor', a large number of cancers were produced in populations within a certain range of the site. In 1957, when the accident and radiation leak occurred, I was fourteen years old and living in Manchester, less than a hundred miles from Sellafield. It is true that Robinson focuses more on leukaemia than on thyroid cancer, and that the most striking incidence of these cancers seems (despite the direction of prevailing winds and the jet stream) to have been in Ireland. Nevertheless, thyroid cancer (which she does also discuss) is known to be caused by exposure to radioactivity, especially in children. And Robinson makes this comment:

> The use of Cumbrian lakes as reservoirs for cities sheds an interesting light on the practice of expressing cancer rates as multiples of regional or national rates. The runoff from the mountains would surely concentrate contaminants in the drinking water of large populations. The nearness of Sellafield to Manchester and Liverpool is seldom alluded to, but there are hundreds of thousands of people living within the range of its effects.

The origins of the Sellafield nuclear plant – originally, and at the time of the 1957 accident, called Windscale – lie in another British-American story. Indeed, the catastrophic failure of the reactor can fairly be

Windscale, 10 October 1957

Atlantic moves

described as a direct outcome of a critical transatlantic event. The 1943 Quebec Agreement between Churchill and Roosevelt had promised British involvement in the Manhattan Project and the United States nuclear programme; many British scientists worked at the atomic bomb laboratory in Los Alamos. The following year, another agreement confirmed Anglo-American co-operation after the war. But in 1946, by which time Churchill and Roosevelt had been replaced by Atlee and Truman, the US Congress passed the Atomic Energy Act (known as the McMahon Act), which prohibited the passing of classified atomic energy to foreign countries. As Lorna Arnold records: 'Britain felt entitled to post-war atomic status and was not prepared to leave the atomic monopoly in American hands. She was determined to create a successful national project both for its own sake and as a powerful lever to gain renewed Anglo-American collaboration.' The consequence was an urgent, and incredibly fast, programme of building and implementation, bypassing any stage of pilot plants. The first weapon test, as a result, took place in 1952. Windscale was established in 1947, and operational two years later. Although Arnold acknowledges the two production piles which constituted Windscale as 'an extraordinary technological achievement for their time', she itemises the causes of the disaster, apparent in retrospect:

There were failures of knowledge and research ... The piles were used for purposes not envisaged when they were designed and lacked adequate instrumentation. There were deficiencies in staffing, organization, management and communications. The whole project was overloaded with too many urgent and competing demands – to expand and extend military production, develop new reactor types, and support an arguably over-ambitious civil power programme.

Reluctance to publish the full findings of the initial inquiry into the accident also had to do with Anglo-American relations: Harold Macmillan, then Prime Minister, did not want to give the Americans any reason to continue to block collaboration on military applications of atomic energy. His diary note for 30 October 1957 records this concern:

The problem remains, how are we to deal with Sir W Penney's report? It has, of course, been prepared with scrupulous honesty and even ruthlessness ... But to publish to the world (especially the Americans) is another thing. The publication of the report, as it stands, might put in jeopardy our chance of getting Congress to agree to the President's proposal.

Even in full that report, published only twenty days after the event, downplayed the problems and actual effects of the radiation leak.

It identified no danger from irradiation or inhalation, and considered the small risk of contamination by ingestion (mainly through milk) minimal, and satisfactorily dealt with. Marilynne Robinson's outrage was about what she saw as a gross understatement of risk and actual harm, and at the time of publication of her book she was challenged on this. The fiftieth anniversary of the accident prompted further thought, with the benefit of new scientific and meteorological research, including the recognition that there were likely to have been more cases of cancer attributable to the leak. Even so, the numbers are small – perhaps 240 rather than 200 cancers (thyroid and breast cancer and leukaemia). And this news cannot help me pin down the blame for my own case:

> 'Several dozen more cancer cases may have to be added to our total', said epidemiologist Professor Richard Wakeford, of Manchester University. However, Wakeford said it was impossible to determine which individual cancer cases might be linked to the incident at Windscale, now called Sellafield. 'We can only say an excess in cancer cases was caused by the fire'.

After all, some of those most closely involved in the event don't seem to need to create a drama of it, even with benefit of hindsight. Marjorie Higham, a chemist at Sellafield, recalls the event:

> I remember the fire, of course. At the time I had a motorbike, this is before I was married. I was going in and out on this motorbike and of course I was wearing a crash hat. I went to Seascale and then along the railway, there's a track between the railway and the sea which we called the cinder track.

> I knew something had gone wrong, but then things did go wrong, so you just don't take any notice. The less you know about it, the less you can tell somebody else. This day I'd got to the building where I worked and I was stopped at the door by the foreman of the industrials, who said, 'If you come in you can't go out.' By this time the plant was being shut down, but nobody had said anything, no notes put down. They'd been trying to keep it quiet for three days. It started on the Wednesday and this would be the Friday. Don't forget we'd been brought up during the war and you accepted things more.

Neville Ramsden acted just as coolly, having been told 'Ey-up, lads, there's smoke coming out the pile chimney!' As he says, he realized then 'obviously not right'. He went home as usual, and went to the cinema, as Thursday was film night.

The point is, though, that this was a story I could tell myself, as both a metaphorical and a literal proof of the need to emigrate. The other side of it – the desire for 'America' as the playing-out of a teenage fantasy of 1950s rock music and American movies – I had always known; I wrote a bit about this in essays on Eddie Cochran, and on England in the 1950s, in my book *Resident Alien*. It just took me thirty years to manage to follow up on it, finally moving to the States in 1988. It was on the point of returning in 2006 (not just to England, but specifically to Manchester) that I found I was willing to rewrite the story. What if the cancer only started in the States? If stress is a possible cause of cancer, then it seems quite likely. My first two years there, when I lived in northern California, contained a rather large quota of stressful events, including the following: the unexpected death of my mother three months after I left England (my father died almost exactly two years later); being in a 7.1 earthquake (Loma Prieta, October 1989, when I was teaching in Santa Cruz, only ten miles from the epicentre); a diagnosis of an ovarian tumour (a week later found to be a misdiagnosis); anxiety about money, since, for the first and only time in my life, I was freelancing and not getting a monthly salary (on leave from my job at the University of Leeds, and spending a couple of years as a peripatetic academic); travelling to too many visiting appointments; involvement in the custody battles of the person I was living with in California. And (not so trivial) living in the least beautiful apartment I've ever had. Was it time to blame everything on America instead?

At about the time of my revisionist thoughts, I reread Richard Hoggart's account of his year in the United States. By coincidence, he spent this year (1956–57) at the University of Rochester, where I taught for a decade, after I left California. Earlier, and just over ten years after his stay in the United States, I knew him for a while at the University of Birmingham, where I was a postgraduate student in sociology, spending most of my time at the Centre for Contemporary Cultural Studies, which he directed and had founded in 1964. It was during his year as a visiting professor in Rochester that his groundbreaking book *The Uses of Literacy* – the primary inspiration for the Centre's founding – was published in England.

For him it was a year off, with his wife and three young children, from his job teaching in the extra-mural department at the University of Hull. I am struck by a number of things in his appealing narrative. In some ways, the city he describes, looking back on the 1950s from the late 1980s, is very much like the one I lived in through the 1990s:

> Rochester – and I can speak only of the Rochester we saw just over thirty years ago – has the friendliness of a medium-sized city which

a Pelican Book   5

The Uses of Literacy

Richard Hoggart

1958 edition of Richard Hoggart's *The Uses of Literacy*

[12]

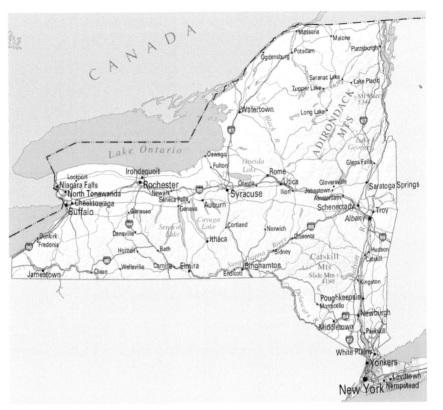

Map of New York state

cannot and does not wish to think of itself as an exciting metropolis; it believes it has more of a community spirit and is safer; it is sensitive to being looked down on by people from the great aggregations, and secretly knows it has better ideas about what makes for a good life: space for private and public gardens (it calls itself the Lilac City), the air coming off Lake Ontario, the Finger Lakes nearby, sufficient good music, exceptionally good provision of films (the Eastman-Kodak museum being there), not much of a race problem or unemployment since its industries are mixed and many of them very much of the late twentieth-century (Eastman-Kodak, Bausch and Lomb, IBM); and those industries civic-minded ... All in all and in general, Rochester is a decent, undramatic city much like Leicester, only much richer.

His account of the University of Rochester is perceptive and sympathetic.

The University of Rochester was a true child of the city in that it was of medium-size by American standards but quite large by British, privately funded and proud of it, academically in some ways modest, in other ways – like Rochester's large industries – of national and international calibre. Its staff and their manners mirrored their institution. Some knew they would move on and many did, regular movement for promotion or for tenure being a feature of the academic life for even near-high-flyers; but during their time at Rochester they did not feel, as some at Hull did, that they were in a backwater and only waiting for a call ... Almost all of them believed ... that we had to be friendly one to another, and the more so because academic life in the States is regarded as more of an odd backwater even than it is in England.

He tells stories about his encounters with colleagues, neighbours and students, always reflecting in interesting ways on the differences between English and American cultures. This is something he is confronted with the minute he sets foot in the country, after crossing the Atlantic on the *Queen Elizabeth*. Arriving to what seemed like a chaotic immigration process, with his young children tired and thirsty, he has this exchange with a customs official:

I asked, in a very polite manner: 'Can you help me, please? I have three children'.

He stared at me callously and answered, before looking down at his papers again, 'Don't blame me, bud. See a doctor'.

Characteristically, Hoggart does not take offence at this – on the contrary, even in speaking he is aware of his 'thin Limey voice', and of the annoying English tendency to 'elliptical speech'. For him, it is an occasion for reflection on cultural difference, with his sympathy aligned, if anything, with the American.

A second encounter, this time with a student, encapsulates cultural difference in a way that seems timeless – as he himself says 'Henry James again, forty years after he died'. It is worth quoting him at length on this. A student comes to see him some weeks into his class on modern English literature, to make, as he puts it 'a statement about plenitude and about the threatened loss of innocence'.

She said something like this: 'I am enjoying your course very much. But it is disturbing me. Let me tell you about my background. I come from [she named a medium-sized town twenty or thirty miles south]. My father is a lawyer; my mother stays home but does a great many good works in the community. So does my father. They are good people and greatly respected. They are loving parents to me and my brothers. We have a pleasant life. In summer we have barbecues with the family, the neighbours, members of our church. In winter we skate on the Lake. I have to say, and I've only realized it after auditing your course, that I've been happy, it's been a happy sort of life. But now I'm shaken. I enjoy hearing you talk about, for example, T.S. Eliot and Graham Greene. I enjoy reading them after the lectures. But there's so much unhappiness, so much cruelty, so much accepting that life is grim and black and sinful. But it hasn't felt like that to us, not at all. And I don't know how to make head or tail of it.'

I searched out a copy of Hoggart's book – one volume of his autobiography – from an internet used-books site, because I had remembered these two stories so clearly, fifteen years after first reading them, and wanted to read them again. When I first came across them, I had just moved to the States, and I took some pleasure in the customs officer's put-down. It was American directness that I wanted, English circumlocution and caution that I felt I needed to abandon (in myself, of course, as much as in how others spoke to me). If Eddie Cochran (an arbitrary example – though I had been to hear him in the Manchester Hippodrome in March 1960) stood for the excitement and freedom of American rock 'n' roll (pathetically imitated by English rockers like Tommy Steele), ways of speech – ways of being – were just as exciting, and just as liberating. I loved the story, told to me quite a few years later by an English friend of mine, living and teaching in the United States, of her father, a famous British composer, being invited to receive an honour at some American campus. When he arrived, she told me, he said something to the effect of 'I don't know why you are giving me this award – I really don't deserve it'. Normal British modesty, and not even, in the end, false modesty – simply expected behaviour. Of course the response should have been 'Nonsense, of course you deserve it!'

But this wasn't England, and so one of the hosts looked confused and said 'Oh, perhaps we have made a mistake'. Or so my friend told me. It makes the point, even if it's clear that the American host was only teasing his distinguished visitor.

And Hoggart's second anecdote, about the student, resonated so strongly with ideas of American openness and optimism and sunniness, a myth to yearn for and to aspire to. You can go for the image (to the radical extent of moving across the Atlantic) while at the same time knowing perfectly well (as any self-respecting sociologist would know) that it *is* a myth – or, perhaps worse, an ideological construction. You can sustain your investment in that myth while also knowing its own dark side, which is denial of actual harm, glossing of real pain, inability to understand – and even enjoy – nuance, complexity, perversity. The difference between Hoggart and me, I now see, is that he didn't feel called upon to take sides. His sensitivity as an observer allowed him to make fun of his own excessively self-effacing culture while seeing both the great strengths and the disconcerting weaknesses of his host society. It seems that it is only when the personal investment in these matters abates that it becomes clear that it isn't a matter of black and white. Sometimes it takes a while to get to that point.

The eulogy for Henry Norr spoke of his 'innate modesty' and it occurs to me now, as I conclude with my anecdote about British modesty in an American context, that I may have accidentally exposed an underlying theme. Or perhaps not so accidentally. Is there a certain 'modesty' in writing memoir through other people's stories? I prefer to think of it, in fact, as obliquity. Of course this has been a story about my own Atlantic moves – both geographical and emotional. If others – Henry Norr, my father, the Sellafield workers, Richard Hoggart – take up more space than me in these pages, perhaps my marginality is a rather immodest device. The people I write about are mobilised by my narrative, and serve the purpose of telling my story.

And yet there isn't 'a story' as such, and perhaps that is the point. David Shields, in his passionate defence of new forms of writing for our contemporary age, says: 'I want books to be equal to the complexity of experience, memory, and thought, not flattening it out with either linear narrative (traditional novel) or smooth recount (standard memoir)'. Ambitious writing, he suggests, 'doesn't resolve contradictions in a spurious harmony but instead embodies the contradictions, pure and uncompromised, in its innermost structure'. His project accords well with the strong antipathy I have long had towards the chronological, coherent account of a life. I cannot particularly claim honourable post-structuralist motives here – refusing to uphold the mythical centred self. Rather, my own resistance has more to do with a kind of constitutional attachment to uncertainty. The openness produced in an interplay of stories, switches of point of view and of opinion, as these stories are navigated, allows the protagonist – glimpsed from time to time, and often at an angle – the liberty to remain unfixed. What Shields describes as the 'standard memoir' tends to proceed in linear fashion, with the chronological story of the life, in which photographs and letters, clearly captioned, may serve as illustration or proof. In another kind of writing, the protagonist takes centre stage only occasionally – perhaps quite rarely – while the play of other narratives and other memories, cross-cut with visual texts, constructs the life in a less tangible way. Somewhere uncertain – perhaps mid-Atlantic – this oblique memoir situates its subject.

Kathleen McEnery, c. 1910

Austerity baby

2: **Provincial matters**

Thirty years before Richard Hoggart lived in Rochester, Kathleen McEnery Cunningham presided at the centre of a lively cultural scene there. In 1914, she had married Francis Cunningham, then secretary and general manager of James Cunningham, Son and Company, a luxury coach- and car-making company. She was probably introduced to Cunningham by his cousin, Rufus Dryer, a good friend of hers in New York and, like her, an artist and a student of Robert Henri at the Art Students League a few years earlier. Before her marriage, she lived in New York, where she was already achieving success as a young artist. Her paintings were exhibited in gallery shows in the city with the work of Stuart Davis, Edward Hopper, George Bellows and other now well-known artists, and two were included in the landmark 1913 Armory Show, known as the major exhibition which introduced European modernism to the United States. In Rochester, she continued to paint – mainly still life works and portraits of her friends and acquaintances.

The city was transformed in the years immediately after McEnery's arrival. I wrote about this a few years ago, in a book about English and American artists outside the mainstream of institutionally accredited 'modern art'.

Economically, the first three decades of the twentieth century had been described as Rochester's golden age, and the centrality of Eastman-Kodak to the city's prosperity had important cultural consequences. The establishment by George Eastman of the Eastman School of Music and the Eastman Theatre in 1922 was the single most important event marking the 'end of provincialism'. Eastman brought musicians, opera directors, and teachers to Rochester from the capitals of Europe and thus virtually single-handedly created the conditions for a new cosmopolitanism in the city ... A lively social and cultural world developed around this group, and McEnery (now Mrs. Francis Cunningham) was central to it.

George Eastman, 1921

As a result of a series of chance events, I spent my last year in Rochester (2000–1) researching McEnery's work and life, interviewing people who remembered her (she died in 1971), and getting to know many of her twenty grandchildren. Of her three children, only Peter Cunningham was still alive, living in northern California. He died in 2003, soon after the close of an exhibition of McEnery's work I had curated in Rochester, which he was too ill to attend. I met him a number of times, in Sausalito, San Francisco and New York, and got some of my best information (and gossip) from him – to be treated cautiously, according to some of his children. Peter Cunningham's account of McEnery's involvement with the conductor Eugene Goossens, who had been brought to Rochester by George Eastman in the 1920s, seems to have been common knowledge though. McEnery painted Goossens's portrait at least twice; one portrait is still in the Eastman School of Music.

Several of the people I spoke to – mainly women in their eighties and nineties – remembered McEnery well, especially in her later years, and had fascinating stories to tell about the salon she ran in her house in Goodman Street (bequeathed to the Rochester Museum and Science Center on her death, and now used as the Center's administrative offices). Belatedly, I came to realise what a fabulous world Rochester must have been in the 1920s, prohibition notwithstanding – indeed, from everything I heard, more or less ignored. The gorgeous villas on East Avenue and nearby, including Eastman's own home, now the George Eastman International Museum of Photography and Film, stand now as a reminder of a way of life for the city's wealthier inhabitants.

Rochester in the 1920s is vividly portrayed in Paul Horgan's charming *roman à clef, The Fault of Angels*. The novel was published in 1933, and won the Harper Prize of 1934. Horgan, who died in 1995, is best known for his fiction and non-fiction writing about the American south-west, winning the Pulitzer Prize for History in 1955 and 1976. He was born in Buffalo, New York, in 1903, and moved with his family to Albuquerque at the age of twelve. After high school in the New Mexico Military Institute, he moved to Rochester as a music student in the new Eastman School of Music, and spent the years 1923 to 1926 in the city, before returning to New Mexico to become the librarian of the Military Institute. As he tells the story, at the age of nineteen he found himself involved in multiple tasks in the new music school and opera company, working with George Eastman's protégé, Vladimir Rosing, a Russian tenor brought to Rochester as director of the school's opera department; and with Rouben Mamoulian, hired in turn by Rosing to teach dramatic action. Horgan's account of his own role, written in 1988 in an appreciation of Mamoulian, gives an idea of the excitement, and also of the rather chaotic nature, of the early years of the 'Rochester Renaissance' – a renaissance almost entirely due to the wealth and cultural enterprise of the city's major figure, George Eastman.

The exciting days of the convening of the company were bounteous with promises for the future. Rosing made an address to the school of music at large in Kilbourn Hall, describing the aims of the

Catalogue for McEnery Exhibition, Rochester, NY 2003

Kathleen McEnery, *Eugene Goossens*, c. 1927

Cunningham residence, 10 S. Goodman Street, Rochester, early twentieth century

Rochester Museum and Science Center, 2001

company and its policies. As a newly enrolled music student, I was in that audience, listening with the same excitement as the members of the company. In all his plans, Rosing mentioned nothing about scenery, an art director, the physical mounting of the operas about to be undertaken. I needed a job to see me through my study of music. I produced overnight a sheaf of drawings for various operas I knew, and took them to him the next day. My authority for this bumptious venture was based wholly on my having planned and painted the scenery for two plays, a year or two before in school. After several hilarious incidents having to do more with me than with Rosing or Mamoulian, but within forty-eight hours, I was engaged to do the designs and paint the scenery for the opera company ... I was then nineteen years old, an unpublished writer, an unexhibited painter, an unheard singer, an unseen actor, and, above all, an unrevealed scenic artist.

In the opera company's second season, Horgan was, he says, 'relieved of my assignment as scenic artist, and a professionally experienced artist brought in'. But the careless mix of amateur and professional involvement – as it now seems to us – continued.

My duties became more various. In effect, I was Mamoulian's Figaro, his general assistant, responsible for any number of details of the productions. At the same time, I was supposed to think up and even write the stage acts for the movie house each week. In a few of them I appeared myself. The job was fascinating, if exhausting. I had an intensive apprenticeship in production, design, acting, singing, writing, musical selection – the blend of the arts that go to make up the vocabulary of the stage. I remember that I was charged with designing make-ups for the productions of the operas, and every time we gave one, it was I who, with Mamoulian himself, 'did' all the major people in their characters, applying grease paint up to the very minute of the curtain.

(The reference to the 'movie house' recalls that the Eastman Theater in its early years was used six nights a week for movies, and the seventh for concerts.)

Horgan developed a close friendship in these years with the composer Nicolas Slonimsky, who also came to Rochester in 1923 as opera coach of the new company. In his amusing – and grandiose – autobiography, Slonimsky, who calls Horgan his 'hagiographer', describes him as a 'kindred soul', and a 'talented painter and illustrator' who also 'wrote facile verse and clever short stories'. In *The Fault of Angels*, Slonimsky is a central character, with the fictional name 'Nicolai Savinsky' (or 'Colya'), a close friend of the protagonist, 'John O'Shaughnessy'. (Horgan's own heritage was German and Irish.) The George Eastman character is easily

Kathleen McEnery, *Woman Seated (Charlotte Whitney Allen)*

Provincial matters

recognisable in 'Henry Ganson', the multi-millionaire who had already given the university of the city of 'Dorchester' a medical school, a dental school, a museum and a library – and now a theatre and music school. The conductor Eugene Goossens is most likely the fictional conductor 'Hubert Regis'. Indeed, in a letter of 26 January 1934, written from New Mexico to Kathleen McEnery in Rochester, Paul Horgan says this: 'I had a most lively and amusing letter from Gene about my book. He said he was amused, and much surprised that I'd taken no more cracks at him than I did!' The novel re-creates the city's social and cultural world, centred on the music school and opera company, and convening in the Corner Club (called by its real name in the novel) for drinks and meals before and after concerts. There doesn't seem to be a McEnery character, but another of the city's *salonnières*, Charlotte Whitney Allen, has much in common with 'Blanche Badger', whose book-lined home is always open to her friends. McEnery painted Charlotte Whitney Allen's portrait a number of times; my favourite of these paintings is now in the Rochester Institute of Technology.

The star of the novel, though, is Nina. A White Russian arrived from Paris in 1924, she is the wife of 'Vladimir Arenkoff' ('Val'), whom the protagonist, John, befriends. Nina is a passionate, flamboyant and beautiful woman, with artistic abilities (or perhaps pretensions). She makes an overwhelming impression on John at their first meeting, and he remains charmed by her, and in love with her, until she and her husband leave for good the following year.

She stared at the gray bare trees outside, whose branches leaned upon the bay window in her turret alcove. She was not tall, but her body was so exquisitely shaped that she gave an impressive hint of tallness. Her face was really oval, pointed at the chin. Her brow and cheeks were pale with underglows of pearly *café au lait*. Her eyes were deep and sad and black, with sparkling whites and definitely curving brows that gave a frank mystery to her countenance. Her mouth was small and inconceivably expressive, even in repose. She had rouged it only at the outline. Her neck was magnificent, slender and full and straight. No jewel diluted its loveliness. Her shoulders went from it with the pride of waves. She was wearing a gown whose chic made the women in Dorchester look dowdy and content to be so. Her hands had long nails and no jewels. This morning she was holding in them a gold comb.

Almost immediately, John has a glimpse of how intensely she experiences every event, and how dramatically she inhabits the world.

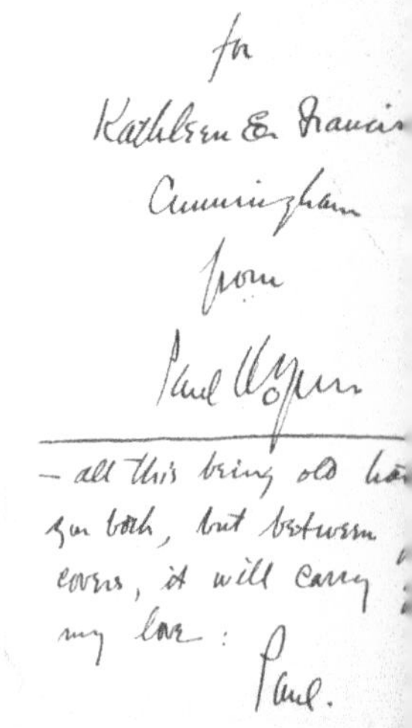
for
Kathleen & Francis
Cunningham
from
Paul Horgan
– all this being old
you both, but between
covers, it will carry
my love:
Paul.

Title page of *The Fault of Angels*, signed by its author

'I do hope you will find it pleasant here,' said John, speaking a little slowly and a little loudly, until he realized that she was not deaf, but only unfamiliar with English.

'Oh, mon Dieu!' she said, and with the greatest dignity began to weep. Her eyes were more brilliant, if anything, behind her tears, and John's astonishment disappeared in admiration of her sadness and its great loveliness.

There is much more weeping, and there are many dramas, in the novel, by the end of which John succeeds in overcoming his crush on this lovely woman, who has spent a good deal of energy in trying her best to improve the lives of several people in the city, sometimes with success, often – most notably in the case of 'Ganson' himself – without.

I had assumed that 'Nina' was entirely an invention of the author's, or, perhaps, a composite of several of the Russians brought to Rochester by Eastman and Rosing. But when I read Horgan's letter to McEnery – the one in which he mentions the letter from Goossens – I realised that not only was she based on a real person but 'Nina' was her real name.

Dear Kathleen,

It was so delightful of you to send me the Nina letter in such a nice letter of your own that I am ashamed to answer you this lately for both. The Ninaisme is so really *like* that I am possessed of the curious conviction that my character in the novel was at times clairvoyant. I only wish it could be savoured by the reviewers who felt I'd poured it on too thickly … that no one could possibly think and talk/write like that. Of course, if only I could have invented such a line as the one in the letter: 'Life is short and life is once': I'd feel that the Harper prize was deserved this year. As it is, I have many doubts as to that.

Do you know, I am very curious to know what (if anything) E.B. thought of the book: and Nina herself, if she's seen it. I sent them a copy long ago in the summertime, care of the Eastman School. But I have heard nothing from them. I am grieved to think I may have offended either of them with the story. Can you tell me anything? Oh, if they felt mockery in it anywhere, I should be awfully sorry. Because it isn't there. Yet I take their silence to mean pique. I hope I'm wrong. Surely they perceive the problem of fiction: the taking of a model and the evolvement of something altogether personal and invented … fictional … from it? I really meant it when I put the 'usual' fiction disclaimer on the reverse of the title page. But no one ever believes that.

Horgan had also given a copy of the book to McEnery and her husband, inscribed inside 'for Kathleen & Francis Cunningham from Paul Horgan – all this being old hat to you both, but between fine covers, it will carry you my love: Paul'.

THE
FAULT
OF
ANGELS

by
Paul
Horgan

Harper & Brothers Publishers
New York and London
1933

So who was Nina, and who was 'E.B.'? If he had sent one copy for the two
of them, it seems likely that E.B. was Nina's husband. My assumption
is that he was Emanuel Balaban, a conductor of the Rochester
Philharmonic Orchestra (a position he shared with Eugene Goossens
in the 1920s). Balaban's wife was indeed called Nina. Horgan's letter
to McEnery ends by asking her to send him a photograph of 'the Nina
portrait' – 'the first one you did … In the gold dress, with the lucent and
lunar hip'. In my research on McEnery, though I was able to see well
over a hundred of her paintings (including one of another beautiful
Russian woman, Katya Leventon, wife of a violinist in the RPO), I hadn't
come across a portrait of this description. Having made the guess that
she was the model for the fictional Nina, though, I then discovered
Bruce Kellner's 2002 literary portrait of Nina Balaban, whom he had
known in New York in the 1950s. A graduate student in the University
of Iowa's writing programme at the time, he decided to spend the
summer of 1956 in New York, sharing an apartment with a friend
from Iowa's theatre department. They came to rent Nina Balaban's
fifth-floor apartment at 6 West 75th Street for $65 a month, while she
summered, and painted, in Woodstock. Here is a Nina thirty years after
Horgan's fictional character.

> Nina was in the doorway, managing to look apprehensive,
> welcoming, imperious, and charming all at the same time. Her eyes
> struck me first, dancing gray eyes, straight across the bottom and
> rounded into half-circles, black-rimmed and batting mascara-heavy
> lashes at us, under mismatched arcs for eyebrows, drawn on in
> high, single lines. Her teeth were white and even, and her hair was a
> reddish nest through which an electric charge might have recently
> surged. She was nut-brown, like soft and weathered leather. At first
> she seemed to be no taller than five feet, gaunt and wizened, and
> then perhaps of medium height and as youthful as we were. Was
> she forty? Sixty? I couldn't tell. She wore huraches on her bare feet
> and an oversized blue wrapper, and under it a plain, soft blouse and
> a fulsome peasant skirt. There were gypsy loops with little rocks
> hanging from them in her earlobes; necklaces of beads, seeds, pods,
> semi-precious stones dangling from her neck; bangles on her wrists.
> The bright crimson staining her lips bled into tiny lines around them.

Older, of course. But also much changed from the unadorned goddess
of Horgan's description. And now 'nut-brown', no longer 'pale, with
underglows of *café au lait*'. One can allow for changing styles, for
the pressures on an older woman, perhaps for the new milieu of the
Woodstock art community where Nina spent her summers – and,
of course, for fiction. Still, Kellner abolishes any doubt about the
real and the fictional Nina. In one of her letters to him, after that first

summer (he sub-leased her apartment again the following summer), she asks him, in her idiosyncratic spelling, if he knew where her copy of *The Fault of Angels* was. 'I can't find a book – "Fault of Angels" by Paul Horgan – This book is very dear to me – it was written about me and by my friend Paul – It is so important to me to have it. Did you tack it?' The following summer, Kellner found the book for her, in her hall closet. But here is something very interesting – and, to me, rather mystifying. While the book was still missing, Kellner offered to try to find a second-hand copy for her.

No, she said, smiling and crying at the same time, another copy would not be the same thing; it was that particular copy that meant so much to her because she and Horgan had been lovers, and every time they'd gone to bed together they'd made a hole with a thumbtack in the binding.

When Kellner asked her about Horgan, she said 'not sadly but wistfully perhaps, "we do not see each ozzer any more longer"'.

But could this possibly be true? The love affair in the novel is clearly unconsummated, and just as clearly one-sided. Nina is devoted to 'Val', her husband. Of course it's fiction. But it seems rather unlikely that the real 'John', Horgan himself, was actually involved with Nina. Moreover, if they made a hole in the binding each time they went to bed together (itself a rather weird-sounding ritual – but who knows?), then it must have been after the book's publication in 1933. By that time, Horgan had long been in Albuquerque, and Nina in New York. (According to Kellner, 'Maestro Balaban had long departed from Nina's life when I knew her'.) Whatever the truth about this affair (and personally I suspect that Nina's wild imagination created it in retrospect), I do wonder whether Horgan's mind was ever put at rest on the question of Nina's, and E.B.'s, reaction to reading the novel.

Although I haven't been able to trace the portrait of Nina described by Paul Horgan, there is a Nina portrait by Kathleen McEnery, owned by one of the artist's grandchildren; this is reproduced on the cover of the exhibition catalogue from 2003. I sent a copy of it to Bruce Kellner, who confirmed that it is very likely Nina Balaban. Another portrait seems to be of Nina; although McEnery did not label the painting, family lore recalls the identity of the sitter. A comparison with a photograph, reproduced in Kellner's book, is also fairly convincing.

The 'Rochester Renaissance' owed a lot, as I have said, to Eastman's wealth and philanthropy. The city of the 1920s is often referred to

Kathleen McEnery, *Portrait of Nina Balaban*

Photograph of Nina Balaban

Austerity baby

as 'Mr Eastman's town'. Amongst other achievements, he brought Martha Graham, then at the beginning of her career, to teach dance movement in the opera company in 1925. But other wealthy denizens of the city participated in the transformation of a quiet provincial city into an exciting cultural centre. Emily Sibley Watson, heir to the Western Union fortune (both through her father, Hiram Sibley, and through her second husband, James Sibley Watson), had founded the city's Memorial Art Gallery in 1913 in memory of her son James Averell, who died of cholera in 1904, at the age of twenty-six. The son of her second marriage, James Sibley Watson Jr, doctor, publisher, avant-garde film-maker, who died in 1982, spent most of his life in Rochester, after studies at Harvard, a short residency in Chicago and a number of years in New York, where he pursued his medical studies at New York University. In 1919 he took over, with Scofield Thayer, the publication and editing of the respected New York-based literary journal *The Dial*. The journal ceased publication in 1929, but it had produced lifelong friendships for Watson (known to everyone as Sibley) and his wife, Hildegarde Lasell. The poet Marianne Moore, who took over the editorship of the journal in its last years, visited them in Rochester, and had a lengthy correspondence with Hildegarde. (Volume 85 of *The Dial*, from 1928, contains two paintings by Kathleen McEnery.)

On his return to Rochester in the late 1920s, Watson became involved in making movies, and with Melville Webber produced two films generally regarded as classics of the avant-garde – *The Fall of the House of Usher* (1928) and *Lot in Sodom* (1933). (In later years, he went back to his career in medicine, working in the University of Rochester's radiology programme, where he helped invent cinefluorography – X-ray motion pictures – which became an important diagnostic process.) Hildegarde, who had been an actress and singer in her early years, played Madeline Usher in the first film and Lot's wife in the second. The architect Herbert Stern, brought in to play the part of Madeline's brother Roderick, looked back at the experience in 1975.

Every time I see the Watson–Webber version of *The Fall of the House of Usher* I am struck anew with wonder and awe. How was Dr. Watson, almost fifty years ago, able to produce a film that is, technically, avant-garde today? I had a part in the film, but all of the trick photography was done behind my back, as it were, and I had no idea that I was taking part in an epoch-making film. Perhaps there were props, but I can't seem to remember them ... I have often wondered why I was chosen for the part. Could it be that Sibley thought of Roderick as a robot and sensed that I might fulfill that role? I took directions from Melville Webber and they were mystifying in the extreme: 'Look weary and at the same time jubilant.' 'Look perplexed and at the same time relaxed.' It was easy to appear weary and perplexed but never for a moment relaxed and jubilant.

The composer, Alec Wilder, who wrote the score for that film, recalls his involvement in *Lot in Sodom* a couple of years later. Another composer wrote the music, but Wilder, who was studying at the Eastman School of Music, helped to find the supporting cast.

> The Sodomites themselves were a bit of a problem for, as is obvious, considering their sexual aberrations, they would be more convincing as Sodomites not only if they were lavishly costumed, but if their physical movements were on the effeminate side.

> So I did a perhaps mean thing: I approached the most effeminate among the Eastman School students and, under some wildly false pretense, persuaded them to come to the 'barn' for a tryout. Unsuspecting of my nefarious plot, they arrived like swallows returning to Capistrano, allowed themselves to be lavishly bedecked and alarmingly maquillaged by Melville Webber, with the great wit and hyperbole that were his special talent ..., and permitted themselves to be photographed in a hysterical, posturing group. But it must have rapidly become clear that their unconventional personalities were being mocked, for they never appeared again. I'm surprised that I had the courage to enter the Eastman School during their subsequent (admittedly justifiable) fury at having been so misled.

In 2001 I interviewed Nancy Watson Dean, who had married James Sibley Watson after Hildegarde's death in 1976. She left her own first husband, to whom she had been married for forty years, to marry Watson, after a long friendship with him and with Hildegarde. After Watson's death, she was married a third time, to a childhood friend, Sterling Dean, in a marriage that lasted fifteen years, until his death in 2000. In preparation for our first meeting, she wrote a five-page memoir, which she read aloud to me when I visited her in January 2001. She spoke about Sibley's involvement with *The Dial*, and about her own early career as a watercolour portraitist of children. She recalled Kathleen McEnery, and had known her children, Joan and Peter, quite well at one time.

> During Hildegarde's heyday, she and 2 other wealthy matrons here entertained often and loosely organized a real coterie. The other 2 matrons were Clayla Ward and Kathleen [McEnery] Cunningham. The scene, in this distinctly conventional city, consisted of several gays (though nothing was said about that), several couples and a number of attractive widows. They met at various locations and were unconventional and merry ...

> Concerts were held every week, and before long I discovered that during intermissions, if you went to a certain hall on the Gibbs St.

side of Eastman theater, Kathleen and Clayla, and often Hildegarde, held court. It was an interestingly dressed, chic crowd. After the concert, it often re-met either at Clayla's, which was a mansion on Grove St. or a restaurant called 'Town & Country' on Gibbs St. across from Eastman Music School ... Another place they gathered was the Corner Club. This was up a flight of stairs in a building just east of the present Carlson Y. The same chic dressers, much gaiety ... All three of the reigning women were witty, amusing and loved their devotees. They knew the latest 'happenings' in Rochester and conversations were interesting.

Although I had the chance to talk to other elderly women who remembered Kathleen McEnery and recalled something of the Rochester of a certain class and cultural circle, I came too late to be able to encounter many recollections of 'the golden age'. Elizabeth Holahan, ninety-seven years old when I interviewed her in 2002, was long-time President of Rochester Historical Society and life-long resident of Rochester. She had worked all her life as a house restorer, amongst other things restoring the house of Eastman's birth in Waterville, NY, and arranging its move to the Genesee County Museum. She remembered all the *grandes dames* of an earlier Rochester, but kept her distance, telling me that, unlike them, she had to work for a living. At some point in our conversation, she went down to her basement, and returned with two small portraits done by Kathleen McEnery – one of her sister, Margaret, who had died young, and one of herself. She told me that she didn't at all want to sit for the portrait – that she was too busy at work – but that Kathleen 'wouldn't take no for an answer'. My conversation with her reminded me that my view of 1920s Rochester was very skewed, to an upper-middle-class and rather privileged sector of the community. But it remains quite fascinating to me. And Miss Holahan (as she was known) was probably my closest connection to that world. As the executive director of the Rochester Historical Society, Ann Salter, said when she died in 2004, this was 'an incredible passing for our community'. 'I was struck by the extraordinary change in life she witnessed – her life spanned a century,' Salter said. 'She'd talk about a party at the George Eastman House, and then it would hit me: George was actually there.'

George Eastman died on 14 March 1932, at the age of seventy-seven. He had been in failing health for some time. After a busy morning of meetings and document-signing at his home, he lay down on his bed and shot himself in the heart. He left a note beside the bed: 'To my friends. My work is done – Why wait? GE.'

Richard Hoggart had described Rochester as 'much like Leicester, only much richer'. A more appropriate comparison for me is Manchester (though here I would have to say 'only less rich'). Once, on a visit home, I phoned Zygmunt Bauman, my old friend and colleague from my years at the University of Leeds. The start of the conversation:

'Hello – where are you phoning from?'

'Manchester.'

'Rochester?'

'No, Manchester.'

Moment's hesitation: 'You went to a lot of trouble just to change one syllable, didn't you?'

Well, that was true in a way, and especially in terms of geographical moves (Birmingham, London, Leeds, York, Leeds again, London again, Berkeley, Rochester – not to mention eight visiting appointments during the California period). Then there were the domestic changes – eighteen homes in the same thirty-year period, not counting the visiting appointments, involving living alone, living with a partner (three times – different partners), collective houses (three times – different cities). But that was the first time it had occurred to me that perhaps I had ended up somewhere similar – only one syllable different. When I was contacted about a job in Rochester, I didn't know anything about the city. I knew I wanted to leave California for the East Coast. I needed a permanent job and a green card, after three years of visiting appointments. And the job, directing a new interdisciplinary graduate programme in visual and cultural studies, seemed perfect for me. I ended up staying ten years, and although eventually I came to feel the limits of life in a provincial city, and moved to New York when the opportunity came up, I loved my time in Rochester and have retained a great affection for the city. In the years after I left, in 2001, and until I moved back to England in 2006, I visited regularly, always staying a night or two and seeing friends and places I used to frequent – restaurants, the Little cinema, the Memorial Art Gallery, the Eastman House. In Rochester, and because of Rochester, I acquired two new 'families' – my colleagues there, and the students in the graduate programme, now in teaching and other posts across the country; and the Cunninghams – Kathleen McEnery's grandchildren (in San Francisco, Boston, Hartford, New Haven, Virginia, Vermont and France). What I came to see, in my last year in Rochester, and on the point of moving to New York, was the real appeal of a provincial community. My own community there – mainly, though not solely, the academic community – was more provisional and precarious, given the mobility of university life. But my discovery that year of Rochester in the 1920s reminded me of the appeal of a certain way of life in the provincial city, in which you would live within easy reach of one another, meet your friends at the same events, frequent a limited (but perfectly adequate) number of places (concert halls, restaurants, cafés). Perhaps I was already in the process of finding my way home – preparing to change back the syllable.

Before I 'discovered' Kathleen McEnery in 1995, she had had a brief moment of visibility in 1987. That was the year the National Museum of Women in the Arts opened in Washington, DC. Two of McEnery's paintings were included in the inaugural show, curated by Eleanor Tufts. She writes this in the catalogue:

> **Kathleen McEnery is one of the discoveries of this exhibition. A whole corpus of impressive works exists in the homes of her children as testament to her painterly accomplishment. Two of her paintings were in the Armory Show of 1913, and her works were exhibited in New York galleries. But after this promising beginning, she yielded to her responsibilities as wife and mother and gave up her artistic commitment.**

> **In 1914 her marriage to Francis E. Cunningham took her to Rochester, New York, where he manufactured in his grandfather's carriage factory the Cunningham automobile, 'the nearest thing to a Rolls-Royce produced in America'. They had a daughter and two sons in the first decade of their marriage, and in 1917 the family moved to a new house, which included a spacious studio.**

The two paintings Tufts included in the 1987 show were *Going to the Bath* (one of the works included in the Armory Show, and now in the National American Art Museum in Washington, DC) and *Breakfast Still Life* (owned by McEnery's grand-daughter in Virginia, and the painting I chose for the front cover of my book *AngloModern*). Eleanor Tufts is wrong about McEnery giving up her art after marriage. (Indeed, an article about her in the Rochester local paper in the 1930s is headed 'Mrs. Cunningham: Real Artist and Real Wife and Mother'.) It's a little surprising that she was left with this impression, since she was in contact with McEnery's son Peter (by correspondence) and daughter Joan (correspondence, and a visit to Joan's home in November 1985). Joan Cunningham Williams, who was married to a diplomat and at that time lived on a farm in Virginia, was herself an artist. She studied in New York and Paris, and was commissioned as a Works Progress Administration (a New Deal agency) artist in 1940, when she painted a mural at Poteau Post Office in Oklahoma. (She wasn't necessarily Eleanor Tufts's most helpful informant, though. In one of her short handwritten notes to Tufts, she has five mistakes about her mother, including date and place of birth and date of death. She also seems to have forgotten, as Tufts politely points out in her reply to another letter, to have included a promised map for Tufts's visit to the farm.)

Eleanor Tufts died in 1991, but I was able to see her papers, including the correspondence with the Cunninghams about McEnery's work, thanks to her colleague at Southern Methodist University, Alessandra Comini, herself a distinguished art historian who has written widely on early twentieth-century German and Austrian art. In her letter to Joan Cunningham Williams (reminding her to send the map), Eleanor Tufts adds a postscript to say 'One or two colleagues may drive with me'. Alessandra Comini was the colleague, as Tufts's later letter of thanks makes clear.

Dear Mr. and Mrs. Williams,

You were absolutely wonderful about showing us the paintings of Kathleen McEnery, and I deeply apologize about our driver's wrenching us away prematurely. Both Professor Comini and I felt very privileged to meet you both, and we reluctantly departed at the insistence of our hostess. We regret terribly missing the opportunity of sitting down and talking with you over the tea which you so graciously offered. Not only could I have heard from you more on the subject of your mother, but here was an opportunity to learn about two women artists. When we started out in the morning from Washington, we had no idea that our hostess was under any deadline to return to Washington, and were shocked to learn this when our time was also abruptly curtailed at Nancy Hale's ...

Both Alessandra and I hope that we might some day return to visit you – next time in a rented car! Since I noticed that you seem to subscribe to *Art News*, you might be interested to look at your September 1985 issue, p. 107, which cites Sandra as an expert on German Expressionism.

As far as I know, they didn't visit Joan Williams again, though the correspondence continued for several months as the NMWA show was planned (and as Eleanor Tufts changed her mind several times about which works by McEnery she wanted to borrow). After her discovery of the artist on this occasion, Tufts included a note about her in the 1989 edition of *American Women Artists*, and contributed a short piece about her for Jules Heller and Nancy G. Heller's *North American Women Artists of the Twentieth Century*; the 1995 edition of the latter book is dedicated to Eleanor Tufts after her death.

I had an email exchange with Alessandra Comini in 2000, when I started writing about McEnery, and sent her a copy of our Rochester catalogue in 2003. Then, as I was beginning work on this book in January 2006, I came across Comini's own memoir, *In Passionate Pursuit*, in the bookstore of the Metropolitan Museum of Art in New York. It relates the story of her life in art and music, from childhood years in Spain and Italy, through studies in New York and California, to teaching at Southern Methodist University, where she has been since 1974. The main 'passionate pursuit' has been of the Austrian artist Egon Schiele, who died at the age of twenty-eight in the flu epidemic of 1918. In the course of her work, Comini has travelled often and energetically, meeting and befriending collectors, scholars and Schiele's own sisters and several of his sitters. But the pursuit has also, unusually for an academic in the twentieth century, been an impressively open-minded one, taking the author from a passion for music (amongst several other early careers, she spent some time as a folk musician, and plays flute and guitar), through a sometimes bewildering variety of research interests. She has published books on Schiele and on Gustav Klimt, but also on images of Beethoven, on 'the visual Wagner', on Mahler, and on women artists and Scandinavian artists. She and Eleanor Tufts joined the SMU faculty at the same time, and found a house together close to the university. When Tufts was invited to curate the inaugural exhibition of the National Museum of Women in the Arts in 1987, Comini was asked to contribute two of the catalogue essays (on sculptors Harriet Hosmer and Elisabet Ney), and she and Tufts travelled together across the country over a period of several years, selecting works for the show. The memoir doesn't mention McEnery, or the visit to Joan Cunningham. (In a personal email, Alessandra Comini told me that until I sent her the quotation from Tufts's letter of thanks she had quite forgotten how furious they were with their driver, who rushed them away too early.)

Alessandra Comini is one of a growing number of women academics writing memoirs. Some of the books, like hers, are accounts of an intellectual or political life, told in personal terms. Other writers have told stories of their lives as Holocaust survivors, or as children of survivors. For some, the nature of memoir and autobiography is the point of the work, which both contributes to the academic study of life-writing and at the same time tells the reader about the author's life. Some writers, confronting serious illness, have been compelled to write about that. I've been very interested in this – not so much the question of why so many women have turned to personal writing, but rather the matter of style. A couple of times, in Rochester and at Columbia University, I taught a graduate seminar on memoir, social history and cultural theory, looking at how life stories are told and how they intersect with broader cultural histories. For me, the best examples of such work – avoiding the kind of self-indulgence that has been referred to as 'moi criticism' – tell more than a personal story. In these, the life is interesting not for its own sake but because it illuminates moments in a social world. Ronald Fraser's In Search of a Past, written in a variety of techniques (personal memory, oral history, psychoanalysis), shows us aspects of country life in England in the interwar years. Carolyn Steedman's memoir, Landscape for a Good Woman, told as intersecting stories of her mother and herself, does the same for working-class life in the north of England. These, I think, are the most interesting kinds of memoirs. Still, each writer must confront the question of how to deal with the personal – how much to tell, how intimate the detail, how to judge the style of writing.

The life as linear, chronological narrative is by now exposed as entirely artificial. Traditional memoirs still take that form, based on the belief that this is how to tell the story of a life – birth, family members, education, adolescence, occupation and so on. It isn't the timeline that's a problem here but the fact, so obvious now, that the choice of events and moments to relate is arbitrary and quite selective. Because of this, writers have told their own stories in various deconstructed modes – confused chronology, changes in voice, interjections of other kinds of plot. A 'life' emerges out of this, but not one packaged and complete. In a final chapter of his book, Richard Hoggart suggests that autobiographical writing must discover 'a shape proper to itself', one which emerges from the material. He wasn't writing with the benefit of knowing more recent critical discussions of 'life-writing', but it's the same point. And, since it is also clear that we rewrite our own stories at different times in our lives, why not give up the pretence of an autobiographical 'truth'? For this reason, I find most appealing those narratives with specific or even eccentric framing devices, permitting only partial views of the 'self'. For example, Janet Berlo has organised her memoir, Quilting Lessons, around her practice as a quilter, describing the art itself, her friends and family, and her life as an art historian and academic.

Deborah Tall's memoir, From Where We Stand, is a lyrical account (she was in fact a poet and a writing teacher) of the Finger Lakes region of upstate New York in which she lived and worked. As the book's jacket explains, she

interweaves her own story with the story of this place: of the tragic Seneca Nation of the Iroquois, whose mythology still clings to the landscape; of the European settlers, who for a while turned the land into the 'breadbasket of the nation' but then, mostly, moved on, leaving behind decaying, hopeless towns; of the many utopians who sensed a spiritual resonance and were inspired – among them the early feminists.

The area, a few miles south-east of Rochester, is one I know well, and so the story has a special appeal. And, as an aside, there is for me another personal connection – on Seneca Lake, where Deborah Tall's college is situated, there is a large US Army Depot, a storage place for bombs, and the place where uranium for the Manhattan Project was kept. Not a nuclear processing plant, but still another rural threat, like Sellafield in the English Lake District.

Nina Balaban left New York sometime after Kellner's acquaintance with her in the 1950s. Born in 1890, she lived to be one hundred and one, and died in 1991. I contacted Bruce Kellner in February 2006, before I left the United States. Not very surprisingly, he still remembered her well. He put me in touch with the artist Sam Spanier, who lived in an arts community and spiritual centre called Matagiri, near Woodstock, New York, which he had founded with his partner Eric Hughes in 1968. We exchanged letters and had a long telephone conversation that same February. He knew Nina Balaban throughout the later decades of her long life – he remembered meeting her on a beach in Provincetown in the 1940s, when, by then in her fifties, she was in a bikini and, according to him, looking many years younger than her age. He recalled that she lived for many years with a sculptor, more than twenty years younger than her. Ten years after Sam Spanier's first meeting with Nina, when Bruce Kellner rented her New York apartment, he couldn't tell if she was forty or sixty. She told Kellner, in 1956, that she wanted to go to Woodstock for the summer to paint. They continued this rental arrangement for two more summers.

Nina moved to Woodstock permanently in the early 1960s. Already established as an artist, she began to specialise in hand-painted ceramic plates. These still turn up from time to time on auction websites. Today – the day I am writing – I find on Amazon a book of her printed covers (at £124 rather too much of an extravagance for me to send for):

Balaban, Nina. Plan zemli. (Russian Edition) New York, National Printing & Publishing Company (1936). 4°. 40 pages. Original printed wrappers with art-deco illustration. The front cover with a small tear and chip. A little dusty. Inscribed by Nina Balaban to Kathleen Cunningham To my dear friend Cathleen – with love from Nina. 5.Feb.36 New York. With the printed dedication for Emanuel Balaban. Text in Russian.

Kathleen Cunningham is, of course, Kathleen McEnery, under her married name.

German-Jewish refugees from Manchester in internment camp,
Isle of Man, 1940 or 1941

Austerity baby

3: Aliens

For my first creative writing group, formed with three colleagues at the South Bank Centre in London in December 1987, I wrote about this photograph, taken in 1940 or 1941. I called the piece 'Image of an alien'.

But the really extraordinary thing about this photo is that he is right in the centre. Not only that. He is framed and displayed by the arch, projected, more than any of the other men, against the pale background of the sky.

It took me a while to understand what was so unsettling about it. I thought it was the dislocating effect of seeing him in the company of men – a different vision of how he might have been before the matriarchy took him over on his return. There is something strange, too, in the evidence that he existed, in a particular place and at a particular moment, before I was born. But now it's perfectly clear that the most disorienting feature of this image is his position of casual centrality. Because for the past forty years he has only appeared at the edges of things, exiled to the margins of the life and the conversations of the family.

I imagine that this was, for him, a position he took with some gratitude. Excluded by culture and language, as well as by natural inhibition and reticence, he was more than content to leave all the Important Things (which included the children) to my mother and her ample extended family. There's only one photo of him holding the baby (me), in which he looks embarrassed and nervous (but with the same shy smile as in this photo). Someone must have told him that for once he had to take a turn in front of the camera.

The photograph is a scene from one year in his life, when he was interned with other refugees in the Isle of Man. The 'internment of aliens' – a peculiar and rather hysterical measure taken by the British government after Dunkirk. He had only been married for four months. But I suspect he really enjoyed the ironic freedom of that year.

This is my father as an alien. He is alien to Britain and to English culture. Surrounded by those who are not alien to him, he is captured in an alien environment. And this image of him as the central figure is one which is entirely alien to me. His existence on the edges of my childhood, his refusal to engage with me or to challenge the matriarchy, constitute the real alienation.

Now this all feels a bit strained, and the theme overstated. But the photo retains its strangeness, so many years after I wrote the piece. My father is the one in the middle of the top row. On the far left of the picture is Heinz Kroch, another refugee, whose company in Eccles, near Manchester (Lankro Chemicals), had hired my father in 1938 and thus enabled his (belated) departure from Germany. I recognise one other person in the photo – Ernst Levi, second from the left at the front, wearing a beret – but remember him only vaguely from my childhood. He also worked at Lankro. (I remember that I had to start the piece with 'But' in order to pretend to myself that I was already in the middle of something – otherwise it would perhaps have been impossible to embark on a writing project of this kind. On the same basis, I think, writing teachers sometimes give the advice that you shouldn't buy a special notebook, but simply use an ordinary school exercise book, in order to make the task less daunting.)

The internment camp my father was sent to in 1940 was Onchan, on the Isle of Man. On the basis of Winston Churchill's notorious order, 'collar the lot!', all enemy aliens still at liberty in Britain were rounded up in June 1940, when invasion by Germany seemed very likely.

My father, who had come to Britain from Germany in February 1938, was a class C 'enemy alien' (recognised as a genuine refugee, and officially designated a 'friendly' enemy alien). The classifications were made by wartime tribunals set up in Britain in 1939. Those classified 'A' were considered to be of highest risk, and likely Nazi sympathisers, and were interned immediately. Category B aliens were not interned at that stage, but their freedom of movement was restricted and they were monitored by the police. Category C aliens were considered no risk, and remained at liberty. By January 1940, 528 enemy aliens had been interned, and about eight thousand placed under restrictions. The majority, of a total of about 75,000 cases, were assessed as category C. In May 1940 Germany invaded the Netherlands, and the Home Office, under pressure from some politicians and some of the media, ordered the arrest and internment of all male German and Austrian aliens between the ages of sixteen and sixty living on the east and south-east coastlines of England and Scotland. The surrender of Holland, and the imminent collapse of Belgium and France in the following days, led to the decision to arrest all category B males later the same month. As the evacuation from Dunkirk began, this was extended, on 27 May, to include German and Austrian women in category B. Finally, the Home Office wrote to all Chief Constables on 31 May, to say that they could intern any German and Austrian men or women of category C 'where there are grounds for doubting the

By virtue of the power vested in me by the

Secretary of State contained in Home Office letter

dated 31st May, 1940, reference Gen. 200/110/5, I hereby

authorise the arrest and internment of _____Arthur_____

_____WOLFF_____ of _____German_____ nationality,

Police Registration Certificate No. 631582, at present

residing at _____No. 30, Snowdon Road, Eccles, Lancs.,_____

and that he be handed over to the Military Authorities.

_____

CHIEF CONSTABLE OF LANCASHIRE.

County Chief Constable's Office,
PRESTON, 11th June, 1940.

Notice of arrest, June 1940

reliability of an individual'. When Italy entered the war on 10 June 1940 Italian enemy aliens were also rounded up for internment, together with any remaining category C German and Austrian aliens under the age of seventy, following prime minister Winston Churchill's order. My father's arrest document is dated the following day. My mother, born in England in 1917, lost her British citizenship on marrying my father four months before his internment. She had to apply for naturalisation to regain her British citizenship in October 1941.

The irrationality of the arrest and internment of aliens, many of them doing valuable work in Britain, is captured in a contemporary newspaper account from Manchester, quoted by François Lafitte in 1940:

> A chemist who has held an important position at a chemical works in the Manchester district for three or four years was dismissed at a moment's notice (his hat and coat were brought out to him: he was not allowed to go to his office to bring them) when the factory was taken over by the Government. Two days later he was interned as an unemployed enemy alien. A highly qualified chemist, who specializes in a branch of industrial chemistry in which qualified men are rare in this country, employed by a firm engaged on sub-contracts for Government orders has been interned ... An 'Aryan' German who has been with the same firm for more than three years and before that was in a German concentration camp as a punishment for having tried to help his Jewish employer when the employer was expropriated by the Nazis ... All the directors and chemists of a works near Manchester engaged on chemical manufacture for the leather industry ... A pathologist in the pathological laboratories of Manchester University. A distinguished German Jewish dentist who had to leave the west coast town where he was practising, and, as he was therefore without a practice, was interned. A young chemistry research student of six years' standing at Manchester University, son of a famous German Jewish doctor.

Lafitte, a young researcher working for Political and Educational Planning at the time, played a crucial role in the opposition to internment. His book on the subject was published as a Penguin Special in November 1940, and sold almost all fifty thousand copies right away. Together with other reports, and persistent questions in Parliament by Eleanor Rathbone, George Strauss, Josiah Wedgwood, Sidney Silverman and others, it produced pressure on the government and by mid-1941 many of the internees had been released. Lafitte went on to a career as a journalist for *The Times*, and, later, as an academic. When I was a sociology student at the University of Birmingham in the 1960s, he was Professor of Social Policy there. I knew him very slightly, but knew nothing then about his early career, and the great impact he had had, as a young man, on my father's situation.

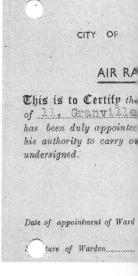

Air Raid Precautions card, November 1943

By July 1940 about 27,000 people had been interned. Many enemy
aliens were also deported to Canada and Australia. That month,
The Arandora Star, a ship carrying 1,500 German and Italian – many
category A – internees to Canada, was torpedoed by a Nazi U-boat;
more than 650 of them lost their lives. Deportees, from all three
categories, arrived in Canada on other boats (the *Ettrick*, the *Sobieski*,
the *Duchess of York*); some were sent to Australia (on the *Dunera*
– whose captain foiled another U-boat attack on 12 July). But the
majority of arrested aliens were interned in a number of special camps
in Britain, primarily on the Isle of Man off the north-west coast of
England. The island (and in some cases the same camps) had been
used for the internment of over thirty thousand enemy aliens in the
First World War. In 1940, there were six camps in Douglas; one in
Onchan, near Douglas; one each in Ramsey and Peel; and women's
camps in Port Erin and Port St Mary. My father was in Onchan camp,
described in this way in a book published by the Manx Museum and
National Trust (*Living with the Wire: Civilian Internment in the Isle of Man
during the Two World Wars*):

> Onchan camp was the third camp to open on the 11th June 1940
> and consisted of 60 houses around Royal Avenue East and West
> in Onchan. The camp held German and Austrian internees until
> July 1941 when it closed. It reopened in September 1941 with Italian
> internees who were held there until November, 1944.

My father, who was given the job of Postmaster, was at Onchan for
twelve months. When he was released, he took with him a letter of
reference, signed (illegibly) by the Camp Supervisor, and stamped
'Onchan Internment Camp Internees Office 31 May 1941'. Addressed
'To whom it may concern', it says:

> It gives me a pleasure to confirm that Dr. Arthur Wolff has been
> working in the Camp Administrations of both Central and Onchan
> Camp for many months. His particular task was the organization
> and direction of the Camp Post Office and in the course of the
> discharge of his functions as Postmaster he proved to be a very able
> administrator. His tact and integrity won him the sympathies of all
> with whom he came into contact, and I am convinced that he will
> succeed wherever the exigencies of the war may require his services.

As far as I know, the exigencies of the war next required him to act
as air raid warden in Manchester, as he returned to his job as an
industrial chemist at Lankro Chemicals (perhaps the same chemical
company cited by Lafitte as losing all its directors to internment the
previous year).

SALFORD.

TIONS.

r Wolfe.
Salford.8.

aid Warden.   *This is
id upon Wardens by the*

Chief Air Raid Warden.

11.43.

Voeff.

Actually, although in many ways the internment of aliens was a shameful episode, fuelled by anti-alienism (and, some have suggested, antisemitism), and although conditions in some of the camps, as Lafitte disclosed, were rather dreadful, the impression I always got was that my father quite enjoyed his time there. There were things to worry about at home. He had managed to bring his elderly parents out of Germany in 1939. His father, who had a weak heart, died later that year. His mother, who barely spoke English, was living with my father's new bride (my mother) and her parents. A terrible dilemma for my father, which he told me about only years later, was whether to write his first letter – only one a fortnight was allowed – to his wife or to his mother. Personally, I had no doubt that he made the right choice in writing to his mother, so recently displaced and widowed, but he said that my mother, a twenty-three-year-old new bride, was upset, and it upset me to realise that he had felt bad about this for years. Still, he seemed to thrive among his fellow aliens. And the camps were amazing places, inhabited by brilliant and talented writers, musicians, scientists. Lafitte, looking back on the internment episode four decades later, starts his 'afterthoughts' in this way:

> The only blessing for which we can thank Britain's rounding up of its 'enemy aliens' in 1940 is that it unintentionally accomplished the genesis of the Amadeus Quartet. After the Second World War this talented and eventually internationally famous group delighted music lovers everywhere for forty years until Peter Schidlof's death ended the partnership in 1987. For it was in a British internment camp that Schidlof, a youth of eighteen, made friends and first attempted to play music with two other gifted young men, Norbert Brainin and Siegmund Nissel. In the Third Reich, from which they had escaped to England, these three had belonged to the great host seen as a threat to the German 'race' and way of life. Seen now by the *British* state as a possible threat to the nation's security in time of war, they found themselves fortuitously confined together – and plucked opportunity from adversity. Growing after the war, with the addition of Martin Lovett, from a threesome into a foursome, they proceeded to enchant the nation's heart and enrich its culture.

Among other distinguished internees, Lafitte names many scientists (including Hermann Bondi, G. V. Lachmann, Hans Motz, Max Perutz, Guido Pontecorvo, Franz Borkenau), social scientists and financiers (Francis Carsten, Jürgen Kuczynski, Claus Moser, Franz Borkenau), lawyers and legal scholars (Sebastian Haffner, Fred Uhlman, Max Grünhut, Fritz Hallgarten), writers, artists, composers, musicians

(Richard Friedenthal, Hans Gal, Kurt Schwitters, John Heartfield, Ludwig Meidner, Egon Wellesz), art historian Ernst Kitzinger, and choreographers Kurt Joss and Sigurd Leeder. Internees in the Isle of Man were able to attend lecture series and concerts and to see exhibitions of work by fellow internees. Fred Uhlman, interned in one of the Douglas camps, recalled the cultural riches on offer.

> But our pride was our marvellous collection of more than thirty university professors and lecturers, mainly from Oxford and Cambridge, some of them men of international reputation. I doubt if one could have found a greater variety of lecturers anywhere else – we had an *embarras de richesse*. What could one do if Professor William Cohn's talk on the Chinese Theatre coincided with Egon Wellesz' Introduction to Byzantine Music? Or Professor Jacobsthal's talk on Greek Literature with Professor Goldmann's on the Etruscan language? Perhaps one felt more inclined to hear Zunz on the Odyssey or Friedenthal on the Shakespearean stage.

> Every evening one could see the same procession of hundreds of internees each carrying his chair to one of the lectures, and the memory of all these men in pursuit of knowledge is one of the most moving and encouraging that I brought back from the strange microcosm in which I lived for so many months.

The artist Hugh Dachinger, in the Mooragh Camp at Ramsey, organised an exhibition in November 1940 of work he had made in an internment camp in Huyton, near Liverpool, and in Ramsey. In Onchan camp artist Jack Bilbo founded the Popular University and organised several exhibitions. The camp paper, *The Onchan Pioneer*, produced by inmates and duplicated for circulation, announced the week's lectures, included sketches and cartoons, summarised the progress of the war and presented short pieces on a range of subjects by internees.

By the time of the 13 April 1941 issue, a start had been made on the gradual release of interns. A short paragraph reports this:

> About half of the 'enemy' aliens who have been under detention in Britain and the Dominions have now been liberated. The latest figures of releases is about 13500. Approximately nearly 1300 of which were Italians. There are still about 5000 detained overseas and between 8000 and 9000 in Britain.

Immediately below are these reports:

> *Compulsory labor in the desert!*

> Internees at the Vermey concentration camp, in France are being conscripted for compulsory labour on the Trans-Sahara-Railway. The first group of 150 has already left. Most of these people have

Cover of *Onchan Pioneer*, 13 April 1941

been undernourished for months in Vermey and it is feared that the compulsory work in the heat of the desert will for many of the prisoners be tantamount to a death sentence.

General Commissioner for Jewish Affairs

The Vichy Government has installed a 'General Commissioner for Jewish Affairs'. M. Xaver Valat, the new commissioner has been given authority to liquidate Jewish property. All measures necessary for the imitation of the anti-Jewish laws of Nazi-Germany are to be prepared.

It is very difficult to imagine the state of mind of internees, many separated from family in Britain, many concerned about friends and family still in Europe, and yet making the best of their imprisonment and participating in daily work and cultural activities. Tony Kushner stresses the negative impact of internment.

To the infirm and elderly refugees, the camps, especially in their earlier days, did create serious physical difficulties ... Nevertheless, the major problem was more psychological, especially to those refugees who had suffered in the German concentration camps during the 1930s. Needing security, instead they were given more barbed wire to face. Although not common, suicides did occur, a sober qualifying factor to the tendency to view internment, a generation later, in almost nostalgic terms.

This wasn't the first time my father had been identified by the state as an 'alien'. In 1933, he was working at ORACEFA – the Oranienburger Chemische Fabrik, twenty miles north of Berlin. The company manufactured sulphuric acid, super-phosphate and a range of organic chemicals for the textile and leather industries. My father had just completed his PhD in chemistry from the University of Berlin, and started work at ORACEFA in February 1930, the day after his final exam. He describes the job in his 1976 memoir.

My title was that of Lab and Works Chemist, and the job was initially concerned with production control. Later I was given the Analytical Department and technical correspondence with foreign representatives and licensees, particularly customers' service and analysis of competitive products. Once every month I spent a day at the Patent Office in Berlin looking for competitors' Patent applications in case we objected.

His introduction to the memoir (a booklet of twenty-four pages, published by a local press in Manchester) is indicative, and typical, of his benign view of the world, one which persisted through the events of the 1930s and 1940s.

Arthur Wolff doctoral dissertation, 1930

Austerity baby

Zur Kenntnis der Parawolframate und einiger Heteropolywolframate

---

Inaugural=Dissertation

zur

Erlangung der Doktorwürde

genehmigt von der

Philosophischen Fakultät

der

Friedrich = Wilhelms = Universität zu Berlin

von

ARTHUR WOLFF

aus Fraulautern

Tag der mündlichen Prüfung: 6. Februar 1930
Tag der Promotion: 4. Juni 1930

Druck: Doktordruck — Graphisches Institut Paul Funk,
Berlin SW 48, Friedrichstr. 231.

Bankverbindungen:
Bank der Arbeiter, Angestellten u.
Beamten A.-G., Berlin S.W. 19
Postscheckkonto: Berlin 521 00
Fernsprecher:
Zehlendorf H 4 Nr. 3445
Drahtanschrift:
Technikerverband, Berlin

Deutscher Techniker=Verband

Reichsgeschäftsstelle

Berlin=Zehlendorf — Schweizerhof

DTB / Berlin=Zehlendorf / „Schweizerhof"	Zeichen:	Tag:	12. 8. 33.
			17. 8. 33.

Herrn
A. Wolff,
Oranienburg b/Bln.
Königsallee 22

Abteilung   3 – Austritt

Streichung I.   63762

Werter Berufskamerad !

Da bei Ihnen die Voraussetzungen in
bezug auf die Arierbestimmungen für die
Übernahme in den "Deutschen Techniker-Verband"
nicht gegeben sind, haben wir die Streichung
Ihres Namens aus unserem Mitgliederregister
mit sofortiger Wirkung vorgenommen.

Mit deutschem Gruss !

Deutscher Techniker-Verband
Reichsgeschäftsstelle
Abteilung 3 – Austritt

Letter from German Technicians' Union, August 1933

Austerity baby

The following pages should be read as a personal purely subjective recollection of the events which concerned me during the last eight years before I emigrated. The emphasis is on memories of events rather than judgment in general.

Surprisingly, after my arrival in this country in 1938, I found it relatively easy to forget the past and rarely looked back. Only in the last few years memories have kept coming back and after forty years seem curiously distant and unreal today. Being sufficiently detached now, I felt an increasing temptation to put some of the episodes, as I remember then, on record, mainly for my own satisfaction, for my family or for anybody else who may be interested.

He is convinced, he goes on, 'that the majority of Germans did not really care for Hitler, or for a long time did not take him seriously', and he acknowledges that he was one of the optimists 'who took events as they came, always deluding themselves that it wasn't so bad'.

Looking back, I don't really regret my own optimism in those days, although later events proved me wrong, it was the only way to be reasonably relaxed and to carry on with the job. I was lucky because nobody who had the power took any action against me personally, and I am aware that my own experience was a very special one. It would, therefore, be wrong for me to generalize as I have known people elsewhere in Germany who were less fortunate and had to face the more violent forms of anti-semitism.

The vignettes that follow are as much about people's kindness as about those colleagues and acquaintances who became enthusiastic Nazis after Hitler came to power in 1933. The Works Director, Dr Kurt Lindner, was arrested early on, and taken to the nearby Sachsenhausen concentration camp, though he was released ten days later. (It was Lindner, by then running a consultancy laboratory in Berlin, who told my father that Heinz Kroch was starting a factory in Manchester, and initiated the contact that allowed my father to leave Germany in 1938.)

When the excitement of the take-over had died down, things had to be re-organised. I was assured again by my superiors that what had happened was only in line with Party instructions and was nothing personal. There was no objection to Jews staying in their jobs as long as they didn't get involved in politics. Ironically, I was soon appointed Production Manager and was able to hold on to this job for a few years. The deterioration of my personal, social and public living conditions came so slowly, in little stages, that it was hardly noticeable. Naturally, thoughts of emigration must have occurred to me from the very beginning, but the changes seemed remote.

Identity cards for
Josef and Bertha
Wolff, March 1939

II.
Grund der Schädigung

3. Kurze Darstellung der Umstände, die die Schädigung verursachten:

I. In der Nacht v.8/9.Nov.1938 drangen Nazis in das Wohnhaus
Rodenerstr.1, zerstoerten saemtliches Mobilar, Einrichtungs-
gegenstaende, Fenster, Laeyden usw. und misshandelten meinen
inzwischen verstorbenen Ehemann.

II. Die Kaufsumme v. 5.300.----Mk. fuer das Wohnhaus Rodenerstrasse 1
wurde vor der Emigration als Judenvermoegen auf Sperrkonto
ueberwiesen und ging verloren.

Section of
restitution claim
form, 1951

Damaged
photographs
of Rosa and
Heinrich Wolff

Austerity baby

The receipt, in August 1933, of a 'friendly letter' from the German Technicians' Union, telling him that in accordance with the regulations about non-Aryans his name had been removed from their register, seems to me to be more than a 'little stage', and certainly noticeable.

Soon after my father left for England, on Kristallnacht (9 November 1938), a Sturmabteilung (the paramilitary wing of the Nazi Party) gang broke into my grandparents' house in Saarlautern, destroying every piece of furniture including the kitchen stove. (Even on this occasion, my father finds some virtue, paying tribute to the local police chief 'who knew my father and simply "forgot" to arrest him on this occasion'.) They already had their new identity cards, with the additional first names 'Israel' and 'Sarah', and the stamp of 'J', compulsory for German Jews as of 1938.

Hans Peter Klauck, historian of the Jews in the region of Saarlouis, sent me copies of documents about the Kristallnacht attack on my grandparents. The detailed information, which I had never seen before, is taken from a restitution claim lodged by my grandmother in 1951. In the document she states that on the night of 8–9 November 1938, Nazis broke into their home and destroyed furniture, fittings, windows and blinds, and physically attacked her husband. She also claims recompense for the cost of their home, which they had been obliged to sell and for which they had never received the money.

She itemises the cost of damage in each room, adding to the destroyed furniture items of kitchenware, lamps, a radio, two mirrors, and – somehow very poignantly – 'a man's coat (stolen)'. Photographs of my grandfather's parents, Heinrich and Rosa Wolff, were also damaged during the attack; the damage is still visible.

Josef Wolff in German army uniform, 1917

Until that point, they had been reluctant to leave Germany. My grandfather, who had fought in the German army in the First World War, could not believe that anyone would want to harm him. He also thought he was too old to move and start a new life. As it happened, my father points out, 'his refusal proved to be a blessing in the end, as all the Saarlautern Jews who had found refuge in France and Holland in 1935, were caught by the German invasion and died during the War'. Then again, the usual silver lining:

> It must, however, be remembered that, as distinct from the hostility of French officials, many Jews, including some relatives of mine, owe their survival to the great number of French people who protected them during the War, often at the risk of their own lives. At least ten of my relatives survived in France, hidden by French people.

On the other hand, many of my father's relatives, on both sides, didn't survive, including his Aunt Leonie. His parents went to stay with

Leonie, Bertha's sister, in Offenburg in Baden, hoping to emigrate from there. My father managed to get visas for his parents and for his uncle and aunt to emigrate to Britain in 1939. His parents arrived in June of that year. Leonie and her husband Sigmund Kahn delayed their departure, and missed the opportunity to leave. Sigmund died in the French internment camp Gurs in December 1940, and Leonie in Auschwitz in September 1942.

Of course what I was also trying to say in that 1987 piece about my father in Onchan camp was something about his 'alien-ness' in my own life. He was so much in the background of things when I was growing up. For one thing, he worked pretty long hours at Lankro in the early postwar years. My youngest sister, eleven years younger than me, says he was much more present in her life as a child. In addition, apart from his widowed mother, who lived with us until I was twelve, he was alone in England, the rest of his surviving family living in France or further away in the United States. My mother's family was large, and very much involved in our everyday lives: her three brothers and their families; her mother and her mother's two unmarried sisters; her father and his many brothers and sisters and their families – almost all of them, like us, in north Manchester. Mainly, though, my father – Arthur – was an extremely reserved man, who seemed to inhabit his life with great contentment and equanimity, but at some remove. He loved classical music, and he loved his garden, to which he devoted most of his leisure hours. I have never known whether his quietness and restraint had something to do with his experiences in Germany, and with the family losses he suffered. Cousins of his in France and the United States, whom I have got to know in the past couple of decades, haven't been able to throw much light on this for me. My cousin Marthe in Metz in France knew him best, though she was a couple of decades younger than him. My cousin Marlyse, a retired anaesthetist in Washington, DC, has only vague memories of him – she was also more than twenty years younger than him. In any case, it has been very strange for me on occasion to come across some evidence of him in the pre-emigration period – or to see him in the Onchan photograph away from the family. In his memoir, he reproduces a photograph of his 'illegal Aryan girlfriend', Charlotte Bohnsted, whom he used to meet secretly. He identifies the photograph as 'Charlotte dressed up for the weekend (Picture taken secretly on the train to Berlin)'. She had been a laboratory assistant at a college in Berlin, and they became friendly after she came to ORACEFA as an analyst. At work, they had to ignore one another, managing to be alone only sometimes in the library. More

Charlotte Bohnsted

Arthur Wolff with unknown woman

Aliens

Bertha Wolff with author as young child

Austerity baby

usually, they met at weekends in cafés or small restaurants in Berlin. 'For quite a while, we met several times a week after dark a few miles outside Oranienburg. This was achieved by leaving the town on our bicycles in opposite directions for a pre-arranged rendezvous.' Once they met away from Berlin.

> I had treatment for duodenal ulcers, and in January 1937 I decided to have a last fling to get away from it for a short time. I went to Silvaplana in Switzerland for a 3 week ski-ing holiday, and Charlotte and I worked out a devious plan to meet secretly outside the Third Reich. We picked the tiny village of Muenster in the south east corner of Switzerland, and after detailed planning and studying timetables we arranged that I would be there on a certain day, travelling 6 hours from Silvaplana by train and coach over a snow covered pass. Independently, Charlotte went on holiday to Austria not far from Muenster. To avoid any suspicion, she went with another girl from the Lab. whom we took into our confidence, and who found it all very exciting. Everything went well and the two of us met at Muenster and spent a whole day there feeling perfectly free for the first time and probably for the last time.

It's quite difficult to imagine this version of my father – the drama, the romance, the fear of that time, and his participation in it all. Just as surprising for me was to come across a photograph of him with an unknown woman, taken in the earlier years, in which he looks so confident and debonair. One of my German American relatives had the picture – she doesn't know who the woman was, or where it was taken.

Of course I also didn't know my father as a young man. He was nearly forty years old when I was born.

Meanwhile, there were other aliens in our midst. My German grandmother, as I said, lived with us for the first twelve years of my life, and had lived with my parents from the beginning of their marriage. I can't begin to grasp the difficulties this must have created for everyone. For my mother, who didn't particularly get on with her mother-in-law, and who anyway must surely have wanted to have my father to herself. For my grandmother, devoted to her son, recently widowed, removed from the rest of her family, having to share the house (not a very large one) with her daughter-in-law. And for my father, who must have felt just as torn as he did when he had to decide which letter to write first from the internment camp. Everyone was very civilised and restrained; and of course in the immediate postwar

Family photograph, Thionville, 1953

Austerity baby

years many other people were putting up with difficult economic and residential circumstances. My sisters and I were never aware of arguments or tensions. But can that really be true? In any case, how strange that it never occurred to us how *alien* our grandmother must have seemed, with her grey hair in a bun, and in her long black dresses, fringed with lace, in the context of Manchester in the mid-twentieth century.

About eighteen months after my younger sister was born, in 1954, we moved to the south side of Manchester, to a bigger, sunnier house; my grandmother had gone the year before to live in a home for elderly German-Jewish refugees nearby.

Since my parents' deaths (my mother on New Year's Eve 1988, my father in January 1991), I have spent a lot of time talking to elderly relatives of theirs. My belated introduction to David Norr, of Scarsdale, New York, whose father's 1909 journal starts this book, is one example – in this case, a cousin (a couple of times removed) on my mother's side. These are the 'Russian' relatives, all descendants of family who left Russia and Bessarabia in the early twentieth century. Some of the 'German' relatives (my father's family), who left Germany in the 1930s, were already known to me, because my father had kept in touch with them. In fact, even though I resumed contact with Marthe Hanau, in Metz, only after my father's death, here I am in a picture with her in 1953. I'm the taller of the two little girls in matching sun dresses. Marthe is third from the left, her face partly in shadow. My mother (not a very flattering photograph) is second from the right, behind my sister Veronica. I am ten; Veronica is nearly eight. The other little girl is Marthe's daughter, Dany.

The line-up is a bit confusing – the man on the far right is my father's cousin Edgar, a cousin on his mother's side. The others are all relatives on his father's side. They had all got together to meet my father and his family on our summer vacation in Europe. The photograph was taken in Thionville in Alsace, and we were on our way to a holiday in Austria. To the left of Marthe are her parents, Josef and Julie Joseph. Behind me is Julie, and next to my mother is Julie's sister Emma. I seem to remember an occasion of great affection, and enormous amounts of food. But, really, to a ten-year-old, these were rather boring older people, who spoke incomprehensible (to me) German and French much of the time, and wore old-fashioned clothes. I wonder how much I registered (and have since forgotten) of the importance of this postwar reunion for my father (who took the picture).

My more recent explorations have been an exercise in rapprochement with the alien. Those uninteresting elderly women, the sisters Julie and Emma, turned out to have had very interesting lives. When she was herself about ten years old, my cousin Marlyse, having left Germany after Hitler came to power (her father had been a judge in Saarbrücken), lived in Metz, in France, first with Julie, Julie's husband Prosper Siesel and his sister Félicie, and then with Emma and her father Daniel (Marlyse's grandfather). Julie and Emma were her aunts, sisters of her father Alfred Levy. In the photograph, Emma is on the left, Julie on the right, and Félicie standing behind Marlyse.

In 1939, when Luxembourg was invaded, and in advance of the German invasion of France in May 1940, Julie, Emma and Félicie, together with Julie's son Marcel, were evacuated to Bar-le-duc in Lorraine, and then to the south of France. Here they lived for a number of years in Capdenac, north of Toulouse, in the unoccupied region. Julie's husband, Prosper Siesel, had died in 1938, and her father Daniel in 1939. At one point, while they were living as refugees in Capdenac, Emma was arrested and taken to the Gurs concentration camp. She was soon released, on the grounds that she was a German national. The fact that she was Jewish seemed not to be the point for the moment, but she was fortunate later to survive the 1942 *rafles* (round-ups) of Jews throughout the region.

Marlyse's own family (parents and brother Theo), who had been living in exile in Luxembourg, were expelled from there in December 1940, and were given an affidavit allowing them to move to France. With thirty kilos of luggage, they travelled to Nancy, via Chalons-sur-Saône, on the demarcation line between occupied and unoccupied France. From there, they took the train to Lyons, and finally reached Capdenac, to join Julie and the others. For a while, Julie supported the entire family, by selling jewellery and other possessions. Soon, Marlyse and her family moved to Villefranche de Rouergue, where there was a better school. Life was very precarious for all of them until the end of the war. There were often local raids, with Jews frequently arrested. Alfred Lévy, Marlyse's father, warned about an impending raid, went into hiding on a nearby farm where he stayed for about a year, occasionally visiting his family at night. On one occasion he was discovered by the authorities at home, and arrested. He was eventually cleared, with the help of the second-in-command at the local gendarmerie, who was secretly active in the Resistance. After the war, Alfred returned to Saarbrücken with his family, and resumed his work as a judge. I think he was the only member of my father's family who went back to Germany after the war. Marlyse completed medical school in Toulouse, and after some years in Strasbourg moved to the United States, where

Emma Levy, Marlyse Levy,
Julie Siesel, with Félicie
Siesel standing, 1930s

she worked as an anaesthetist until her retirement. For more than twenty years after that, she worked as a highly respected docent at the Freer and Sackler Galleries in Washington, DC. Julie and Emma returned to Thionville after the war, which is where I met them in 1953 when I was ten years old. Julie died in the early 1970s, and Emma a few years later. Julie's only son, Marcel Siesel, who was involved in the French Resistance, had been captured and executed by the Nazis during the war.

Another German in Manchester, arriving by way of a different kind of history than my father's, was the footballer Bert Trautmann. Rather fancifully, I like to think he may somehow have been connected with the artist Fritz Trautmann, born of German parents in Wisconsin, and a member of Kathleen McEnery's circle in Rochester. Her fascinating portrait of him is in the Memorial Art Gallery there.

Kathleen McEnery,
Fritz Trautmann, 1927

But I have absolutely no evidence for it, and it is not very likely. Bert Trautmann (actually Bernd Carl Trautmann) was born in Bremen in 1923, and after a time in the Hitler Youth he served in the German army in Russia and then France during the Second World War. When he was captured by the British, apparently he was greeted with the words (which may be the only kind of link I can make to his Rochester namesake) 'Hello Fritz, fancy a cup of tea?'. Declining the offer of repatriation when the war ended, he became the star goalkeeper of Manchester City Football Club. He overcame strong protests, especially from Jewish groups, to become one of the city's most popular players. In 2004 he was made an OBE for his work for Anglo-German relations. He lived for many years near Valencia in Spain, and died there on 19 July 2013. I haven't much interest in football, but even I remember the 1956 FA Cup Final between Manchester City and Birmingham City. Manchester City won; the reason I (and thousands of others) remember it is because Bert Trautmann broke his neck fifteen minutes before the end of the game, in a collision with another player. He played to the end, and the broken neck was diagnosed only three days later. This was a major media event, and it made him even more of a star. Manchester City has always been – in a fairly abstract way – my family's team. In a city where the competing team, Manchester United, was often higher-profile, and especially after their own tragedy, when seven players died in a plane crash in Munich on 6 February 1958, we were proud to be associated with a certain kind of heroism. Of course at the time (aged thirteen) I knew nothing about Trautmann's and my father's parallel – and entirely different – routes from Germany to England, nor about their separate internments in different kinds of 'alien' camps.

I was an alien myself for eighteen years, and an official one after March 1992. I gave one of my books the title *Resident Alien,* and in the introductory chapter wrote briefly about the experience of acquiring my green card – my permanent resident status. Although there were complex reasons for my decision to move to the United States in 1988, there is something about continuing the family tradition of alienness that I have enjoyed. I am the third generation of aliens in my family. Before my father and his parents came to Britain as aliens in the late 1930s, and before he was interned as an alien (indeed as an 'enemy alien') in 1940, my mother's family had done the same thirty years earlier. The 1905 Aliens Act in Britain was clearly, if not explicitly, designed to restrict the immigration of Jews from Eastern Europe. Tony Kushner and others have suggested an antisemitic element to this anti-alienism at the time, just as other scholars have exposed antisemitic prejudices in the resistance to the acceptance of Jewish refugees into Britain in the 1930s. (David Cesarani has also documented the admission of many Ukrainian, Latvian and Estonian war criminals to Britain after the war.) My mother's parents, quite young children at the time, did gain admittance to Britain, and settled in Manchester, where they met and married. It was her father, my grandfather, Maurice Noar, who welcomed the American cousin in 1909. The ways in which Jews in general have remained 'alien' in Britain (still, after all, a country with an established church) is a much bigger question, and the focus of a proliferation of excellent studies over the past twenty years.

In the end, I decided to break the pattern. Although I would have been permitted to keep my green card indefinitely, as long as I visited the States regularly, I made the decision, which seemed to be as much an emotional as a practical one, to forfeit it when I left in June 2006 and came home.

Anna Atkins, *Cyanotype of British fern*, 1853

Austerity baby

4: Colour (mainly blue)

My conversion to blue occurred in May 2005, in the attic of a stone
    terraced house in the Crookes area of Sheffield. My sister and I had an
    appointment there with a Colour Me Beautiful consultant, who worked
    from her home. The stairs up to the top floor opened directly into a large
    open room, full of bales of material, swatches of samples, and bottles
    and pots of cosmetics. CMB promises a personal transformation. On its
    current website, it proclaims that 'wearing colours that complement your
    colouring can make you look healthier, more vibrant and younger'. The
    consultant establishes what your dominant colouring is, and how this
    determines what clothes and make-up you should wear. I was identified
    as a 'cool winter' person; the little folder of twenty-nine swatches of
    material I came away with is dominated by teal, periwinkle, aqua, and
    royal, medium and Chinese blues, together with reds and greens with
    blue tints, and the instruction to go for an 'overall look' of blues (with
    eye pencils in 'marine'). On the few occasions in the past I had deviated
    from black and other neutral colours in my clothing choice, I had never
    even considered blue. It turned out to be excellent advice. And outside
    the world of fashion, I already knew quite a bit about the history of the
    colour in Western art.

Cennino Cennini, early fifteenth century: 'Ultra marine blue is a colour
    illustrious, beautiful, and most perfect, beyond all other colours; one
    could not say anything about it, or do anything with it, that its quality
    would not still surpass.'

Goethe, 1810: 'As the upper sky and distant mountains appear blue, so
    a blue surface seems to retire from us. But as we readily follow an
    agreeable object that flies from us, so we love to contemplate blue, not
    because it advances to us, but because it draws us after it.'

Kandinsky, 1911: 'Blue is the typical heavenly colour. The ultimate feeling
    it creates is one of rest. When it sinks almost to black, it echoes a grief
    that is hardly human.'

Yves Klein, 1957: 'What is blue? Blue is the invisible becoming visible ...
    Blue has no dimensions. It "is" beyond the dimensions of which other
    colors partake.'

William Gass, 1976: 'Praise is due blue, the preference of the bee.'

Julia Kristeva, 1977: 'Thus all colors, but blue in particular, would have a noncentered or decentering effect, lessening both object identification and phenomenal fixation. They thereby return the subject to the archaic moment of its dialectic, that is, before the fixed, specular "I".'

Derek Jarman, 1993: 'Blue transcends the solemn geography of human limits.'

Press release, 10 December 2007: 'Pantone, Inc., the global authority on color and provider of professional color standards for the design industries, selected PANTONE 18–3943 Blue Iris, a beautifully balanced blue-purple, as the color of the year for 2008. Combining the stable and calming aspects of blue with the mystical and spiritual qualities of purple, Blue Iris satisfies the need for reassurance in a complex world, while adding a hint of mystery and excitement.'

Pantone 18-3943 Blue Iris

And, for good measure (and perhaps rather surprisingly), Michel Pastoureau, 2000:

'All of the studies focusing on the "favorite color" question conducted since World War I show, with striking regularity, that more than half the people polled in Western Europe and the United States indicate that blue is their favorite color.'

Ideas about the effects of a certain colour, its associations and symbolism, are far from uniform cross-culturally. In addition, the *naming* of colours is almost impossible to clarify for earlier periods and for other cultures. It is not simply a problem of translation from another language, as Michel Pastoureau has explained:

> It is difficult to determine which Greek or Latin words designate blue because both languages lack basic, recurring terms for it, whereas white, red, and black are clearly named. In Greek, whose color lexicon did not stabilize for many centuries, the words most commonly used for blue are *glaukos* and *kyaneos* ... During the classical era, kyaneos meant a dark color: deep blue, violet, brown, and black. In fact, it evokes more the 'feeling' of the color than its actual hue. The term *glaukos*, which existed in the Archaic period and was much used by Homer, can refer to gray, blue, and sometimes even yellow or brown.

Philip Ball tells us that blue and yellow are categorised together in some Slavic languages as well as in other languages in northern Japan, East Nigeria and among some northern Californian Native Americans.

And in Western Europe since the medieval period there are plenty of examples of shifting meanings of colour terms. According to John Gage, the medieval colour terms *bloi* and *caeruleus* could each refer to blue or yellow, perhaps because of the technologies that produced them, in which mid-stage colours are transformed into others. All these authors are careful to warn us that unnamed colours are not necessarily unseen; or, rather, that the distinctions our language makes may be just as visible to those whose words do not identify and differentiate in the same way. Linguistic difference does, though, have implications for the use and status of particular colours in that culture. And it does remind us that our own categorisations and hierarchies (primary, secondary, complementary) are in an important sense arbitrary. Wittgenstein said as much in 1950, when he insisted that identification of colour is always a language-game.

If the identification and recognition of colour cannot be assumed across place and time, then neither can any intrinsic meaning or symbolism of a colour. Blue, says Pastoureau, was considered a warm colour in medieval and Renaissance Europe, and only began to be seen as cool in the seventeenth century. Kandinsky, mapping out his theories of the spiritual qualities of colour and colours, believed that blue was associated with the circle (red with the square, yellow with the triangle); his contemporary Adolph Hoelzel, on the other hand, had thought red circular, blue rectangular, as did the artist Oskar Schlemmer. William Gass (*On Being Blue*) and Alexander Theroux (*The Primary Colors*) each free-associate for pages on the meanings and associations of the colour. The radically diverse associations of colours with shapes and meanings lead John Gage to conclude that 'colour symbolism has always remained inescapably local and contextual'.

And yet it is possible that there are pre-social factors in play. Colour itself is the effect of the electromagnetic field of light on the eye, where different sets of retinal photoreceptors are receptive to different wave lengths. Blue, with a wave length of 420 nanometers, has a higher frequency than green, red and yellow. Julia Kristeva suggests that this quality of blue produces a special reception, which she explores in relation to frescos by Giotto in Padua:

> Blue is the first color to strike the visitor as he enters into the semidarkness of the Arena Chapel ... The delicate, chromatic nuances of the Padua frescoes barely stand out against this luminous blue. One's first impression of Giotto's painting is of a colored substance, rather than form or architecture; one is struck by the light that is generated, catching the eye because of the color blue. Such a blue takes hold of the viewer at the extreme limit of visual perception.

In this way, blue has a particular 'decentring effect', engaging with the viewer at some pre-linguistic, pre-conscious level. I don't know how to assess this kind of claim against the overwhelming historical evidence of cultural relativism in colour perception (that, combined with my own prejudice in favour of sociological accounts). But in a 2011 BBC programme, *Horizon*, on the theme of colour (and entitled 'Do you see what I see?') proposed very specific qualities of blue – presumably intrinsic rather than culturally specific – in which, interestingly, blue is perceived once again as a 'warm' colour. Experiments with restaurant décor found that diners perked up in the late evening in blue rooms. Scientists on the programme explained that we have photosensitive cells which are receptive only to blue, and which send the body a signal to wake up. Further, they argued that the colour blue digs into our earliest evolutionary consciousness, since primitive one-cell organisms can detect only blue and yellow; red and green reception came later, as new receptors developed in the eye.

This business of meaning and symbolism turns out to be rather tricky, though I am inclined to default to my rather automatic resistance to such universal, socio-biological claims – at least until persuaded otherwise. We are on safer ground, though, in looking at the clear evidence for the changing *importance* of blue throughout the history of Western culture. This history is nicely summarised by Colm Tóibín, in a 2004 catalogue essay for a Dublin exhibition called 'Blue': 'Blue was the banished orphan who lived to take the throne'. He bases this on his reading of Gage, Pastoureau and others who have recorded the fortunes of blue, in art and in textile dyeing, over two millennia. It is primarily a history of the availability, and therefore cost, of materials. It is a history of plants – woad and indigo – and minerals – lapis lazuli, azurite, cobalt – and, later of the invention of synthetic blues. It is also very much a social history, linked not just to the discovery and extraction of colours but to navigation and trade routes, relations between nations and, especially in the case of indigo, the patterns of colonial power. For example, Philip Ball points out that the highly valued blue, lapis lazuli (also known as ultramarine, because it came from 'beyond the sea'), was more common in Italy than in northern Europe during the Renaissance, because it arrived from Afghanistan and elsewhere through Italian ports.

Michael Baxandall's classic social history of Italian painting gives a marvellous insight into how the value and price of the precious mineral played out in the fifteenth century, in the detail of a 1485 contract for Domenico Ghirlandaio's *Adoration of the Magi* (in the Spedale degli

Innocenti in Florence). The Prior of the Spedale specifies clearly that the artist 'must colour the panel at his own expense with good colours and with powdered gold on such ornaments as demand it, with any other expense incurred on the same panel, and the blue must be ultramarine of the value about four florins the ounce'. Baxandall explains:

[67]

> After gold and silver, ultramarine was the most expensive and difficult colour the painter used. There were cheap and dear grades and there were even cheaper substitutes, generally referred to as German blue. (Ultramarine was made from powdered lapis lazuli expensively imported from the Levant; the powder was soaked several times to draw off the colour and the first yield – a rich violet blue – was the best and most expensive. German blue was just carbonate of copper; it was less splendid in its colour and, much more seriously, unstable in use, particularly in fresco.) To avoid being let down about blues, clients specified ultramarine; more prudent clients stipulated a particular grade – ultramarine at one or two or four florins an ounce.

The fortunes of lapis lazuli in the history of art are entirely to do with its cost of extraction and transport, and its rarity, just as the fortunes of indigo in the history of textile dyeing are inextricably linked to Europe's role in India and, later, America and the West Indies. In the West, although there were alternatives to lapis lazuli for artists, in particular the cheaper mineral azurite, it was ultramarine that was the most prized blue. The colour blue itself, rather insignificant in earlier periods, emerged in the twelfth century as a highly fashionable and desirable colour, manifested most clearly in the new practice of rendering the robes of the Virgin in ultramarine. Blue became a royal and noble colour, in painting and in heraldry. By the seventeenth century blue had taken its place as a primary colour, displacing the white-red-black triad which, according to Pastoureau, 'had been the focal point of Western color systems since antiquity (if not before)'.

Orange: blue's complementary colour, and absolutely banned by my CMB adviser in Sheffield. Nevertheless, it inserts itself here as something to be confronted, representing a memory as uncongenial to me as the colour itself. Early 1979 – I'm not sure of the exact date. By then, there were only three of us still living in a collective house in Leeds, after a falling-out the previous autumn, during my three-month absence in the United States. Complicated personal relations, sexual politics and other problems I was kept informed about – I assume it must have been by letter, since there was no email then and I don't recall many phone calls. It was a large, four-storey terraced house, five minutes from the university where three of us worked, and still 'inner city' enough to have been very affordable (£10,000, as I recall) in 1975. Most recently it had been used as a children's home, and perhaps because of that there were bathrooms on three of its four floors. The lower ground floor comprised a living room and a large kitchen/dining room, with a door out to the small garden at the back. We spent most of our time, together with many visiting friends, round the table in that room. But now the house would soon be sold and we would each be living somewhere else. Before that, though, was orange – in the form of a line of washing hanging one morning in the basement kitchen/dining room, announcing our housemate's expected decision that she had joined the Bhagwan. A shared domestic life – five adults and two children – begun four years earlier, tailed off rather pathetically at that point. As for the colour – the new sannyasin, who left for India soon after the washing episode, wrote in her 2007 memoir:

Someone once asked Bhagwan why we had to wear orange. He explained it was the traditional colour for sannyas, the colour of sunrise signalling the dawning of a new age. But I think it was to mark us out, to force us into each other's arms, as who else would willingly walk down the street next to someone swathed in such a deadly colour.

All this is now more than thirty years ago, and no doubt none of us remembers the details. Still, coming across a memory which bears little relation to my own has something of a shock effect. In the same book, she writes about the time, a couple of years earlier, when she had come to live in our house:

I applied to join a neo-Marxist socialist-feminist commune. After an interview where I wore my badges of revolutionary slogans, dropped in the names of my most right-on mates, mentioned the conferences I'd attended, the barricades I'd fought at, I was in.

Applied? Interview? Political requirements? And four people (one had recently left) as a 'neo-Marxist socialist-feminist commune'? We were really just a group of friends, with no particular shared political activities – two men, two women, some of us colleagues, two with kids who lived half the week with us and half with their fathers, nearby. The account has no connection at all with my memory of our household.

And I also try to square my memory of the orange-dyeing moment with that of her son, then aged three, who lived with us part of each week. His name was Tim Guest (Timmy in those days), and many years later he wrote a wonderful and moving book, *My Life in Orange*, about his early years in the Bhagwan's communes in India, England and the United States.

'A vivid and moving account of a remarkable childhood' ANDREW MILLER

My Life in Orange

TIM GUEST

St. John's Terrace, Leeds, 1975

Cover of Tim Guest's *My Life in Orange*

Tim Guest as a young child,
with his mother, Leeds, c. 1977

Colour (mainly blue)

Three weeks after hearing his voice on tape, my mother posted her letter to Bhagwan. That afternoon, upstairs playing with my Lego, I heard a loud splash. I went down to investigate. My mother was in our bathroom, her arms stained orange up to the elbows, sloshing all her clothes around in the bath, which was filled to the brim with warm water and orange dye. Later that evening she wrung her clothes out and hung them by the fire – to my delight, they left permanent orange stains on the fireguards – and from then on, she wore only orange.

An old friend from the Leeds days got in touch in 2004, to tell me that 'Timmy' had written a book which was getting a lot of publicity. That is how I found out that he had become a journalist and writer. Although I lived with him and his mother only for a couple of years, and haven't seen either of them since 1980, I read the book with great interest and have reread it several times since. It is a beautiful, generous, heart-breaking story, an account of the disasters of communal life based on a strange (and later discredited) spiritualism, sexual freedom and chaotic disorder for the children involved. John Lahr, the *New Yorker* critic, called it one of the best autobiographies of the decade. Elaine Showalter, reviewing the book in *The Guardian*, says that this 'calm, meditative, and even lyrical memoir is a testament to his recovery'. Certainly he became a very successful writer. The particular memory doesn't fit though. For one thing, he and his mother had a bedroom each and a bathroom they shared all on one floor, so he wouldn't have gone down to investigate. Also, we didn't have open fires anywhere in the house, so I can't see how there could have been fireguards. Of course it doesn't matter. But I hoped to get in touch one day, and compare memories. This didn't ever happen.

Tim Guest's second book, *Second Lives*, was published in 2007. It is an ethnographic study (if this isn't a contradiction) of virtual communities and of the entrepreneurs who created those worlds, and it too was very well received by critics and readers. Later, some noticed the continuities between the two books, the recurring damage, perhaps the impossibility of full recovery. Guest himself (it seems a little strange not to call him Tim) hints at it, without making this a big deal in the book – indeed, only on page 246, though he alludes to the connection briefly throughout:

When I was four, my mother and I moved into the communes of her guru – a bearded man-god who promised ecstasy and delivered mainly absence. I was supposed to be the child of the commune, not of my mother ... In the communes that bore Bhagwan's name, she and her friends danced, rolled their heads, swayed their arms, beat cushions, broke down their social conditioning and set themselves free. Meanwhile, we children filled our lives as best we could with the things we found around us.

I filled the space with my imagination ... By chance, I had uncovered the purpose of the imagination: to conquer absence. Our dreams give us a lens through which to examine what we lack – just as virtual worlds do.

In 2004, he wrote a short personal essay for the *New York Times* magazine about his fear of commitment, his desire to marry and his deep resistance to taking this step and particularly to having children. His girlfriend of five years is keen for them to buy a house, and she wants to start a family. He knows that his resistance has everything to do with his own suffering as a child of the Bhagwan's communes, and some sort of fear that his own children might suffer. He ends on a tentatively optimistic note, deciding to go ahead with the house and to try to leave his childhood behind: 'Maybe it's time to let go of my grievances, to grow up, to give some new little person a chance to be young.' In fact he got married in October 2008, to a woman he met at the Notting Hill carnival in 2006. Ten months after the wedding, his new wife found him dead in bed, at the age of thirty-four. The first obituaries reported an unexplained death, with suggestions that the cause was a heart attack or a stroke. In an essay in the *Observer* in March the following year, Elizabeth Day tells the full story – of his early life, his recovery through writing, his periods of drink and drug-taking, and his eventual marriage. He died of an overdose of morphine. Day speaks to his family and friends and his wife Jo, and concludes that although this was almost certainly not a suicide 'it seemed none the less as if his commune experience had cast a long shadow and he was never entirely sure whether to embrace its legacy or try to escape it'.

I am touched by the fact that this lovely writer (and, by all accounts, lovely person) has a connection, before his troubles really began, with a moment in my own life. The moment before orange.

What is a complementary colour? The combination of the two other primaries (so here, red plus yellow as complementary to blue). Or (the Newtonian version), the colour which, combined with its primary, makes white in coloured light, grey in coloured paint. Or, on the colour circle we have employed since the seventeenth century, the colour directly opposite its primary. Or, the colour of the after-image through closed eyes after staring at its primary. One might think that a primary and its complementary constitute a colour clash to be avoided. But many artists have realised that they may enhance one another when placed together – Delacroix, the Impressionists, van Gogh. According to John Gage, 'throughout the nineteenth century complementary contrast was widely regarded as the most harmonious because it constituted a union of all three primary colours'. I suppose what goes for fashion advice simply doesn't apply in the same way in aesthetic, and technical, decisions about painting. But my prejudice against orange, from my blue vantage point, apparently needs a bit more thought. A quick internet search turns up a range of companies, mostly in the design and technology industries, which capitalise on the combination of opposites: BlueOrange software consulting, Blue Orange Signs, Blueorange web technologies, Blueorange IT, Blue Orange Marketing, as well as a Blue Orange theatre (and a play, by Joe Penhall, called *Blue/Orange*, about race and mental illness, in which a patient maintains that oranges are blue). It seems that the clash is seen as productive and dynamic, just as the juxtaposition may be striking and beautiful in a work of art.

It may, on the other hand, turn into the grey that is the unavoidable blur when juxtaposition becomes total merger. As David Bomford and Ashok Roy record, Michel-Eugène Chevreul, director of dyeing at the Gobelins tapestry workshop in the mid-nineteenth century, promoted the use of complementary colours, but 'warned that colours that mutually enhance each other can also cancel each other out if too intimately mixed: as an example, he wrote of threads in a tapestry that would appear merely grey if adjacent complementaries were too closely woven'. This became a problem in Seurat's pointillist technique, where 'uncalculated greyness' surrounded the points of colour in some paintings. But here I want to put in a word for greyness, calculated or otherwise. In the field of art, the case is made by Gerhard Richter:

Vincent van Gogh,
Van Gogh's Chair, 1888

> [Grey] makes no statement whatever ... it evokes neither feelings nor associations; it is really neither visible nor invisible. Its inconspicuousness gives it the capacity to mediate, to make visible in a positively illusionistic way, like a photograph. To me, grey is the welcome and only possible equivalent for indifference, non-commitment, absence of opinion, absence of shape.

In his grisaille paintings, often blurry as well as monochrome, this 'absence of opinion' compels our own reflections, whether they are the series of works about the Baader-Meinhof group or the painting based on a photograph of an aunt of his, a schizophrenic killed in a euthanasia camp by the Nazis. There is a certain moral imperative in the way in which refusal of colour presents us with the image. The 'indifference' of the image evokes quite the opposite, I think, in the viewer, namely the insistence that we think for ourselves.

Gerhard Richter,
Tante Marianne, 1965

Gerhard Richter, *Abstract
Painting* (Grey), 2002

Colour (mainly blue)

Now that I have navigated the threat of orange by merging it with blue, the grey I am left with is a colour with which I have a great affinity. (As it happens, though this is incidental, there are also three shades of grey in my CMB personal colour guide.) That 'capacity to mediate' which Richter alludes to is very compelling, and if we substitute 'uncertainty' for 'indifference' then I feel sure this describes an important lifelong value of mine, though one I have only recently come to recognise, articulate and defend. My last book was called *The Aesthetics of Uncertainty*, and its project was to refuse certainties – especially uncritical, unconsidered certainties – in favour of an aesthetics (and an ethics) willing to start from a position of not-knowing. The open-minded negotiation of meaning and of value, in dialogue with others and with other points-of-view, is for me a particularly attractive feature of some contemporary political and theoretical trends. So if grey stands for that – one could say the avoidance of colour, the mediation of black and white keeping things fluid and not quite certain – it is an appropriate metaphor. But this is not about avoiding responsibility, nor is it a kind of postmodern relativism. Rather (to stay with the colour model) the image, confronting us in grey and perhaps also blurred, makes us think differently about its moral and political content, as well as its nature *as* painting and representation – a familiar avant-garde strategy. When I think about it, too, my academic life over more than thirty-five years was always somewhere between disciplines – sociology, cultural studies, art history, aesthetics – and institutionally nearly always in an interdisciplinary unit or project. A scholarly dilettantism (shared with many colleagues and friends over the years – that has been the trend in our corner of the humanities and the social sciences) which is another crucial kind of uncertainty. Grey Studies, maybe.

Primo Levi's concept of the 'grey zone' of moral behaviour is not unrelated to this project of principled negotiation, though his subjects are acting out of what Lawrence Langer has called 'choiceless choices'. These are the Kapos and Sonderkommandos of the Nazi concentration camps, many of them Jews and all of them prisoners, who operated as functionaries and thus, in a sense, as collaborators, helping to run the camps. He writes at length too about Chaim Rumkowski, elder of the ghetto of Lodz, who mediated between the Gestapo and the inhabitants of the ghetto. Levi identifies a hierarchy of collaboration, from 'those whose concurrence in the guilt was minimal and for whom coercion was of the highest degree' to those who took more powerful roles and, at the extreme, those who performed them willingly and with cruelty. But he refuses to condemn any of them. 'How would each of us behave if driven by necessity and at the same time lured by seduction?' he asks. This impossible situation constitutes the grey zone:

> The harsher the oppression, the more widespread among the oppressed is the willingness, with all its infinite nuances and motivations, to collaborate: terror, ideological seduction, servile imitation of the victor, myopic desire for any power whatsoever, even though ridiculously circumscribed in space and time, cowardice, and, finally, lucid calculation aimed at eluding the imposed orders and order. All these motives, singly or combined, have come into play in the creation of this gray zone, whose components are bonded together by the wish to preserve and consolidate established privilege vis-à-vis those without privilege.

Levi included himself among those in the grey zone, exploring his residual feelings of guilt in an essay on shame. Still, he is less concerned to identify and judge levels of collaboration than to insist on the recognition of circumstances of confusion and ambiguity. Scholars of the Holocaust have since shown how many 'grey zone' areas there were outside the camp and the ghetto – in industry, in the church, in the French detention centres, even in the area of postwar Holocaust restitution. The Holocaust is always the extreme case taken in discussions of ethics and morality, not always usefully if it is intended as a generic example. But I do think that the concept of the grey zone, somewhat downgraded from its stark and terrifying existence in Primo Levi's experience, memory and testimony, is one we should retain, as an injunction against simplistic and unconsidered judgement.

I don't think any of this is disloyal to blue. After all, as Philip Ball tells us, in Classical literature the distinction between grey and blue was not at all clear. Blue was not then recognised as a colour in its own right, and was considered a colour related to black – 'a kind of grey'.

When I was thirteen, my life changed from black and white to technicolour. This, though obviously metaphorical, at some level feels literally true. We moved house that year (1956), from a semi-detached house in north Manchester to a larger, detached house in south Manchester, and my memories of the earlier period seem to have no colour in them at all. Certainly the house was darker and gloomier. The new house had bigger rooms, more windows and a larger garden, and it was in an area with many more trees. I had also recently moved from an inner-city lower-middle-class/working-class primary school to a solidly middle-class direct-grant girls' high school, which in retrospect also somehow feels like a lightening, and a coming-into-colour.

Class photograph, Temple primary school, Cheetham Hill, Manchester, c. 1951

Class photograph, Manchester High School for Girls, 1955.

Austerity baby

There is of course one obvious explanation for this chromaticising of my
memory. Colour photography was newly available at this time. When
I look through our old family photo albums, everything is black and
white – in fact right through into the early 1960s. And then, around
1956, the occasional colour photo turns up. Here is one of my sisters
and me, inexplicably inserted among pages of black-and-white photos,
dated 1956 on the back.

The effect is something like the 1998 film *Pleasantville*, in which a teenage
brother and sister are transported through their television set into
the black-and-white world of a 1950s sitcom, a world which gradually
takes on touches of colour as its inhabitants discover emotions,
freedom from rigid social conventions, and sexual liberation. I mean
the surprising – and at first – fleeting appearance of colour in my black-
and-white world. And as with the movie, I suppose I am talking about a
kind of liberation, which colour seems to connote.

Author with her sisters,
1956

At the cinema too we were now seeing more films in colour. Although
Technicolor itself dates from the 1920s and 1930s, and home movies
had used colour film for a while, it was only in the 1950s that colour
film became widespread, after a successful 1950 anti-trust case against
Technicolor and the simultaneous development of lower-cost colour
film. Eastman Color was crucial here, and so twenty years after his
death, and still forty years before I came to his city, where I lived for ten
years, George Eastman of Rochester, New York, already figured in my
life. Steve Neale has traced the history of Technicolor:

> In fact, the value of colour to the film industry fluctuated during the
> 1950s and 1960s as the relationship of the industry to television, and
> as the importance of colour within television, themselves shifted and
> changed. The use of colour in film production increased steadily from
> 1935 to 1955, accelerating in particular during the early 1950s until
> colour films comprised some 50 per cent of total US output ... It was
> only during the mid-1960s, when television had converted to colour,
> that the use of colour in the cinema became virtually universal.

We know very well that a switch to colour within a film (*The Wizard of
Oz* is the obvious example) can signify transition into a fantasy world,
or at least a different world. In Wim Wenders's *Wings of Desire* the
coming-into-colour signifies the angels' full immersion in the 'real'
world of everyday life. So the effect of adjusting from black-and-white
films to the new colour cinema must have been something similar.
In a context in which reality has been conventionally represented in
black and white, the introduction of colour was bound to register a
kind of exotic shift. The history of colour cinema and its technologies
is a fairly new, and fast expanding, field in film studies, but I haven't

found anything yet that discusses the particular effects on audiences of that moment of relearning how 'the real' may be represented. (These days we tend to consider black-and-white footage, whether documentary or fictional, as 'authentic' in a certain way.) Of course what I am really interested in here is the reverse effect: the possibility that the immersion in cinematic colour has transformational power in our everyday lives and, more particularly, our memories. My strong suspicion is that my idea that the world became colourful in 1956 was mediated by a visual imagination radically reorganised by photographs and the movies. The introduction of colour television in Britain in 1967 no doubt reinforced the effect.

I think there is another, more personal, factor in my emergence into Technicolor. Just before we moved house in 1956, my grandmother, my father's mother, had moved into a retirement home. She had lived with my parents since their marriage, and therefore with me for my whole life. Widowed within six months of her arrival as a refugee from Germany in 1939, far from any members of her family apart from her son, she did not have many options. In our very discreet and calm household – no fights or arguments, no strong emotions, certainly no mention of unpleasant things – this all seemed like a 'normal' arrangement. I didn't even consider, until much later, that this may have been a rather ghastly situation for both my mother and my grandmother. I also had absolutely no knowledge then of the probable cause of my grandmother's sadness – the loss of many family members, including her sister Leonie, in the Holocaust. Now I am absolutely sure that the new 'lightness' (colour) after the move was very much to do with a general sense of release – not just the absence of my grandmother (who was, it is true, a rather dark and brooding presence, and always dressed in dark colours) but more particularly the lifting of my mother's depression. After sixteen years of marriage, she was living with just her husband and daughters – including a new baby girl, born in November 1954. I think I am right that from the age of thirteen I was no longer living in black and white.

The Oranienburg company outside Berlin, where my father worked before emigration, was the twentieth-century descendant of one started by the chemist Friedlieb Ferdinand Runge, mentioned briefly in my father's short memoir:

A famous German chemist called Runge worked here on the same premises where later a chemical works was built. He was a distinguished scientist of the early 19th century, who discovered a large number of basic chemicals, among them phenol, aniline and atropin. He also discovered caffeine from a box of coffee beans which Goethe gave him as a curiosity. In 1832 he started a chemical company producing the first candles from stearin. This firm, after a number of name changes, became the Oranienburger Chemische Fabrik, ORACEFA or OCF for short, the company for which I worked. The house in which Runge had lived and worked was a well-preserved museum piece on the premises of the company, which was always very proud of its historical background.

Friedlieb Ferdinand Runge
(1794–1867)

Birthplace of F.F. Runge

As I have discovered more recently, in connection with my developing interest in Manchester's history in textile production, Runge was the first to produce synthetic blue, the product of his researches on coal tar in 1833. He named it 'cyanol', blue oil. Its other name, given by a researcher in 1841 who had produced the same substance by treating indigo with caustic potash, was aniline. This was the beginning of the aniline dye industry, so crucial in textile production through the nineteenth century. The person generally credited with the discovery of aniline dyes is William Perkin, who in 1856, at the age of eighteen, produced, in the course of his experiments with coal-tar aniline, the first usable synthetic colour – mauve. After this, the possibilities of synthetic colour expanded, and the new colours multiplied. They were enthusiastically taken up by the thriving textile industry. Perkin went on to discover and market other dyes, and received many honours, including a knighthood. He retired a very wealthy man. But Runge, with one or two other earlier researchers, is there in the background, as Simon Garfield relates:

By the time Perkin found mauve, aniline had been linked with colorants and colour-producing reactions for thirty years. The liquid had first been discovered by the Prussian chemist Otto Unverdorben in 1826, one of several products isolated from the distillation of natural vegetable indigo. Some years later the chemist Friedlieb Runge obtained it from the distillation of coal-tar, and found it gave a blue colour when combined with chloride of lime. But such colours were considered to have no practical use.

Colours, especially blues, had been synthesised artificially for many years – millennia, in fact. Egyptian blue was in use before 2000 BC; according to Philip Ball, this was a blend of calcium oxide, copper oxide and silica. In the early eighteenth century, a scientist called Johann Jacob Diesbach, trying to make red paint, accidentally produced a new blue. This mixture, iron ferrocyanide, was named Prussian blue. Over a hundred years later, Prussian blue was to prove of great importance in Japan, where it was known as *berorin-ai*. Hokusai's iconic, and greatly influential, 1831 print *The Great Wave* uses three shades of Prussian blue for the water and indigo blue for the outlines and the text.

But what was radically new was the growing understanding of the structure and composition of the materials – in other words, the rise of the chemical industry. Later, other dyes were added to aniline dyes – alizarin (a red from the madder plant) and azo dyes. And through those nineteenth-century decades the traffic between Germany and England was particularly fascinating (a subject, of course, of personal interest to me, given my father's experiences a century later). The first great chemists were in Germany, and notably at Justus Liebig's laboratory at the University of Giessen. Simon Garfield quotes Liebig's own assessment of England's deficiencies in the early part of the century, speaking at the British Association meeting in 1837: 'England is not the land of science ... There is only widespread dilettantism, their chemists are ashamed to be known by that name because it has been assumed by the apothecaries, who are despised.' The establishment of the Royal College of Chemistry in London in 1845 was inspired by Liebig's lectures, whose fans included the prime minister, Robert Peel, 'who expressed personal interest due to his family's involvement in calico printing'. The first director of the College was August Wilhelm von Hofmann, who had studied in Giessen. By the 1860s German scientists were moving to England, and specifically to Manchester and its surrounds, employed by textile companies to develop their dyes. Hofmann predicted that England would become 'at no distant date ... the greatest colour producing country in the world'. Hofmann continued: 'nay, by the strangest of revolutions, she may, ere long, send her coal-derived blues to indigo-growing India, her tar-distilled crimson to cochineal-producing Mexico and her fossil substitutes for quercitron and safflower to China and Japan'. In fact this was already the case by the time he wrote this, in his report on the 1862 International Exhibition in London.

The story of blue ends, for now, in Manchester, which suits me very well. Some of the most important chemists lived and worked here in the mid- to late nineteenth century: Lyon Playfair, Frederick Crace-Calvert, Henry Edward Schunck, Heinrich Caro, Ivan Levinstein, Charles Dreyfus. Some started their employment in the textile industry, often brought over from the Continent by the calico printers or simply deciding to come because of the opportunities linked to the industry. Some started, or joined, laboratories in the new Owens College (later the University of Manchester). And some started their own chemical factories (Roberts, Dale and Co., Clayton Aniline, Levinstein & Sons). New colours were discovered and produced in Manchester,

Katsushika Hokusai, *Under the Wave off Kanagawa*, c. 1831

Colour (mainly blue)

Blue steps, Panarea, Aeolian Islands

Austerity baby

including Manchester Brown and Manchester Yellow in the 1860s. As R. Brightman put it in 1957, 'Manchester can fairly claim to be the home of the first attempts to synthesise new dyestuffs to meet the growing demands of the expanding textile industry for fresh supplies of colour, and speedier and simpler methods of applying them'. There are also, in these developments, some blues in Manchester, for example Ivan Levinstein's Blackley Blue of 1869–70. Robert Kargon records Crace-Calvert taking out patents in the 1860s for new colouring matters, including Azurine (blue) from aniline and its homologues.

In 1938, my father's belated departure from Germany was possible because of a new chemical company, Lankro Chemicals, founded in Manchester by another German-Jewish refugee. Heinz Kroch had known my father at university in Freiburg and gave him the job which enabled him to emigrate. It was not a company involved in work for textile production, but its very existence was due, I think, to the history of the chemical industry in Manchester.

I like the sound of Friedlieb Ferdinand Runge, of whom my father seemed so proud. Esther Leslie devotes quite a few pages to him in her fascinating book on nature, art and chemistry, *Synthetic Worlds*. As well as the famous discovery of aniline dye (and a reminder of the story about Goethe and the coffee beans) we learn he was criticised by Hegel, in his doctoral viva, for not theorising properly 'in a philosophical manner' (though he did pass the exam); that as a populariser of science he wrote manuals for many different trade groups, as well as a series of letters for housewives; that an acquaintance visited him and found him 'with hair in long curls hanging down to his shoulders ... with one hand he was filtering a precipitation, while the other was stirring a few potatoes, which were boiling over a chemical lamp'. He continued to do many experiments and make many discoveries in colour chemistry and he developed a notion that there is a 'drive to formation' (*Bildungstrieb*) – a sort of life-force – in chemicals, shown in the images which form when chemical solutions are dropped on to paper. These images he considered a 'painterly art', and he clearly took pleasure in their beauty at the same time as observing their structures and effects. The long-term effects of his 1833 discovery of cyanol were the guarantee of another kind of beauty – the deep blues of calico in Manchester, and of fabrics around the world.

Janet Ann.   25.3.43.

    Arrived a few days after schedule
at 6.10 am. Thursday. Very tiny,
ugly + thin – folds of skin without
any fat.   Weighed 6lbs. 14 ozs.
She improved rapidly however – or
maybe I just got more used to
her, but even so when we went
home (5/4/43) she wasn't very
beautiful.
    She gained weight very quickly
+ was soon looking very sweet
+ lovely – not only my opinion. On
the 25th April she gave her first
real smile (not wind) + smiled
quite frequently after that, but only
when she felt like, especially when
Arthur whistled.
    On the 25th May she was

Diary page, March 1943

Austerity baby

5: Austerity baby

I seem not to have made such a good impression when I arrived, at least not on my mother. She started keeping a baby diary on 5 July 1943, just over three months after I was born.

> Arrived a few days after schedule at 6.10 am Thursday. Very tiny, ugly and thin – folds of skin without any fat. Weighed 6lbs. 4ozs. She improved rapidly however – or maybe I just got more used to her, but even so when we went home (5/4/43) she wasn't very beautiful.

> She gained weight very quickly & was soon looking very sweet and lovely – not only my opinion …

> From starting off as a real Austerity baby, war time model, she soon became lovely and plump. She lost the long black hair she first had, and soon got over a moth eaten period, and got a fresh lot of black hair (Arthur suspects that it is really dark brown.)

Author as a baby

Even allowing for my family's style of humour, which often involves affectionate insult, I'm afraid I really was a bit of a disappointment. Even as I improved, she adds, on the next page, 'The only thing missing is the curl'. Judging by one rather startling photo of me as a baby, she tried to set my hair with curlers at least once to remedy that problem.

Luckily, I was learning to be Good, and learning very early.

> She does seem to be a good baby – soon got used to sleeping through the night, but used to yell regularly every evening until she found the pleasure of sucking her thumb, since when she has soothed herself to sleep. The main trouble is that if she is naughty & cries (it is wonderful that as soon as someone goes to her pram she stops crying and laughs) she seems very badtempered & sometimes can't catch her breath.

The diary records many details of feeding, bathing, weaning and teething, as well as the baby's interactions with various adults. First words at nine months. And how about this for verbal skills (not to mention sucking up to the grown-ups)? We were on holiday in Blackpool, June 1944, and I was fifteen months old.

> Janet behaved exceedingly well the whole time, settled down quickly & quite happy. First evening cried when put in cot, so I thought I would stay with her till she slept, but she wanted to play

Tuesday October 11th
I have got a teacher and she is very
very lovele her name is
miss macdonerld

Monday October 17th
esterday I went to Belvuw
and my frend and my sister wet
as well and we ser all the
animls we ser too elifnts
and for bares and liernes and
agrs and the snaks and
the muncies and the
zebrs

Tuesday sebember sevn
I ber not no Any tes to day

Pages of child's diary, 1949

Austerity baby

with me, so I left her and she yelled two minutes – no more – then settled off to sleep. Was delighted to find us in the same room in morning – stood up saying 'Mama dear how are you. Dada dear how are you, Mama dear, Dada dear' etc. till we had to take her in our bed – but when we screened her off it was all right.

In general, I think I have been all right when screened off. More importantly, I learned valuable lessons about approved behaviour. My school diary from 1949 (age six):

> I have got a teacher and she is very very lovele her name is miss macdonerld.

I didn't get a star for that entry, which should have taught me that flattery gets you nowhere. A couple of years later, at my second primary school when I was eight or nine, my school report from Mr Hurst says 'If I had a class full of Janets, what a wonderful class that would be'. I think my parents were very pleased with that one. It's many years ago, but I am pretty sure that underneath the pleasure at such praise and, even more, at my parents' approval, was an extremely faint, much suppressed, feeling of rebellion against this Compulsory Goodness. I wonder if I was rather envious when my sister's school report, at age eight, said 'Veronica is the biggest nuisance in the class!'

Occasionally there are signs of genuine enthusiasm in my diary, as on Monday 17 October after a day at the zoo:

> Yestrday I went to Belvuw and my frend and my sister went as well and we ser all the animls we ser too elifnts and for bares and liernes and tagrs and the snaks and the muncies and the zebrs

More usually, the entries are dutiful and, somehow, trying too hard to please. Sometimes it was just too much.

> **Tuesday September 27th**
>
> I do not no any nes today

Book plates in volumes I still have on my shelf testify to the continuation of a careful, obedient and dutiful childhood.

Half a century later it has become possible to understand something of the complex familial, social and psycho-dynamic aspects of what now seem, in retrospect, to be rather sad successes.

SCHOOL PRIZE FOR
PROGRESS
AWARDED TO
Janet Wolff
Upper IV alpha

a. M. Bozman.
HEADMISTRESS

CHAIRMAN OF THE
GOVERNORS

DATE July 1957

**MANCHESTER
HIGH SCHOOL FOR GIRLS**

MANCHEST
OF B
RELIG

PR

Prize bookplates

Austerity baby

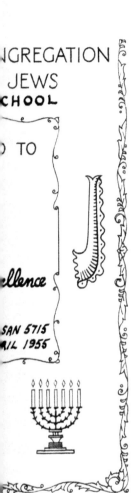

NGREGATION
JEWS
CHOOL

) TO

llence

SAN 5715
RIL 1955

MANCHESTER CONGREGATION
OF BRITISH JEWS

PRESENTED

TO

JANET WOLFF

For regular Sabbath
attendance.

P.Selvin Goldberg,
Rabbi.

Cyril Lever, P.Warden.

MOWBRAYS BOOKSHOP, MANCHESTER

The British journalist Anne Karpf, daughter of Holocaust survivors, has written movingly about her anxious childhood in London. Her parents came to England from Poland in 1947, each having lived through terrible events in the preceding years. Her mother, a concert pianist, was in Płaszów and Auschwitz camps – her first husband and other family members died during those years. Her father, who also lost close relatives, was held in camps in Russia for some time. Karpf's book, *The War After*, explores the ways in which her parents' history has affected her own life, in particular the 'primary ontological insecurity' she recognises on reading R.D. Laing and the (psycho)somatic disorders that plagued her from childhood – chronic sinusitis and severe eczema. Mary Cappello, an American writer and academic from an Italian immigrant background, tells a similar story, discussing the 'ways that we inherit the pain or deformation caused by the material or laboring conditions of our forbears' and linking her own chest pains to those of both her father and her grandfather. In her case, the inherited injury – actual and psychic – relates to the poverty and shame of earlier generations. For Anne Karpf – closer to home for me – a review of the psychoanalytic research on children of survivors makes sense of a good deal of her years of anxiety, her feeling that she had to protect her parents, her inability to separate from them (especially her mother) and the need to be good and do well in school. My father was a refugee, not a concentration camp survivor, but many of his relatives died in the Holocaust, including his mother's brother and sister and their spouses, and his father's two siblings, one with her husband. It seems very likely that the same disturbances pervaded our postwar lives. From some of the studies Karpf reviews:

The Holocaust, it was claimed, had become the unconscious organising principle for the second generation, shaping both their internal reality and interpersonal relationships.

The parents and children often develop extreme symbiotic ties; the parents don't encourage the child's autonomy, and experience the normal process of separation and individuation in their offspring as a threat and an acute narcissistic injury to the family.

[The] studies appeared to show that children of survivors left their parents' homes later than other young adults, and after they'd left remained in close contact with their parents.

Perhaps the first of these was true for me. I suspect the second may have been too. Certainly the third – I didn't leave home until I was twenty-two, and then only because my younger sister had left the year before, and so had already broken up the protected space. (At the same time, like Karpf herself, I find myself very ambivalent about, and quite resistant to, the notion of 'second-generation survivors', the idea of inherited trauma, and, especially, any idea of claiming 'victim' status by those – like me – who grew up in safe, comfortable and fairly privileged environments.)

Anne Karpf always had the feeling that it was her mission to take care of her parents, and to protect them from (mostly imagined) harm. 'Our parents depicted the world as so unsafe that we gathered it was best to lie low and hold back: if you avoided attracting attention, you might escape a backlash.' In this context, success at school operated as a kind of reassuring gift to her parents: 'From a very young age I knew that through achieving I could bring something very special to my parents. I took them my feats ... School and extracurricular success was something with which to nourish them, an infinite balm.'

And later too: 'As I got older my compulsion to repair didn't diminish. Just as I'd brought them my academic achievements at school, when I became a journalist I'd render them my articles. My accomplishments seemed earmarked, a direct debit to keep them well.' It is an interesting psycho-dynamic explanation of the anxious need to do well.

As Mary Cappello's three-generation story suggests, too, the history of damage may have a longer reach. Earlier Jewish immigrants to Manchester, fleeing the pogroms and other hardships in Eastern Europe, also passed on the habits of fear and suspicion, as illustrated in Howard Jacobson's comic novel of Anglo-Jewish life, *Coming from Behind*:

> It is pretty well established now that the Gestapo was never fully operational in Manchester in the 1950's. But that did not prevent Sefton Goldberg's early years from seeming every bit as fraught as Anne Frank's. The faintest rustle in the porch used to be enough to throw the Goldberg household into scenes of such unforgettably terrifying confusion that even now, whenever his doorbell rang, Sefton Goldberg wanted to throw himself under a table and wait with thumping heart, just as he did then, for his mother to peer through infinitesimally parted curtains at the retreating back of the milkman or someone collecting for the NSPCC and assure him that the coast was clear.

This north Manchester family, none of them refugees from Nazism but, one presumes, second-generation East Europeans, reconfigures its fear into the most recent genocidal threat. Another fictional Jewish mother from north Manchester, created by Maisie Mosco in her *Almonds and Raisins* trilogy, manifests the same generic suspicion of the outside world.

'Oy,' Mr. Greenberg sighed, wrapping the haddock in a week-old *Yiddish Gazette* from the pile of discarded newspapers his customers saved for him. 'You remind me of my wife, Mrs. Lipkin. She won't let me have the wireless on loud, in case it disturbs our Christian neighbours. It wouldn't matter if we lived next door to *Yidden*, she always says.' He smiled wryly. 'All these years our people have been in England and we're still trying not to offend anyone.'

❧❧❧

Cheetham Hill, a mile and a half north of Manchester city centre, has long been a multi-ethnic community. Today its population includes South Asian, East Asian, African, Caribbean and Eastern European communities. At the beginning of the nineteenth century, Cheetham was a separate township from Manchester, amalgamated into the Borough of Manchester in 1838, and becoming part of the north Manchester township in 1896. From the 1830s, wealthy merchants, bankers and manufacturers began to build homes in Cheetham Hill, an area protected by its elevation from the pollution of industry. As Bill Williams, historian of Manchester Jewry, records, this included Dutch and German Jewish merchants, who had come to England in connection with the textile industry. 'By the Census of 1841, at least seventy-six Jewish persons were engaged in the Manchester cotton trade – forty-six as merchants, or perhaps commission agents, and twenty as commercial clerks.' The area in those years, according to one source, was 'a pleasant and genteel place in which to live'. It had been largely rural, local occupations being primarily smallholdings and cottage industries associated with textile production. As Manchester and its surrounding region were transformed by the industrial revolution, this particular area remained, for a time, protected from the worst effects, as Monty Dobkin's history of Broughton and Cheetham Hill records:

Manchester soon became very populous: people left the villages, seeking work, and then Irish immigrants flooded in as cheap labour. But Broughton, Cheetham Hill and Prestwich were very little affected by this aspect of the Industrial Revolution, as these areas had been chosen by the Manchester merchants for their country homes. They joined the landed gentry by purchasing large estates and building spacious mansions in private parks, yet they were within driving distance of their warehouses and factories. As these areas lacked many of the facilities which had attracted the first factories, they were kept free of industry and of other great changes, so preserving the way of life which the merchants and landowners wanted for their own enjoyment. Thus the early character of these districts as residential suburbs was established.

In the second half of the century this changed radically as building progressed – public buildings like the Cheetham Town Hall of 1853–55 (now the Saffron Eastern Cuisine restaurant), family houses and artisans' homes. Strangeways and Red Bank, areas adjacent to Cheetham, and on the outskirts of the city centre, were developed as industrial sites, with growing numbers of workshops and factories established. When Jews from Eastern Europe began to arrive in large numbers in the late nineteenth century, they settled in these areas, setting up small businesses as tailors, merchants, cabinet makers, jewellers, glaziers and waterproof makers. Typically they lived near their business premises. Within a generation, a move further north into Cheetham Hill, or neighbouring Broughton, and at a distance from the workplace, represented notable success. By then Cheetham Hill was no longer the elegant preserve of a wealthy elite it had been before 1850.

This geographical upward mobility features too in Maisie Mosco's trilogy, which traces two immigrant families through three generations. David Sandberg, born in 1897 and a child when his family comes to Manchester from Russia, has done well in the tailoring business, and in the early 1920s moves the short distance north with his wife.

The house he and Bessie had chosen for their home ... was pleasantly situated near the Bellott Street park, in Cheetham Hill. No factories darkened the skyline here. The park was minute, but its greenness heaven to behold and the terraced houses were set back from the street, each in its own patch of garden. Cheetham Hill was the new ghetto, but apart from its predominantly Jewish residents bore no resemblance to the grey vista of Strangeways. To David it was the first rung of the ladder he had set out to climb.

On the marriage certificate – 4 March 1914 – of my grandparents, the address of my grandmother, Rebecca Gertler, is given as 3 Bellott Street. She married Maurice Noar, my grandfather, who five years earlier had waited to meet his American cousin, Henry Norr, at the station. His address is given as 107 Bignor Street, also in Cheetham.

In the fictional world, David Sandberg's prediction proves correct. Cheetham Hill is indeed the 'first rung of the ladder'. By 1943, David and his brother, with their families, are living in Prestwich, near Bury Old Road (David with aspirations one day to move to Alderley Edge in Cheshire). His story illustrates the development of the Jewish communities of Crumpsall, Prestwich and Broughton Park by mid-century. In a parallel narrative of mobility, Howard Spring's fabulous creation of 1934, Rachel Rosing, devotes her life to escaping her origins in Cheetham Hill, through seduction and marriage. Later, on the spur of the moment, she decides to board a tram to Cheetham Hill.

Why not once more? ... Probably, she thought, I shall never see
Cheetham Hill again if I don't see it to-night ... She clambered to a
top deck. The tram was full; the windows were all shut. Every seat
was occupied. In almost every mouth was a pipe or cigarette. The
atmosphere was stinking and the windows were opaque with the
condensed breath of the travellers ... To Rachel, after even so short
an absence, it seemed odious and brutal. These trams were galleys,
bringing slaves to and from their chains.

She alights at Derby Street.

She turned to the left when she came to the street where for so long
she had lived. It stretched before her in all its dreadful blank inanity.
Save for the street lamps that burned here and there, the darkness
was almost without relief. Behind a cheap curtain from time to time
she saw a dim light burning. For the most part, she knew, the people
lived in their kitchens at the back. She thought of the kitchen in which
she herself had made shift to live. She walked the entire length of the
street with the thought of it in her heart like the memory of a foul
disease from which she had incredibly escaped. Then she walked back
again and came to a halt outside the familiar door. She looked at it,
fascinated, allowing her hatred to consume her.

Her particular loathing of her place of origin is also felt (though they don't
discuss it) by the wealthy owner of a chain of tea-shops she entices
into marriage, Maurice Bannerman (once called Morris Fahnemann),
who recalls 'how he loathed the squalor of Cheetham Hill'. But earlier
– and perhaps for my great-grandparents by 1914 – Bellott Street in
Cheetham Hill must have seemed such an elegant address after the
early immigrant years in Strangeways.

Five years after my own parents' marriage in February 1940, they moved
(with me, aged two) from Cheetham Hill to Bury Old Road – again that
short but crucial distance to the north. We lived there until I was thirteen.
My mother's parents lived in the same street, six houses away. My father's
mother lived with us. Two of my mother's three brothers lived nearby.
My grandfather's many brothers and sisters, and their children, were
also in north Manchester, as were my grandmother's two unmarried
sisters, until they moved to Blackpool later, and several of her cousins.
A lot of family, and with one exception all of it on my mother's side.

It occurs to me that the narrative of internalisation of anxiety, made
manifest in obedience and achievement, as Anne Karpf so convincingly
shows, must have predated me. I am sure there is a story to be told
about my mother's early years, her 'ghetto' experience and, in this

context, her relationship to her own mother, Rebecca Noar, née Gertler. I am quite persuaded by Alice Miller's account of the origins of the need for approval, achieved typically by the external measures of good behaviour and scholarly success. In *The Drama of the Gifted Child* (also published under the titles *The Drama of Being a Child* and *Prisoners of Childhood*), Miller traces this to the problematic relationship with a mother who is herself 'narcissistically deprived', and whose emotional insecurity translates into an inability to regard her child apart from his or her responses to her needs. The child will construct a 'false self', suppressing desires and emotions in favour of approved behaviour and achievements.

> With two exceptions, the mothers of all my patients had a narcissistic disturbance, were extremely insecure, and often suffered from depression. The child, an only one or often the first-born, was the narcissistically cathected object. What these mothers had once failed to find in their own mothers they were able to find in their children: someone at their disposal who can be used as an echo, who can be controlled, is completely centered on them, will never desert them, and offers full attention and admiration. If the child's demands become too great (as once did those of her own mother), she is no longer so defenseless and will not allow herself to be tyrannized: she can bring the child up in such a way that he neither cries nor disturbs her. At last she can make sure that she receives consideration and respect.

The extremes of what Miller calls 'grandiosity and depression' which often characterise such patients, with the consequent risk of the collapse of self-esteem, are not my own experience. But what rings true is the compulsion to succeed, to do well, to find ways to sue for approval, perhaps in place of the kind of acceptance – independent of any achievements – that this kind of damaged mother is unable to provide. When I consider my own mother's life now it becomes easier to understand the many strikes against the very possibility for her of emotional security and self-esteem. Overdetermined, once again, by the familial atmosphere of inherited anxiety and then, later, by a marriage invaded from the beginning by the constant presence of her alien mother-in-law, the scene was, I am sure, compounded and set by the family dynamic.

Rebecca (Becky) Gertler, born in Russia in 1890, died in Manchester the day before her ninety-first birthday, on 6 August 1981. Maurice Noar, whom she had married in 1914, had died on 27 February 1969, at the age of eighty-two. His profession is given variously on the documents:

Maurice and
Rebecca Noar

Jack, Ralph and
Rosabelle Noar

Rosabelle Noar

Austerity baby

as tailor on his marriage certificate (and 'tailor (master)' on my mother's birth certificate), then 'manager (textile factory) (retired)' on his death certificate, and 'commercial traveller (retired)' where he is named on my grandmother's death certificate. His father, Joseph Noar, had been a tailor in St Petersburg, making uniforms for the Czar's officers; his tailoring skills, we assume, gained him the residence permit to live in the city, outside the Pale of Settlement created in 1791 by Catherine the Great as the territory for Russian Jews. As already related in an earlier chapter, he emigrated to England in 1886 at the age of forty-six and settled in Manchester, accompanied by his oldest son and soon followed by his wife, Bella, and his six other children, including Maurice. At about the same time, his two brothers – Joshua and Jacob – emigrated to the United States, followed by their only sister, Lizzie, who had first gone to Manchester and then moved to the United States in about 1910. Jacob was the father of Henry Norr, with whom my narrative began.

I know less about my grandmother's history. It seems she was born in Bessarabia at the western edge of the Pale of Settlement and now part of Romania. There were rumours in the family that she was related to the artist Mark Gertler (one of the reasons I took an interest in his work and have written about him), but his family came to England from Galicia in the Austro-Hungarian Empire. In fact Gertler was born in London, in 1891, but the family returned to Galicia before he was one year old, returning to London, this time for good, in 1896. Probably the idea of a family connection is a myth. In any case, I recall reluctance even to discuss it, because of Mark Gertler's perceived bohemianism and his association with those immoral members of the Bloomsbury Group. By all accounts, my grandmother, who was quite beautiful, was rather spoiled, first by her parents, then by her two younger sisters, Mary and Rosie, and later by her husband. Although we were in and out of her house, a two-minute walk from our own, throughout my childhood, she was not really actively involved with her grandchildren, unlike Maurice, who often joined us on holidays in Blackpool or north Wales, turns up in many of the family photos and is mentioned in letters we wrote to our parents when they were away. My retrospective understanding (construction?) of her role as a mother is that she preferred her three sons to her daughter, Rosabelle. My mother, born in 1917, was the second child in the family of four – adored by her brothers but kept at a distance by Becky.

In what turns out to be a somewhat uncanny experience (a sort of *déjà vu* in retrospect), I read her school reports from Central Municipal High School for Girls in Manchester, age fifteen to seventeen. Lots of good marks (it seems that B was a high mark in those days – 1933–34). Plenty of complimentary, if bland, comments: good, very good, reliable, works well, continues to do good work, excellent. Interestingly, she got marks of eighty per cent or more for German, and I reflect now how that choice of subject – if it was a choice – would transform her life within five years . Higher education was out of the question for working-class and lower-middle-class children in the prewar period, especially for girls, and she went to work at Imperial Chemical Industries as a shorthand and copy typist in July 1934. This choice also turned out to be fortuitous, as it gave her the experience in the chemical industry which made her a good candidate when she applied to Lankro Chemicals, in December 1936, for the job of secretary to Heinz Kroch, a German refugee then establishing this new firm in Eccles. Her testimonial from ICI emphasises her work with technical reports, and adds 'She types German well', which must have been caught Dr Kroch's eye at the time.

> 'The Limes'
> Crescent Road
> Crumpsall
> Manchester 8
> 18 December 1936

The Advertiser,
E228,
Evening News.

Dear Sir,

I wish to apply for the position offered by you in tonight's "Evening News".

I am nearly twenty years of age, and have obtained my Matriculation Certificate, passing in German, French, English, History, Geography, Mathematics and Art.

I am an experienced shorthand typist and have a good knowledge of bookkeeping, filing and card index systems, general office routine, etcetera.

I enclose a copy of my testimonial from the Imperial Chemical Industries Limited, the temporary staff of which firm I joined in April 1934, and was made permanent there on 1st July 1934.

Should you consider my application and grant me an interview I could call upon you on any day between 1.0 p.m. and 2.0 p.m., when I should be pleased to furnish any further particulars you may require.

> Yours faithfully,
> (Miss) Rosabelle Noar.

Central High School report, Manchester, December 1933

Letter of reference, November 1936

IMPERIAL CHEMICAL INDUSTRIES LIMITED.

DYESTUFFS GROUP

(COMPRISING BRITISH DYESTUFFS CORPORATION LTD., THE BRITISH ALIZARINE CO. LTD., SCOTTISH DYES LTD., AND OLIVER WILKINS & CO. LTD.)

TELEPHONE:
CHEETHAM HILL 1460.

TELEGRAMS:
BRIDYCOR, MANCHESTER.

CODES:
A.B.C. (5TH & 6TH), LIEBERS,
BENTLEY'S, MARCONI,
INTERNATIONAL.

Reply to be addressed to
Imperial Chemical Industries Ltd.,
Dyestuffs Group.

Secretary's Department.

OUR REF. BAF/AS.

YOUR REF.

HEXAGON HOUSE,

BLACKLEY,

MANCHESTER, 9.

LETTERS TO P.O. BOX 42.

4th November, 1936.

TO WHOM IT MAY CONCERN.

    - Miss Rosabelle Noar has been in our service as Shorthand and Copy Typist from July 1934 up to this time. Her work has been mostly concerned with technical reports and general correspondence, and has given entire satisfaction. She types German well. Her ability and intelligence are of a high order, and we expected her soon to be promoted to a post of higher responsibility. We are sorry to lose her services.

IMPERIAL CHEMICAL INDUSTRIES LIMITED.
(DYESTUFFS GROUP).

For Secretary.

22/12/36
1·15 PM

"The Limes",
Crescent Road,
Crumpsall,
Manchester
18th December 19

The Advertiser,
E 228,
"Evening News".

Dear Sir,
I wish to apply for the position offered by you in to-night' "Evening News".

I am nearly twenty years of age, and have obtained my Matriculation certificate, passing in German, French, English, History, Geography, Mathematics and Ar

I am an experienced Shorthand typist and have a go knowledge of bookkeeping, filing and card index systems, general office routine, etcetera.

I enclose a copy of my testimonial from the Imperial

Job application, December 1936

Austerity baby

Chemical Industries Limited, the temporary staff of which firm, I joined in April 1934, and was made permanent there on 1st July 1934.

Should you consider my application and grant me an interview I could call upon you on any day between 1.0 p.m and 2.0 p.m, when I should be pleased to furnish any further particulars you may require.

Yours faithfully.

(Miss) Rosabelle Noor,

Bentcliffe Works
Salters Lane
Eccles/Lancs.
Febr.9th.37.

Miss Rosabel Noar
Limes
Crescent Road
Crumpsall
Manchester 8

Dear Miss Noar,

Referring to your phone-call yesterday I expect you
at 9 o'clock at the worksoffice on Monday, the 15th instant.
I confirm your salary will be 50.-shillings the week
and I shall pay in addition half the amount for the Health-Insurance
and the Unemployment-Insurance.

Yours faithfully,

F. Heinz Kroch

קול ששון וקול שמחה קול חתן וקול כלה

Mr. & Mrs. Maurice Noar
request the pleasure of the company of

at the marriage of their daughter

Rosabelle
to
Dr. Arthur Wolff

on Sunday, 11th February, 1940.
Ceremony at 3 o'clock.
Reception, 4 till 7 o'clock,
at the Higher Crumpsall Synagogue,
Bury Old Road, Manchester.

Bride's Address: Bridegroom's Address:
36, Park Road,   50, Snowden Road,
H. Crumpsall, Manchester 8.   Eccles, Manchester.

R.S.V.P. on or before February 1st, 1940.

Job appointment letter, February 1937

Wedding invitation, February 1940

Rosabelle and Arthur Wolff wedding photograph, February 1940

Austerity baby

Bentcliffe Works
Salters Lane
Eccles/Lancs.
Febr.9th.37.

Miss Rosabel Noar
Limes
Crescent Road
Crumpsall
Manchester 8.

Dear Miss Noar,

Referring to your phone-call yesterday I expect you at 9 o'clock at the worksoffice on Monday, the 15th instant.

I confirm your salary will be 50.- shillings the week and I shall pay in addition half the amount for the Health-Insurance and the Unemployment-Insurance.

Yours faithfully,
F. Heinz Kroch.

The following year, Kroch offered a job to Arthur Wolff, a young chemist desperate to leave Germany. In this way, my parents met. They married in February 1940. Three months later, my father was arrested as an 'enemy alien', and interned in the Isle of Man for a year, together with Heinz Kroch and other German refugees working at Lankro Chemicals. My mother, having lost her British citizenship on marrying an enemy alien, was granted leave to resume British nationality in October 1941 (in a document headed 'Certificate of Naturalisation granted to a woman who was at birth a British subject and is married to a subject of a State at war with His Majesty').

It's hard to imagine what the war years were like for my mother. I know she continued to work at Lankro until July 1942. Two of her brothers were in the army, and at some point saw active service, Ralph in India and Jack in Burma. Her new husband was safe, but interned for – as far as they knew – an indefinite period in May 1940. And wartime Manchester was itself an extremely unsafe place. At the start of the war, in 1939, over two hundred thousand children and young mothers had been evacuated to the countryside from Manchester, Salford and Stretford. Large surface shelters were built in Piccadilly Gardens and elsewhere in the city centre, and Anderson shelters were put up in many private gardens; by the end of October 1939, about 2,250,000 Andersons had been distributed nationally, free of charge. The heaviest bombing raids on Manchester occurred on 22 and 23 December 1940, mostly – but not only – in the city centre.

The devastation within a square mile of Albert Square had to be seen to be believed. No less than 165 warehouses, 150 offices, five banks and 200 other business premises had either been destroyed or sufficiently damaged to make them unusable until repairs had been carried out. A further 300 warehouses, 220 offices, twenty banks, and 500 other business premises had been damaged to a lesser degree. Manchester's death toll over the two days stood at 376 with many hundreds injured. 30,000 houses had been damaged, many extensively, and 5,049 people made homeless by the raids were distributed around twenty-eight Rest Centres.

In addition, 197 were killed in Salford and 106 in Stretford, with similar extensive damage to homes and other properties. Another heavy bombing raid occurred on 1 June 1941 in Manchester and Salford, when fourteen nurses at Salford Royal Infirmary were among those killed. A log of Manchester and District Air Raid Alerts for 1940–45 records many alerts in residential areas, including Chorlton, Didsbury and Sale, and actual bombs in Heaton Park, north Manchester (just beyond Cheetham Hill and Crumpsall), in September 1940. It records the bombing of Didsbury and Prestwich in October and November that year, though with no casualties, and continuing small bombing raids through 1942. In all, nearly 1,500 died in the greater Manchester area during the air raids of 1940 to 1942. And behind all this day-to-day anxiety about survival was the real threat of invasion after the fall of France – the motivation also behind the internment of aliens who posed no danger to the country. Virginia Nicholson, in her study of the lives of women during the Second World War, notes the devastating impact on morale of that critical moment:

The 'it couldn't happen to us' feeling had evaporated. The reality of fear is very evident in contemporary accounts, many of which suggest women reacting to events with a sense of utter impotence. 'Is it any good fighting? Is it any good living at all?' reflected one young diarist ... On that day Nella Last was listening to the radio too, in Barrow-in-Furness; the announcement left her close to breakdown as she felt all her courage and faith in the future ebb away ... The racking anguish left Nella hardly able to stand. She dragged herself to the medicine cupboard, got out some smelling salts, doused her neck and shoulders with cold water and howled like a child.

Compounding these difficulties were more practical ones. Rationing of food and clothing started in January 1940, of petrol a little earlier. Coal rationing began on 1 October 1939. Prices and taxes on goods went up, luxuries were out of the question. 'Silk stockings became a thing of the past for many women who were forced to resort to staining their legs with gravy browning.' My father returned in May 1941 to a real austerity Manchester. Less than two years later, I arrived – austerity baby, wartime model.

You don't come across the name Rosabelle very often. It's the title of a poem by Sir Walter Scott, published in 1805 – a sad tale of a lady who drowns in the Firth of Forth.

> O listen, listen, ladies gay!
> No haughty feat of arms I tell;
> Soft is the note, and sad the lay
> That mourns the lovely Rosabelle.

It is also the title of a poem written in 1846 by William Bell Scott. The spelling here is 'Rosabell' (close to Heinz Kroch's misspelling in his invitation to my mother for a job interview in 1937). William Bell Scott explains, 'I was persuaded to alter the name to Mary Anne, as more indicative of the humble rank of my heroine' – despite which, the poem is always published under its original name. This is more of a Victorian story, about an innocent country girl led astray in the city and lost to her youthful lover.

> Long he sat, few words were said,
> Though oft he fain would speak:
> 'Ah, have you news of Rosabell?'
> The mother cried at last,
> Her frail hand on his stalwart arm.
> And when he spoke, his words, alas,
> Were but an echo of her fears.

Following the usual nineteenth-century trajectory of this narrative, the last stanzas suggest an illegitimate baby and imminent death by drowning: 'And every lamp on every street / Shall light their wet feet down to death'. I am pretty sure that my grandparents were not inspired by either poem in naming my mother. It's possible that her name was a mistake on the part of the registrar, who combined her first and second names into one (Rosa and Bella). Certainly her Hebrew name (required for synagogue purposes and reproduced on her wedding certificate) was Raisie Baille, and according to Jewish custom at least one of these names would have been after a deceased family member – probably her paternal grandmother, Bella. Her English birth certificate has Rosabella. She was always known as Rosabelle.

And yet there is a link – rather fanciful, perhaps – with the William Bell Scott poem, which I relate to my mother via a painting by the Pre-

Dante Gabriel Rossetti, *Found*, begun 1859

Austerity baby

Raphaelite artist Dante Gabriel Rossetti. It is an unfinished work, entitled *Found*, begun in 1859 and now in the Delaware Art Museum.

Rossetti returned to the painting a number of times, still adding new details in 1881, the year before his death. There are early sketches for it – an 1853 drawing, now in the British Museum, another pen and ink drawing of 1855, now in the Birmingham City Museum and Art Gallery, a detail study (of the woman's head) of 1856–61, also in the Birmingham Gallery, and a small oil version, begun in 1853, now in the Tullie House Museum and Art Gallery in Carlisle. This early painting was promised to Rossetti's patron, the Belfast shipowner Francis McCracken. It was left radically incomplete, with only the wall, the calf and cart, and the head of the woman painted. The whole middle section and lower right quadrant are blank. In 1859 the work was recommissioned by James Leathart (for 350 guineas), at which point Rossetti added the head to the Carlisle version and (probably) transferred all completed elements to the larger canvas now in Delaware. After a long break, the commission was abandoned in 1867, to be revived in 1869 with a new patron – William Graham – who recommissioned the painting for £800. Rossetti enlarged the canvas by adding a central strip and including the figure of the man. After sporadic attempts to work on the painting in the 1870s, Rossetti finished the figures in 1881. The background remained incomplete. Graham's estate sold the work in 1886, and in 1892 it was sold again, to Samuel Bancroft, a textile mill owner from Delaware. It was donated to the Delaware Art Museum from Bancroft's estate in 1935, with the rest of his substantial Pre-Raphaelite collection.

The painting is unique among Rossetti's works in its focus on a contemporary theme. He is best known for his symbolic and mythological works: medieval revivalist scenes (*Dante's Dream at the Time of the Death of Beatrice*, now in the Walker Art Gallery, Liverpool, *The Girlhood of Mary Virgin*, Tate Britain) and the later idealised portraits of women (*Beata Beatrix*, Tate Britain, *Lady Lilith*, Delaware Art Museum, *Astarte Syriaca*, Manchester City Art Gallery). And yet, as several commentators have pointed out, *Found* is the only work of his to follow the guiding principles of the Pre-Raphaelite Brotherhood, which Rossetti founded in 1848 together with William Holman Hunt and John Everett Millais, namely close attention to nature and realistic representation, returning to ideas and techniques which predated the high Renaissance. For Millais and Hunt, the PRB doctrine also meant engaging with modern moral issues. It has been suggested that Rossetti's lack of art training contributed to his avoidance of contemporary scenes, and that the difficulty he continued to find in dealing with perspective and placement in *Found* may explain his inability to complete it. And yet Rossetti's passionate interest in the theme, and his long-standing fascination with its personal and moral story, is attested to in letters to his family and to others, as well as in the compulsion to return to the painting over a period of nearly thirty years. The fact that the model for the woman's face, first introduced in the Carlisle oil sketch, was his mistress Fanny Cornforth, whom he had met in 1858, compounded the personal aspect of the theme. Like the woman portrayed in *Found*, Fanny Cornforth was a country girl who had turned to prostitution in the city.

The girl is also Rosabell(e). Rossetti was very taken with William Bell Scott's poem, the story of the country girl gone astray. It seems he tried, unsuccessfully, to persuade Scott to change his poem to include a scene in which her childhood sweetheart finds her again in the city, in her degraded state. This was in 1853, when Rossetti visited Scott in Newcastle. He himself had written a poem of epic length on the theme, entitled *Jenny*, in 1847–48 (published in 1870 and then in a later edition in 1881).

> Jenny, you know the city now.
> A child can tell the tale there, how
> Some things which are not yet enroll'd
> In market-lists are bought and sold
> Even till the early Sunday light,
> When Saturday night is market-night
> Everywhere, be it dry or wet,
> And market-night in the Haymarket.
> Our learned London children know,
> Poor Jenny, all your pride and woe;
> Have seen your lifted silken skirt
> Advertise dainties through the dirt;
> Have seen your coach-wheels splash rebuke
> On virtue ...

Jenny did not encounter her lost early love either, any more than Rosabell does in Scott's poem, though in a sonnet Rossetti composed to accompany *Found* in 1881 the encounter does take place. The poem concludes:

> Ah! gave not these two hearts their mutual pledge,
> Under one mantle sheltered 'neath the hedge
> In gloaming courtship? And O God! To-day
> He only knows he holds her; – but what part
> Can life now take? She cries in her locked heart, –
> 'Leave me – I do not know you – go away!'

William Holman Hunt, *The Awakening Conscience*, 1853

The theme of the 'fallen woman' is a familiar one in Victorian Britain, from Thomas Hardy's *Tess of the D'Urbervilles* and Elizabeth Gaskell's novel *Ruth* to the many paintings depicting the familiar narrative: innocence, seduction, prostitution and, finally, death by drowning. One of the best known of these paintings is Holman Hunt's *The Awakening Conscience* of 1853, shown at the Royal Academy in 1854 – a painting multiply coded to register both the sin and the moment of its recognition.

In a letter to Hunt, Rossetti is keen to point out that he had already taken up the theme before he saw Hunt's version, and his earlier exchanges with William Bell Scott support this. To Hunt he wrote in 1855: 'The subject had been sometime designed before you left England and will be thought, by anyone who sees it ... to follow in the wake of your "Awakened Conscience", but not by yourself, as you know I had long had in view subjects taking the same direction as my present one.' In Rossetti's version, the encounter between the fallen woman and the country boy is crucial. He describes it in the same letter to Hunt:

> The picture represents a London street at dawn, with the lamps still lighted along a bridge which forms the distant background. A drover has left his cart standing in the middle of the road (in which, i.e., the cart, stands baa-ing a calf tied on its way to market), and has run a little way after a girl who has passed him, wandering in the streets. He had just come up with her and she, recognizing him, has sunk under her shame upon her knees, against the wall of a raised churchyard in the foreground, while he stands holding her hands as he seized them, half in bewilderment and half guarding her from doing herself a hurt. These are the chief things in the picture which is to be called 'Found' and for which my sister Maria has found me a most lovely motto from Jeremiah: 'I remember Thee, the kindness of thy youth, the love of thine espousals'.

The theme is not one for our times – the morality archaic, the sentimentality outmoded, the melodrama anachronistic for the modern viewer. And, it is probably not necessary to point out, my mother was not a fallen woman. Yet I have always felt it was more than just the coincidence of the name that drew me to this work. The title itself – *Found* – presented itself to me as somehow symbolic of what I would have hoped for her, as if all the large and small injuries, of family, culture, gender, history, which rendered her 'lost' could perhaps be remedied. In the end, and especially retroactively, it is clear that this was an impossible task. And, of course, the painting, unlike Holman Hunt's version, is not a story of redemption at all. The 'finding' involved is tragic ('leave me ... go away'). It is with rather a leap of faith, and without Rossetti's permission, that we might write a happy ending for Jenny/Rosabell.

In a substantial and perceptive essay on the Rossetti painting, Nochlin concludes by reading across the grain to position the artist himself as 'fallen'. She points out that Rossetti made the analogy between being an artist and being a prostitute, in a letter to Ford Madox Brown in 1873: 'I have often said ... that to be an artist is just the same thing as to be a whore, as far as dependence on the whims and fancies of individuals is concerned'. A poet as well as a painter, he said more than once that he rated his poetry more highly than his painting. He came to feel that he was debasing himself and his talent, especially later in his life when he was obliged to produce replicas to increase his income. Nochlin's suggestion is that 'this sense of moral failure, of "selling out", or perhaps of "overselling", hangs over the troubled history of *Found* and at least in part accounts for its unfinished state'. She reads the painting, in the end, as 'less a key to Rossetti's ultimate feelings about sex, women, salvation, or the self than as evidence of the deep-seated conflicts and contradictions he experienced about all of them'. If she is right, that we might consider *Found*, in its themes and its problematic production history, as 'a document of unfulfilled aspirations', then I find it returns me to Rosabelle, to promising school reports and excellent job references, and to the rather sad reality of the forces – family dynamics, social pressures, historical events – that blocked their fulfilment. A minor local tragedy of mother (and daughter) in austerity times.

CAMPAIGNER
FAMILY ALLOWANCE
ELEANOR RATHBONE

56

Royal Mail stamp, 2008

Austerity baby

6: Tante Leonie

I had always assumed that my sister Eleanor was named after Eleanor Rathbone, to whom my father was always grateful for her role in support of refugees in Britain in 1940. Rathbone is best known for her long campaign for family allowances. A special issue Royal Mail stamp (56p) in her honour was issued in 2008, together with stamps for five other 'Women of Distinction', describing her as 'Campaigner, Family Allowance'.

It was a campaign that she pursued for many decades, beginning in 1917 and culminating in the Family Allowance Act of 1945, a year before her death. From her earliest years in politics, initially as a Liverpool City councillor from 1909 to 1935, she had taken up feminist causes, including women's suffrage, payments to seamen's wives, pensions for widows and, later, the situation of women and children in India. She was elected to Parliament in 1929 as one of the two MPs for the Combined English Universities (a two-member constituency added in 1918 to give representation to the new provincial universities and lasting until 1950), and was as dedicated and energetic a campaigner on the national level as she had been earlier in the north-west. Nancy Astor – the first woman in Parliament – commended Rathbone on her success in family allowance legislation: 'It is very difficult, when we look at the hon. Lady the Member for the English Universities, to think of her as a revolutionary, but she is, and it is her work, and her vision and courage, that have really brought us where we are to-day.' When Rathbone died, in January 1946, the *Manchester Guardian* wrote: 'No Parliamentary career has been more useful and fruitful'. Her work on behalf of refugees from Nazism, important though that was, is rarely highlighted in accounts of her life.

Leonie Kahn

It is just as likely, though, that my sister was named after my grandmother's sister, Leonie. Or perhaps it was a fortuitous double naming for her and for Eleanor Rathbone.

Leonie Kahn, née Schwarz, was born in Busenberg, in the Palatinate region of south-west Germany, on 30 August 1891. She was the youngest of the seven children of Sara Apfel and Jakob Schwarz.

Leonie had two older sisters – Rosa, born in 1872, and Bertha (my grandmother), born in 1874. Of her four brothers, two – Louis and Max – emigrated to the United States in the late nineteenth century. Their success in business in New York – and their continuing loyalty to family remaining in Germany – was to prove critical in the following decades. Max Schwarz was fourteen when he left Germany for the United States, eventually setting up a lace business. He funded my father's university education at Freiburg University in the 1920s; my grandfather, Josef Wolff, a cattle dealer in a small town in the Saar region, would not have had the resources to do so. After the National Socialists took power, Louis Schwarz sponsored the immigration of his nephew, Albert, to New York. Albert, the son of Max's and Louis's brother Alfred, arrived in New York in 1938 at the age of fifteen. He was the only one of his immediate family to survive the Holocaust. Louis's brother Max sponsored his niece, Eri – Leonie's only child – who arrived in New York on the USS *President Roosevelt* on 31 July 1937, at the age of twenty-four. She found work as a baby nurse for a family, and in 1940 married William Cohen, another refugee, known always as Willy. After the war, their last name was changed to Cole. I visited Eri and her family in Mahwah, New Jersey, in 1978. I knew nothing then of her torment in the early 1940s, as she tried to arrange for her mother, Leonie, to escape from Europe. For years, all I knew was that Leonie had died in the Holocaust, probably in Auschwitz. She was declared dead on 8 May 1945. With the help of Eri's daughter, Paulette, in Massachusetts, and my colleague Jean-Marc Dreyfus, scholar of the Holocaust, I have been able to discover more about those last months and years, and, in learning about her personal tragedy, have understood something of the terrible contingencies of life and death – and life or death – in Germany and occupied Europe during the war.

On 24 May 1912, Leonie married Sigmund Kahn from Offenburg in Baden, not far from her home in the Palatinate. They ran a dry goods store in Offenburg, at Hauptstrasse 85a. Eri, their only child, was born on 4 June 1913. This photo of the family also includes Leonie's mother, my great-grandmother, Sara Schwarz, on a visit to Offenburg in 1918.

These days there is a memorial stone – a Stolperstein – outside the shop in Leonie's name, another for Sigmund at their later address. The Stolpersteine, or 'stumbling stones', designed by Gunter Demnig, are commemorative brass plaques in the pavement outside the last known address of victims of the Holocaust. They are now in over six hundred towns in Germany, Austria and six other countries.

I know very little about Leonie's life in Offenburg, or about how their lives changed after the National Socialists came to power in January 1933.

Sara Schwarz,
Sigmund, Eri and
Leonie Kahn,
Offenburg 1918

Hauptstraße
85a, Offenburg,
September 2014

Memorial stone
for Leonie Kahn,
Offenburg

Tante Leonie

By 1937, they were at a different address (Hildastrasse 57a). On 10 November 1938, the day after Kristallnacht, Sigmund was arrested and sent to Dachau; he was released on the 22nd. By then, as my father records in his short memoir, it had become imperative for those family members still in Germany to try to leave. His parents decided to emigrate shortly after the attack on their home on Kristallnacht. They moved to Offenburg in March 1939, to stay with Leonie and her husband before emigration. This photograph was probably taken during those months. My grandparents are seated on the left; Sigmund standing on the left; Leonie seated furthest right. Also in the photo are the Kahns' friends, Fanny and Jakob Maier. Of this group of six people, only my grandparents survived the Holocaust.

My grandparents left for England in June 1939. (Once again, my father records his gratitude – to the British government for allowing entry to the refugees, and to the British Consul in Frankfurt, who 'deserves to be remembered for the kindness with which he treated my parents when he interviewed them'.) Leonie and Sigmund remained behind. My father had succeeded in getting visas for them to come to England as well as his parents. In a letter dated 25 March 1939 he tells them he has found a larger house to rent, which would accommodate them as well as his parents. He urges them not to delay their departure even for one further day. But in a letter of 18 June 1939 to their daughter Eri in New York Sigmund says that they will need three months to get ready. On 9 July he writes that their preparations are very slow, and they won't be able to leave before September. And then, I assume, the war intervened.

On 22 October 1940 Leonie and her husband were arrested, taken from their home and transported to the border with France. They were given a very short time to prepare, and were permitted to take very little luggage and just 100 Reichsmark each. From the border, they were taken by the French police to Gurs, an internment camp in the Basses-Pyrénées, in the far south-west of the country. They were among 6,538 Jews from Baden-Württemberg who, together with 1,125 from the neighbouring Saar and Palatinate regions, were expelled from Germany and sent into Vichy France. The Jews from Baden were sent to Gurs; the Saar and Palatinate Jews to the Rivesaltes camp, in the Pyrénées-Orientales. This deportation – the only one by the Nazi regime to the west, not the east – was the so-called Wagner-Bürckel-Aktion, after the two zealous Gauleiters (Nazi Party regional leaders) who engineered it. Robert Wagner was Gauleiter for Baden (and then also Alsace, after that region was annexed to the Third Reich in June 1940). Josef Bürckel had been responsible for organising the

Josef and Bertha Wolff, Sigmund Kahn, Fanny Maier,
Jakob Maier, Leonie Kahn, Offenburg (1939)

Tante Leonie

1935 plebiscite in the Saar, in which ninety per cent of the inhabitants voted to rejoin Germany. The Saar territory, taken from Germany after the First World War, was administered by the League of Nations for a fifteen-year term, which came to an end in 1935. By 1940, Bürckel was Gauleiter for the Palatinate, the Saar and (after June 1940) the newly annexed part of Lorraine. As a strategy in the regime's antisemitic policies, and before the first formulation sometime in autumn 1941 of the extermination aims of the 'final solution', the expulsion of German (as opposed to foreign) Jews was something new in October 1940, and Wagner and Bürckel, in this co-ordinated action across their regions, complied enthusiastically with Hitler's directive. Wagner wrote proudly to Berlin on 23 October: 'Baden is als erster Gau judenfrei' (Baden is the first district free of Jews). Known for his continuing activities on behalf of the regime as the 'butcher of Alsace', Wagner was tried in Strasbourg in 1946, and executed by firing squad. It is possible that Bürckel (who may have been responsible for the deportation of other relatives of my grandmother's, who had remained in the Palatinate when Leonie moved to Baden, or of my grandfather's in the Saar) would have met the same fate, except that he died in what seem to be mysterious circumstances on 28 September 1944. His death certificate records illness, but suicide, or murder by the SS, remain rumours about his demise.

After three days and nights, the Baden Jews reached Gurs, arriving on 25 October 1940. The train took them to the nearest station, at Oloron Sainte-Marie, from where they were taken in open trucks the ten miles to Gurs. Lisa Fittko, another refugee interned in Gurs in May and June of that year, records her first impressions, on getting off the train:

> The train stopped, doors were unlocked, we got off. There were trains on other tracks as far as one could see, and more arriving ... We walked over a narrow bridge. Basque farmwives stood on both sides, their hostile eyes staring at us. Scrawny, malevolent features atop columnar forms, clad in black from chin to ankle. They spat wordlessly and threw stones at us ... Beyond the bridge the spitting and the stone throwing ceased. Trucks were waiting for us. We drove down a long road, and then we saw the endless extent of the camp – the bare, bleak earth and the barracks.

The camp had been established in 1939 to accommodate Republican refugees from Spain after Franco's victory. In May 1940 the French government also interned so-called 'undesirables' there – ordinary prisoners and citizens of enemy countries. After the armistice between

France and Germany the following month, many of these prisoners were released or transferred, and control of the camp was handed over from military to civil command. Just over three thousand people were interned there by the time the Baden Jews arrived in October. As Claude Laharie records, the population of the camp tripled overnight at that point, to a total of 9,847. Conditions at Gurs were dire, and during the winter of 1940 to 1941 were at their worst. Susan Zuccotti quotes the president of the Jewish community of Mannheim, writing after the war to describe his group's arrival:

> Soaked by the rain, shivering with cold, exhausted by the long voyage, the flock was pushed in indescribable disorder into empty barracks, without benches, without straw, without mattresses. Collapsed against their bundles, many old people spent the night. Barracks 25 meters long and 5 meters wide … would shelter, during the long months ahead, 75 women or 80 men, according to the haphazard distribution of that first night.

Another survivor, quoted by Ruth Schwertfeger, gives her first impression of the camp:

> There it lay, all gloomy, with the individual îlots [blocks] separated from one another by three-tiered barbed wire. No bushes, no trees, only a few tufts of grass growing in the heavy soil that had been transformed into a sea of mud after days of rain. Men were separated from women and children and housed in separate îlots. About 60–80 people were crammed into one barrack, body against body. We stored whatever meager goods we had at our head where we slept. After a few days we were able to fill straw sacks for sleeping bags which seemed like a luxury to us … It simply didn't stop raining. The mud became a huge problem for us.

The barracks were extremely primitive; food rations were barely enough; the internees had to contend with severe cold, with lack of medical provision and with horrendously muddy conditions, particularly difficult for the many elderly among them. Another survivor writes: 'Days, weeks, months go by. Every minute becomes an hour for us, every hour an eternity. The barracks are dark, since there are no windows, no light of day … Desperate hunger dominates our thoughts and emotions … Watery soup twice a day and a little bread ration.'

Over a thousand internees died in Gurs in the three years from October 1940; 611 of those died in the first four months, October 1940 to January 1941. Conditions improved somewhat after that, largely thanks to the commitment of dozens of welfare organisations. Internees themselves organised systems of self-help, including buying food from local farmers and on the black market. From March 1941, the old and the ill were transferred to better-equipped camps, with medical facilities. Amazingly enough, cultural activities emerged – music, art, theatre, writing – to the extent that, as Laharie puts it, the camp was one of the most brilliant cultural centres in the south-west of France. Reading this, of course, I thought about my father's internment in the Isle of Man in 1940, where art flourished in the camps. Indeed Laharie has edited another volume, subtitled 'l'art derrière les barbelés', matching the book I have from the Isle of Man, *Art Behind Barbed Wire*. (Lisa Fittko also recalled women spending hours on their toilette and make-up, when she was in Gurs in May 1940.) Against this, we must recall that in 1942 and 1943 there were six deportation convoys to Auschwitz from Gurs, and that many others were transferred to other camps and also did not survive.

Among the letters Paulette still has, received by her mother Eri from Leonie, is the only one written on a typewriter (and therefore the only one I was able to read – for those handwritten in old-fashioned German script I needed to employ a scholar of the language). It is written on a single page, and is from three women, including Leonie, to their daughters in New York. It was clearly written very soon after arrival in Gurs. The women explain that they are writing together because they haven't got enough money for postage. The first and longest part of the letter is written by Leonie's sister-in-law Meta (wife of Sigmund's brother, Bernhard) to her daughter Trudel.

Dear Trudel,

As you will have heard, on 22 October we suddenly had to leave Offenburg. We could each take 100 marks, and whatever was most necessary. Five policemen were there, and gave us an hour. In the consternation, we took all the wrong things. Papa has only what he is wearing, and I don't have much more. We were on the journey for 4 days and are now in southern France on the Spanish border. We are accommodated in wooden barracks, and we lie on straw on the floor with two blankets. Of course we can't undress. Food is very primitive, in the morning a cup of coffee, at midday a plate of soup, and the same in the evening. They are supposed to organize a canteen in the coming days, perhaps we will get what we need then. Send some money, as we are lacking in everything ... I can endure it here, even if our stay lasts longer, but Papa already seems very ill, he had an accident with his arm and it took hours until we could get a doctor. There are very few doctors here among so many people. Men and women are of course separated, but Uncle Sigmund is, thank God, with Papa and is helping him ... There is no medicine at all, apart from what people packed in their hurry ... Do what you can, to get us out of here ... Approach the consulate in Marseilles.

The conditions here are terrible, you can't imagine. The toilets are awful. I hope we can survive this terrible time. Of course many people die every day, since all were brought here, whether old or ill. I hope this letter reaches you safe and legible. Many warm greetings and kisses. Your mother.

There follows a short paragraph from Fanny Maier to her family, telling of the sixty-hour unbroken train journey. Poignantly she says that the thought of seeing their loved ones soon lightens their stay, and that they don't let their courage fail. She reports that there are visiting hours with the men, in the neighbouring barracks. This, I assume is the Fanny Maier from the Offenburg photo. She was to remain Leonie's close companion through the following two years.

Leonie has little room to add her note to Eri and Willy:

Dear Eri & Willy,

From what is written above, you will understand everything. So far we are well, and hope to remain so. The fathers are also together in a barracks and we have already seen them and spoken with them. They send their love. Aunt Rosa and Leo and family are also here, and Aunt Friedel's sister from Gailingen, which you should tell Friedl, dear Eri. We are not far from Limoges and Grenoble, perhaps someone can visit us sometime. Warm greetings and kisses. Mother.

The return address, at Gurs, is typed at the bottom. There was, indeed, a postal service at Gurs, and the exchange of letters with relatives overseas, though presumably with censorship, seems to have been quite active. Laharie reports that there were between five thousand and eight thousand letters a day, though the service was extremely slow. Packages were also received. In one letter, dated 13 October 1941, Eri writes to Leonie about what she has sent her in one package, via the Red Cross in Lisbon. (I have assumed that Paulette has this letter because Eri kept a copy – or perhaps it never got sent. All the correspondence we have otherwise is, for obvious reasons, from Leonie and not to her.) A telegram from Leonie says she is in good health, but has not had news for six weeks, and the money sent in December has not yet arrived. (The 26 3 at the top of the telegram, from Gurs, may mean 26 March 1941.)

There is one telegram, written in French, which raises an intriguing question. I can't tell for sure whether it's from Leonie or to her – her name and the Gurs address appear above the message. It instructs the reader to write immediately to Herman Herz at the Hotel Windsor in Nice, referring to Monsieur Siesel. 'He will help you.' It adds '2200 francs with Aunt Martha are for you'. It's unclear which person will

Liebe Eri & Willy! Aus obigem Schreiben erseht Ihr alles. Wir sind so-
weit gesund & hoffen , dass wir es weiter bleiben.Die Papas sind auch
beisammen in einer Baracke & wir haben sie schon gesehen & gesprochen.
Sie lassen grüssen. Tante Rosa & Leo & Familie sind auch da,ebenso die
Schwester von Tante Friedel aus Gailingen, was Du l. Eri Friedl mit-
teilen sollst. Wir sind nicht sehr weit von Limoges & Grenoble, vielleicht besucht uns mal jemand. Herzliche Grüsse & Küsse   Mutter

UNsere Adresse ist Meta Kahn   Camp de Gurs   Jlot J.I   Baraque 2

Basses- Pyrenées   Süd- Frankreich

Extract of letter,
October 1940

Western Union
cablegram

Julie, Marcel and
Prosper Siesel

Austerity baby

WESTERN
UNION

CLASS OF SERVICE

This is a full-rate Telegram or Cable-gram unless its de-ferred character is in-dicated by a suitable symbol above or pre-ceding the address.

1201

(06).

SYMBOLS

DL = Day Letter
NL = Night Letter
LC = Deferred Cable
NLT = Cable Night Letter
Ship Radiogram

R. B. WHITE
PRESIDENT

NEWCOMB CARLTON
CHAIRMAN OF THE BOARD

J. C. WILLEVER
FIRST VICE-PRESIDENT

The filing time shown in the date line on telegrams and day letters is STANDARD TIME at point of origin.   Time of receipt is STANDARD TIME at point of destination

NY3 VIA RCA=CD CAMPDEGURS 17 DEC 10

NLT LOUIS SCHWARTZ=

CENTRAL AVE 876 WOODMERE NEWYORK=

PREVENIR ERI WILLY SIGMUND DECEDE LETTRE SUIT=

LEONIE SETURMANN.

876.

THE COMPANY WILL APPRECIATE SUGGESTIONS FROM ITS PATRONS CONCERNING ITS SERVICE

CERTIFICAT DE DECES

N° 250

Je soussigné Docteur LACLAU, Médecin Chef du Camp de GURS (B. P.), certifie avoir constaté le décès de l'interné _Kahn Sigmund_ né le _11.6a.1876_ à _Offenburg_ fils de _____ et de _____

Décédé ce jour _2.12.1940_ à _heures_ à l'Infirmerie Hôpital du Camp des suites de _Cachexie_

Gurs le _____ 1940

Tante Leonie

help, and how. And I have no idea why it was written in French, if it was between Eri and Leonie, who wrote in German. Since it addresses 'vous' (plural, or polite form – so not Eri to Leonie), it must be Leonie's telegram to her family. Is it possible that this is my cousin, Marcel Siesel, who was in the French Resistance? Marcel was the son of Julie – my father's cousin whom we visited in 1953 and who is standing behind me in that photograph. The same Julie who, I later found out, my cousin Marlyse lived with for a time in exile in Thionville. She was married to a doctor, Proper Siesel, and Marcel was their only child.

I don't know what Marcel's activities were in the Resistance, but he is recorded as having been caught and imprisoned in Toulouse with fourteen others. After an escape attempt, during which a German officer was killed, they were transported to Miremont and executed by firing squad on 2 June 1944. He was thirty-six years old. If he was the M. Siesel referred to in the telegram, was it a coincidence? He was not related to Leonie – he was my cousin on my grandfather's side. Nevertheless, it may be that there were strong connections among the Jews on either side of the German–French border of Alsace-Lorraine and Baden/Saar/Palatinate, and these were here being mobilised in an attempt to assist Leonie. I don't suppose I will ever know.

Leonie remained at Gurs until December 1941 – over a year. But Sigmund, her husband, was among the early casualties. He died on 1 December 1940, barely five weeks after their arrival at the camp. That month, eight people died each day in Gurs. There is a telegram from Leonie, sent to her brother Louis. (At least I think so – but what is the 'Seturmann' after her name? Another Leonie? There is no record of a Leonie Seturmann in online lists of victims, in France or Germany. And again – why in French?)

Sigmund Kahn's grave, Gurs

Sigmund's brother, Bernhard, whose poor health his wife Meta reported in that early letter from Gurs, survived the camp, but not the war. The German *Gedenbuch*, online, records a Bernhard Kahn from Offenburg, deported to Gurs on 22 October 1940, deported to Auschwitz on 14 August 1942, murdered in Auschwitz on 23 December 1943. A Fanny Maier from Diersburg, a village near Offenburg, and probably the person who wrote in the same letter (and on that last garden photograph from Offenburg), is recorded as deported to Auschwitz on 17 August 1942, together with her husband, Jakob Maier. Tanta Rosa, Leonie's older sister, mentioned in her short paragraph in the letter, eventually managed through a series of unlikely events to get to the United States, where she

Memorial stones for
Leo and Meta Levy

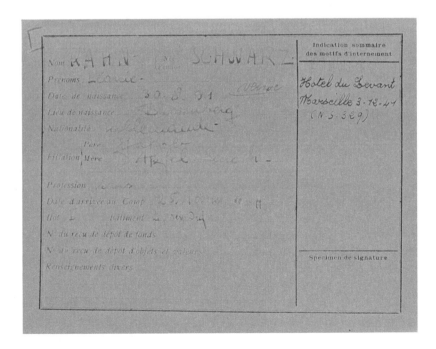

Internment card,
Leonie Kahn,
December 1941

Tante Leonie

lived the rest of her life. But Rosa's son, Leo Levy, and his wife, Meta Levy, both died in Auschwitz. There are Stolpersteine in their names in the Palatinate village of Busenberg, where Rosa, Leonie and the other five siblings (including my grandmother) were born, and where Rosa had remained after her marriage.

‿◦◦◦‿

In December 1941, Leonie received permission to move to Marseilles, to await emigration. She was installed in the Hotel du Levant, one of a small number of detention hotels used to house women refugees and children who were preparing to emigrate. Refugees were permitted to go to Marseilles once they had received their foreign visas. The men were in nearby Les Milles detention camp.

Nearly two thousand internees left Gurs to be located at centres of emigration, most of them during 1941. Thirty per cent of these (580 people) failed to emigrate, and were returned to Gurs. It seems that until 1 July 1941 anyone who got to Marseilles was able to get a US visa, and then just had to await embarcation. But after that date it became a good deal harder, largely because the United States changed the process of application and granted fewer visas. Overall, according to Donna F. Ryan, 1941 was 'the zenith of emigration' from Marseilles. Claude Laharie writes that 1,506 people left Gurs for Marseilles before 1 July 1941, but only 258 in the following six months. Leonie was among that number, arriving at the end of the year. Here she spent several months, trying to get her documents in order to leave and to join her daughter in New York.

There are many letters from this period, from Leonie to her daughter Eri in New York. From them I learned something about Leonie's fourth brother Julius. (Max and Louis were the two long based in New York; Alfred was deported from Düsseldorf on 10 November 1941 to Minsk, where he was murdered.) Julius Schwarz was now living in France – Leonie mentions his being in Limoges at some point. She also refers once or twice to help she is receiving (unspecified) from Edgar and Emmy, who were two of Julius's three children. (Edgar is on the right of that 1953 photo shown in Chapter 3; Emmy I met much later, in May 1993, on a visit to Strasbourg with my sister.) All of that branch of the family survived the war. She says she has had a visit from Ernst, who was happy he would receive his papers soon, and that she thinks it is high time he made it out, after all he had been through.

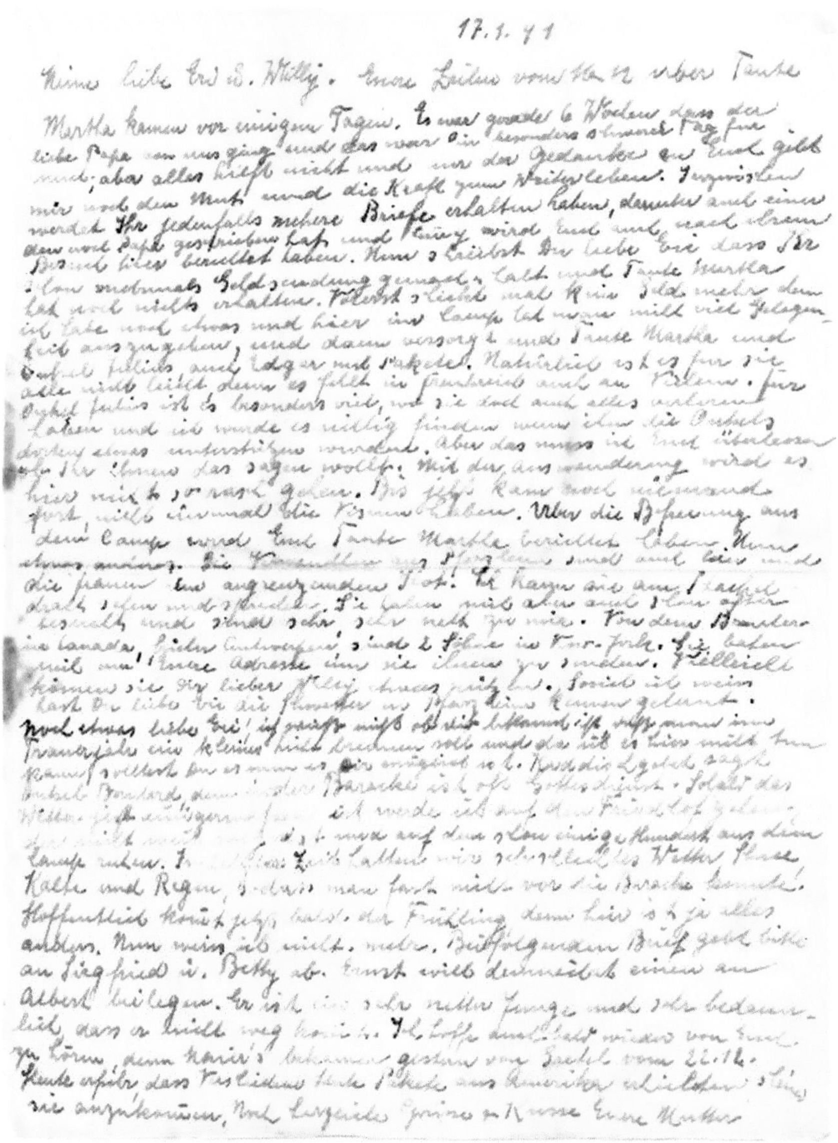

17.1.41

Meine liebe Eri u. Willy. Eure Zeilen vom [illegible] über Tante
Martha kamen vor einigen Tagen. Es war gerade 6 Wochen dass der
liebe Papa von uns ging und das war ein besonders schwerer Tag für
mich; aber alles hilft nicht und nur der Gedanke an Euch gibt
mir noch den Mut und die Kraft zum Weiterleben. Inzwischen
werdet Ihr jedenfalls mehrere Briefe erhalten haben, darunter auch einen
den noch Papa geschrieben hat und [illegible] wird Euch auch nach seinem
Besuch hier berichtet haben. Nun schreibst Du liebe Eri dass Ihr
schon mehrmals Geldsendung gemacht hat und Tante Martha
hat noch nichts erhalten. Vielleicht schickt mal kein Geld mehr denn
ich habe noch etwas und hier im Camp hat man nicht viel Gelegen-
heit auszugeben, und dann versorgt uns Tante Martha und
Onkel Julius auch Edgar mit Paketen. Natürlich ist es für sie
alle nicht leicht denn es fehlt in Frankreich auch an Vielem. Für
Onkel Julius ist es besonders viel, wo sie doch auch alles verloren
haben und ich würde es richtig finden wenn ihm die Onkels
[illegible] etwas unterstützen würden. Aber das muss ich Euch überlassen
ob Ihr Ihnen das sagen wollt. Mit der Auswanderung wird es
hier nicht so rasch gehen. Bis jetzt kam noch niemand
fort, nicht einmal die Visum haben. Über die Befreiung aus
dem Camp wird Euch Tante Martha berichtet haben. Nun
etwas anderes. Die Verwandten aus Pforzheim sind auch hier und
die Frauen im angrenzenden Ilot. Ich kann sie am Stachel-
draht sehen und sprechen. Sie haben mich aber auch schon öfter
besucht und sind sehr, sehr nett zu mir. Von dem Bruder
in Canada, früher Antwerpen, sind 2 Söhne in New-York. Sie haben
mich um Eure Adresse um sie Ihnen zu senden. Vielleicht
können sie Dir lieber Willy etwas nützlich. Soviel ich weiss
hast Du liebe Eri die Schwester in Pforzheim kennen gelernt.
Noch etwas liebe Eri, ich weiss nicht ob dir bekannt ist, dass man im
Trauerjahr ein kleines Licht brennen soll und da ich es hier nicht kann
[illegible] vielleicht Du es nun es für mich [illegible]. Auch die Zedakah sagt
Onkel Bernhard, denn in der Baracke ist oft Gottesdienst. Sobald das
Wetter [illegible] ich werde ich auf den Friedhof gehen;
[illegible] auf dem schon einige Hundert aus dem
Camp ruhen. In letzter Zeit hatten wir schrecklich schlechtes Wetter, Kälte
Kälte und Regen, so dass man fast nicht vor die Baracke konnte!
Hoffentlich kommt jetzt bald der Frühling denn hier ist ja alles
anders. Nun weiss ich nicht mehr. Beifolgenden Brief gebt bitte
an Siegfried u. Betty ab. Ernst will demnächst einen an
Albert beilegen. Er ist ein sehr netter Junge und sehr bedauer-
lich, dass er nicht weg kommt. Ich hoffe auch bald wieder von Euch
zu hören, denn Marie's bekamen gestern von Sachs vom 22.12.
Heute erfuhr dass Verschiedene hier Pakete aus Amerika erhielten. [illegible]
sie anzuerkennen. Noch herzliche Grüsse u. Küsse Eure Mutter

Letter from Leonie Kahn, 17 January 1941

Hauptstraße
49, Busenberg,
Germany, c. 1910

Memorial stones
for Alfred Schwarz
and family,
Busenberg,
Germany

Austerity baby

Later (7 June) she reports that he is still waiting impatiently for his papers. I think this was cousin Ernst, brother of Albert (in New York) and son of Alfred. This Ernst did not survive. His other two brothers died with their parents after deportation to Minsk. Ernst had left Germany in 1939, released after two months' imprisonment in Dachau. It seems that an aunt and uncle in Alsace refused to take him in, and eventually he was arrested. We have two different accounts of how he died. The records on the official German website (*Gedenkbuch* for victims of National Socialism) show that he was interned in 1940 in Saint Cyprien camp, and deported to Auschwitz from Drancy camp on 17 August 1942. A document in Albert's family, compiled by a local historian of Busenberg, records that he was first interned in Gurs camp in the Pyrenees, then in 'St. Cyre', and that he was shot trying to escape to Spain in 1943. In Busenberg, outside the house of my great-grandparents (or rather the house that was built to replace it in 1990) are Stolpersteine to Alfred, his wife, and three of his sons.

Leonie also says she has received money from Eri via the Quakers. On 7 June 1942 she summarises the numerous letters, packages and amounts of money she has received. She says (on 4 May 1942) that when she first arrived in Marseilles she thought she would be able to continue her travels relatively quickly; now she doesn't know how long it would still be. She says, in the same letter, that they have got used to their new lives, even including the bed bugs at night. On 25 May she tells Eri that though she had been sad on what would have been her thirtieth wedding anniversary the previous day, they had made a *Kirschenplotzer* (cherry cake) as a holiday treat for Pfingsten (Whitsuntide). Vegetables and fruit are in good supply, though strawberries and cherries are too expensive. In her 7 June letter, she says that Tante Meta (I assume Bernhard's wife) will be leaving soon. I don't know why Bernhard isn't mentioned, unless he had already been transferred elsewhere, or was perhaps still in Gurs. In any case, Meta did not leave, and did not survive. Leonie adds that one day it will be her turn to leave – that she can survive until then.

Leonie lived in Marseilles throughout the period from December 1941 to August 1942. All the letters from those months have the Marseilles address. The Hotel du Levant was at rue Fauchier 36, on the edge of the Old Town (Le Panier), to the north of the port, a region, according to a tourist website for Marseilles, whose 'labyrinthine warren was a haven for Resistance fighters, Jews and Communists'. The letters give a detailed account of her daily life there – the funds she receives, the women she shares a room with, her special relationship with her old Offenburg friend, Fanny Maier, with whom she goes shopping for food. According to Donna F. Ryan, discipline at the hotels was fairly lenient, and residents could come and go quite freely each day. A good deal of time would have been spent trying to assemble the necessary documents, from the United States consulate but also from other consulates (for transit visas) and from the prefecture in Marseilles. This involved frequent visits, and often hours of waiting. Financial support, and provision of food, was provided for the refugees by several organisations, including HICEM (the international Jewish relief agency), the Unitarian Service Committee (Boston) and the American Friends Service Committee (Quakers). The last letter is dated 7 June 1942.

Together with Meta Kahn, her sister-in-law, and Leo and Meta Levy, her nephew and his wife (son of her sister Rosa), on 13 September 1942 Leonie was on a transport from Rivesaltes camp in the south to Drancy transit camp, near Paris. From there, on 16 September, they were deported on convoy number thirty-three to Auschwitz. (From the first, on 27 March 1942, to the last on 17 August 1944, there were seventy-four convoys from France, each containing about one thousand men, women and children.) In early August 1942 the Nazi regime called for the expulsion of foreign Jews from the unoccupied zone of France, for deportation to the east; the Vichy regime had already agreed, a month earlier, to deport Jews from both zones. By early September more than 27,000 Jews had been deported from all of France. In the south, many were taken on 6 and 8 August from the internment camps (Gurs, Les Milles, Rivesaltes, Le Vernet, Noé). Women and children were brought into the camps from the internment hotels in Marseilles, including the Levant, but I think Leonie was probably not caught in that round-up, on 2 August, since those refugees were taken to Les Milles and were on a transport to Drancy and Auschwitz on 11 August. On 13 August, two hundred women from the Hotel Bompard and Hotel du Levant were taken to Les Milles camp, for deportation. On 10 September, 420 men, women and children were transferred from Les Milles to Rivesaltes. As Leonie's name is on a transport list from Rivesaltes camp to Drancy, I am guessing she was among that number. Or it's possible she was taken a bit later, in the great round-up which began on 26 August. Fanny was on convoy number twenty, a month earlier. Leo and Meta Levy, Leonie's nephew and his wife, were on the same convoy as Leonie.

Convoy thirty-three probably reached Auschwitz on 19 September 1942, three days after leaving Drancy. Of the 1,003 people on the transport, 856 were gassed immediately on arrival. A hundred and forty-seven people were selected to work; it's very unlikely that Leonie, at the age of fifty-one, was one of them. In any case, only

Page from transport list, Convoy 33 to Auschwitz, 16 September 1942

219-	ISAAC Simon	23.11.12	Danzichoise
220-	ISAY Harry	7.4.87	Allemande
221-	JACHMANN Louis	20.1.92	"
222-	JANKELEWICZ Simon	19.1.00	Polonaise
223-	JANKIELEWICZ Sara	1904-	"
224-	JAULUS Alfred	16.8.92	Allemande
225-	JOEL Siegfried	19.1.02	Autrichienne
226-	JOCHSBERGER Sigriff	5.9.83	Allemande
227-	KAHN Frieda	7.7.95	"
228-	KAHN Hans	8.7.26	"
229-	KAHN Léonie	30.6.91	"
230-	KAHN Léopold	25.5.82	"
231-	~~KAHN Martin~~	31.12.98	"
232-	KAHN Meta	19.5.86	"
233-	KAHN Richard	23.11.95	"
234-	KAHN Wolff	12.9.23	Polonaise
235-	KAHANE Simai	26.12.90	"
236-	KALMA Godels	10.1.00	"
237-	KALMA Chana	25.5.00	"
238-	KALTMANN Hélène	16.11.06	"
239-	KAMLUT Jacob	1.4.06	"
240-	KANTOROWICZ Joséphine	16.4.12	Autrichienne

one woman (and thirty-seven men) from that transport survived to the end of the war.

I doubt that Leonie's chances would have been good even if she had escaped the August round-up. The Germans occupied the southern zone on 11 November 1942, and the arrests and deportations continued through 1943 and beyond. In addition, any legal departures from France were prohibited by the end of 1942. Some were able to leave illegally, especially across the Pyrenees into Spain, as many had done earlier in the war. As we have already seen, by the second half of 1941 it was already more difficult to obtain US visas. But even with a visa and an affidavit from the United States, with financial guarantee, the attempt to leave Marseilles for the United States was so complicated as to seem quite surreal. Apart from, of course, securing passage on a boat, would-be travellers needed a refugee certificate if originally from Germany, a certificate of release from any French camp they had lived in, an exit visa from France, a note of safe conduct and transit visas for countries to be travelled through – usually Spain and Portugal, as many boats left from Lisbon. Frequently some of the documents expired while a refugee was still trying to assemble others.

Anna Seghers recreates brilliantly the world of 1940 Marseilles and its impossible logic in her novel *Transit*. Seghers herself, a German-Jewish writer, was living in France in 1940, and was able to sail from Marseilles to Mexico in March 1941 (on a ship that included among its passengers Claude Lévi-Strauss and André Breton). The characters in her novel are, for the most part, not so lucky. The narrator, rather detached and not himself particularly concerned to leave Marseilles, meets an orchestra conductor, who has been offered a position in Venezuela. The conductor explains his predicament:

> He had to start the new position in Caracas before the end of the year. He had already had a work contract before and because of the contract, a visa, and because of the visa, a transit visa, but it took so long for the exit visa to be issued that the transit visa expired in the meantime, and after that the visa and after that the contract. Last week he was issued an exit visa, and he was now anxiously waiting for an extension of his contract, which would mean he could then get an extension of his visa. And that would be a prerequisite for his being awarded a new transit visa.

The next time they meet, the conductor tells the narrator that he had just got his exit visa – but half a week too late, because his Venezuelan visa had just expired. To renew that, he now needs the orchestra to renew his contract, which must be arranged within a month, before his exit visa expires again. 'He laughed and walked on. His pace was that of an old man, and I thought he would never make it across the Canebière, not to mention other countries and other seas.' In the end, just on the point of presenting the last of his essential documents at the American Consulate, where he needed a transit visa, the orchestra conductor is overwhelmed by a last-minute panic about whether he has the requisite number of photographs (twelve), and he collapses and dies.

Walter Benjamin arrived in Marseilles from Paris at the end of August 1940, soon after the fall of France and the June armistice. Max Horkheimer, his one-time colleague at the Frankfurt School, had arranged an emergency visa for him to the United States. By late September he hadn't managed to assemble all the necessary documents, and decided to take the illegal route over the Pyrenees, after which a train would have transported him and others to Lisbon, for emigration. His story is well known. The crossing, on a route taken two weeks earlier by Heinrich and Golo Mann, Frank Werfel, Alma Mahler-Werfel and others, went well. On the other side, they were told by the Spanish police that their transit visas were no longer valid. In fear of being returned to France, and of probable arrest and deportation, Benjamin took his own life. Arthur Koestler was also in Marseilles in August 1940, after three and a half months in Le Vernet internment camp, whose horrendous conditions, recalling those of Gurs, he describes in his memoir *Scum of the Earth*. In Marseilles he met Benjamin, who had been a neighbour of his in Paris and someone with whom he had played poker. Benjamin asked 'If anything goes wrong, have you got anything to take?', and then shared with him the sixty-two sedative tablets he had managed to procure. As it happened, Koestler was only in Marseilles for a couple of weeks. He escaped by boat, via Oran and then Casablanca, and finally by fishing boat to Lisbon and on to London. Unlike Benjamin, he did not need the morphine pills. Forty-three years later, though, he died in a suicide pact with his wife, Cynthia. His suicide note gives the reason: Parkinson's disease and a type of leukaemia. Her appended note simply says she cannot live without him.

There is a special irony in recalling the dark period of 1940 in Marseilles. For Benjamin, it had earlier been a city of great appeal. He wrote two short sketches of the city, in 1929 and 1932, observations of characters, streets, buildings, encounters. The second especially, 'Hashish in Marseilles', is a wonderful account of experiencing the city, in a bar,

Eleanor Wolff,
Mémorial de la
Shoah, Paris,
April 2013

Austerity baby

a restaurant and the streets, while stoned on the drug. Just two lovely passages – lovely, too, in revealing such an unusual aspect of the writer:

> I strolled along the quay and read, one after another, the names of the boats tied up there. As I did so, an incomprehensible gaiety came over me, and I smiled in turn at all the Christian names of France. The love promised to these boats by their names seemed wonderfully beautiful and touching to me. Only one of them, *Aero II*, which reminded me of aerial warfare, I passed by without cordiality, exactly as, in the bar that I had just left, my gaze had been obliged to pass over certain excessively deformed countenances.

> A deeply submerged feeling of happiness that came over me afterward, on a square off the Cannebière where the rue Paradis opens onto a park, is more difficult to recall than everything that went before.

Graeme Gilloch has pointed out that, for all their focus on the northern cities – Berlin, Paris, Vienna – the writers on or of modernity retained a fascination with the cities of the south. Georg Simmel wrote about Rome, Florence and Venice; and Siegfried Kracauer, who had also been a refugee in Marseilles in 1940–41, escaping through Spain and Portugal and then by boat to New York, wrote a number of earlier pieces about the city. The images he invokes are unsettling and uncanny, especially the old woman in 'Apparition on the Cannebière', and the dreamlike quality of Marseilles is by no means entirely benign. But the innocence of visits in the 1920s provides, in retrospect, a shocking contrast with the place Anna Seghers describes as 'the edge of our world'.

If my sister Eleanor, who was born in 1954, was called after my great-aunt Leonie, it was probably lucky for her that this was never said explicitly. There is an extensive literature now on the effects on children of Holocaust survivors of these transmitted traumas, including Eva Hoffman's *After Such Knowledge*, Helen Epstein's *Children of the Holocaust* and Aaron Hass's *In the Shadow of the Holocaust*. Dina Wardi has focused on a particular group, whom she has called 'memorial candles'. These are children named after relatives who did not survive – in some cases even conceived and received as replacements for those lost. Wardi's work as a psychotherapist was for many years with these 'children of the Holocaust', whose inheritance of these memories and expectations often produced serious psychic disturbances. In our case, though, the youngest of the three sisters, who only ever knew the 'technicolour' world, was probably least affected by this suppressed knowledge. If she was named for Leonie, it was by then, nine years after the end of the war, more by way of a gesture, in the tradition of Jewish naming after deceased relatives, than a cry of pain, or of hope, and hence a heavy burden. Though there is a photograph of her at the Mémorial de la Shoah in Paris, where I had asked her to look for Leonie's name on the memorial wall, on a visit in April 2013. And some of my information about Gurs, including the photograph of Sigmund's grave, came from my sister Veronica – also, by coincidence, on holiday in south-west France in summer the same year.

It happens that I have been thinking recently about sibling relationships, and particularly about relations between sisters. Juliet Mitchell has pointed out that the lateral relations between siblings represent the great omission in psychoanalytic theory which, following Freud, has privileged the vertical relationship between parent and child. Barely considered is what she describes as the 'catastrophic moment of displacement', when the small child is confronted with a new baby. The combination of love and murderous hate which is the likely response to this arrival, at a moment when the child's own sense of identity as 'the baby' disintegrates, must play out through childhood and beyond. Interesting to consider, then, is the great difference between a welcome or unwelcome intrusion for a two-year-old child and the arrival of another sister ten years later. The classic psychoanalytic emphasis on the first years of life leaves open questions about the effects on a twelve-year-old of new family dynamics. And if Juliet Mitchell has been the first to urge us to consider sibling relations, her turn to the 'lateral' invites further reflections on extended groups – for example, the particular configuration of three sisters.

Author with sister Veronica

Author with sister Eleanor

I don't remember ever hearing anything about my grandmother's other sister, Rosa. I now know that she lived until a very old age in New York. Her great-granddaughter Judy has a photo taken sometime around 1962, of Rosa with Judy and her younger sister, aged about four and two. And I have a photo of her with my cousin Paulette (Leonie's granddaughter), also taken in New York but a few years earlier.

Here it is framed by the red check tablecloth at a café in Strasbourg, when Paulette and I, with her husband Dean, travelled to Busenberg and Offenburg together in September 2014. If I have the correct date of birth for Rosa, the oldest of the seven Schwarz siblings – 1872 – that would make her around ninety in the photo. The story of how she got to the United States is an amazing one – the happy counterpart to Leonie's story. They were in Gurs together late in 1940. Rosa was transferred from camp to camp in the following months

Rosa Levy, with
Paulette

Leonie Kahn, Rosa
Levy, Bertha Wolff

Tante Leonie

– to Rivesaltes in March 1941, then to Nexon in October 1942 – with the 'viellards, invalides et incurables'. It seems that being classed this way saved her from deportation to Auschwitz. She was twenty years older than her sister Leonie, and one would assume more clearly a candidate for extermination. But my colleague Jean-Marc Dreyfus reminds me that the pretence of the deportations was of a transfer for work, something out of the question for a woman of seventy. In this way, she remained in Nexon until March 1943, when she was transferred one last time, to Masseube camp. She was still there when the war ended. At some point after that she was able to join her surviving son, Siegfried, in New York.

My parents did not keep any letters, so I don't know whether my grandmother, Bertha, continued to correspond with her surviving siblings – Rosa, Max and Louis in New York, and Julius in France. There must have been contact, since we went to visit surviving German relatives in France in 1953, and I'm sure my parents met them more often. Knowing nothing, including my grandmother's feelings about her sisters Leonie and Rosa, it is quite pointless imagining parallels with myself and my sisters, for many reasons: they also had four brothers, which complicated the family relations; they lived geographically apart after marriage, even before the war and the Nazi oppression drove them in many directions; and cultures of the family, and of personal relationships, were certainly entirely different a hundred years ago. Still – I look at this prelapsarian photograph of the three of them, and cannot help becoming immersed again in their presence and their loss.

Eleanor Rathbone worked closely in alliance with different men in her various campaigns – Victor Gollancz on the refugee question, Ernest Simon on housing issues, for instance. But her pre-eminent involvement, in her life as well as her politics, was with women, beginning in her years in Liverpool, where she became involved with the Victorian Settlement, a residential house for women social workers. Here she met Elizabeth Macadam, who came to Liverpool as warden of the Settlement in 1902; they were to become life partners, first while living in Liverpool and later in London. Rathbone was also very close to her mother and her two sisters, Elsie – actually a half-sister, more than twenty years older than her – and Evie. (The three-sister scenario again – here with an additional four brothers and four half-brothers.) She had worked closely with her father, the Liverpool merchant and great philanthropist William Rathbone, and wrote a memoir of her father in 1905, three years after his death (a book which, as her biographer Susan Pedersen points out, omits any mention of his wife and children). Eleanor had returned in 1896 to live at home after university in Oxford, and continued to live with her mother, Emily, and her older half-sister Elsie. After Emily died, in 1918, Elsie and Eleanor moved to another home; Elsie died less than two years later. From that date, Eleanor spent more and more of her time in London, in the house she and Elizabeth Macadam had bought together in 1919. She remained close to her married sister Evie (though according to Pedersen, 'Evie had never much liked Elizabeth').

Given her political commitments and achievements, her lifelong involvement in feminist campaigns, and her own life choices, it is unsurprising that writers on Eleanor Rathbone have focused on her work in these areas. But according to Susan Cohen, this has been at the expense of her equally important contributions in other areas, and notably on behalf of refugees and internees. (She is somewhat unfair to Pedersen, who has plenty to say about these campaigns.) Known amongst friends as the 'MP for refugees', Rathbone was also referred to by another MP as 'the patron saint of refugees'. She was among the first to register concern about Hitler's accession to power in 1933, and was concerned throughout the war, and particularly from 1942, with the fate of the Jews in Europe, campaigning against restrictions on entry of refugees and writing an impassioned pamphlet, 'Rescue the perishing', in April 1943. With regard to refugees in England, she took up the cause against the internment of aliens, asking eighty questions on the topic in the House of Commons. On 10 July 1940, she participated in a six-hour parliamentary debate on refugees and aliens. She twice visited internment camps in the Isle of Man in 1941. The pressure she put on the government was fierce and relentless; her immersion in these campaigns exhausted her. Indeed, her sister Evie later said that she thought the rescue campaign killed her, as she was in poor health for the remaining few years of her life.

Reading about Eleanor Rathbone has produced a certain sense of *déjà vu* for me. I realised I was repeating a sequence of attachment and reaction which I had been through ten years earlier, when doing research on the American artist Kathleen McEnery Cunningham. I spent a number of years finding out about her life, meeting her son and several of her grandchildren (her two other children were no longer alive), discovering many of her paintings, writing about her and curating an exhibition of her work and advising on a second exhibition. I fairly quickly fell in love with her – with her work, with

Sir James Gunn, *Eleanor Florence Rathbone*, 1933

Austerity baby

a stunning photograph and an equally stunning self-portrait, with the glamour of her life in Rochester in the 1920s. Then I was obliged gradually to modify my ideal image of her, as I interviewed many people who had known her, including family members, and as she became rather more real, with – inevitably – some less charming characteristics (arrogance, snobbery, a certain coldness – at least as seen by some). In the end, I was still a fan and an admirer, though with the knowledge that if we had ever met it might not have gone too well. And with Eleanor Rathbone it was the same. I began with great enthusiasm, and also with an image. I sent away for a small copy of her portrait, from the National Portrait Gallery, which I framed and put on the filing cabinet next to my desk.

When it was proposed that the portrait be commissioned, the modest Rathbone – who later refused a DBE – said 'A spinster does not want to gaze on her own portrait in her own home'.

Soon I was beginning to wish I hadn't read the biographies and the commentaries, as I learned about her tendencies to patriotism and imperialism, her interest in eugenics, her somewhat anti-Arab Zionism, her Western arrogance with regard to Indian women in her campaigns with them. And her personality – excessive 'confidence in her own judgment', a 'difficult colleague', 'inflexibility', 'lack of warmth', a certain puritanism. (And – obviously on a different level of importance – her terrible dress sense, and general lack of interest in clothes – her 'shapeless black dresses'.) But of course my retrospective judgements are anachronistic. Perhaps more importantly, she and I don't have to be friends, any more than I have to be friends with Kathleen McEnery. In the end, it seems easy and uncomplicated for me to share my father's admiration and gratitude, and all the more for having learned so much about her life of dedication and selflessness. And, although it was no help to Leonie, who needed equivalent campaigns in the United States, it is good to remember the woman Susan Pedersen refers to as 'the most significant non-Jewish campaigner for "rescue"'.

Rose Hill, Didsbury, Manchester

Austerity baby

7: Houses and barns

The technicolour place I moved to in 1956 at the age of thirteen was Didsbury, in south Manchester. Fifty-five years later, in February 2011, I returned to live there. My apartment, in a late nineteenth-century mansion called Lawnhurst, is a few minutes' walk from the house where I lived in my teens. Less than five miles from the centre of Manchester, Didsbury, listed as a small hamlet in the thirteenth century, was still more or less rural until the mid-nineteenth century. Its main shopping street is still referred to as 'the village' – indeed the metro system, newly expanded further south in May 2013, named the local stop 'Didsbury Village'. By the eighteenth century Didsbury was described as a township. The suburb was integrated into the city in 1904 and has long been part of the continuous urban spread of Manchester, while retaining its green character. The river Mersey runs along the southern boundary of the area and there is a large conservation area – Didsbury St James – and a twenty-one-acre botanical garden and park, Fletcher Moss, as well as two smaller parks.

The renowned radio producer and broadcaster Olive Shapley lived in Didsbury for nearly forty years, twenty-eight of them – from 1953 – in a large house called Rose Hill, in Millgate Lane. Now another Didsbury street, Olive Shapley Avenue, is named after her. She worked at the BBC in the 1930s, organising *Children's Hour* programming in Manchester and also producing innovative documentaries on industrial work, homelessness and other social topics, pioneering in their subject matter and style. After a period in London and New York with her husband she returned to Manchester, from where she presented *Woman's Hour*, broadcasting later on Radio Manchester as well. After the death of her second husband she stayed at Rose Hill, turning it into a refuge for unmarried mothers and their babies in the 1960s, and later, in the late 1970s, for Vietnamese refugees.

With a national profile, and a job that took her to London frequently, Shapley retained her deep love for Manchester, and particularly Didsbury. This is from her autobiography, published in 1996, three years before her death:

> A lot of the attractiveness of Didsbury lies in its proximity to the river and its abundance of trees, which are mostly mature and beautiful, some being known and prized individually. All this enhances the

feeling of being much further than five miles from Manchester's centre and the industry which created the city's wealth. Didsbury also has two very special parks – the Old Parsonage, with its orchid house, and Fletcher Moss, which has an alpine garden on a south-facing slope. The Old Parsonage itself housed for a long time an attractive small art gallery, with some paintings by Turner and Augustus John and one tiny Constable sketch.

But it is, of course, people who create a neighbourhood, and during the sixty years I have known Didsbury it has always been blessed with a great variety of people of all income levels and occupations ... It has had a sizeable Jewish community since the last century due to Sephardic settlement when the city was cotton king of the world. It has also always attracted teachers, journalists, writers, musicians and others in the entertainment world, including the BBC ... If you believe in the 'genius loci', the spirit of a place, then the Didsburys of this country are well worth preserving.

My high-school friend Jennifer Black, who lived nearby when we at school, sent me an email with her memories of Olive and the house:

Olive Shapley moved into Rose Hill in the 1950s, with her 2nd husband, Christopher Gorton, and her 3 children by her first marriage to John Salt, a BBC person – Dan, Nicky and Christina. Kingston Road, at the back of Rose Hill, was bursting with children because the 7 houses there belonged to Shirley Institute [the Cotton, Silk and Man-made Fibres Research Association] and were rented to senior people. Olive's children quickly discovered us and we all played together, with Olive's huge garden a big bonus! I remember when it was very hot and she came out and sprayed water on us all from a hose – and on Pierre, the huge dog (I don't like dogs but he was always well behaved) – we took our clothes off first! that was the kind of thing we learned from her – running around naked in her garden was normal. She owned the first TV in the road and invited us all to come over via the back door at 5 pm every day for children's programmes. We sat in a huddle, mostly on the floor, in a shabby downstairs room. My ideals of a family home come direct from her – piles of books everywhere, untidy rooms, big kitchen where we did crazy baking things. She was such an important role model for me. She used to talk to me about books, and I remember proudly that I had been reading my way through John Buchan and I heard her on Radio 4 – must have a been a section of *Children's Hour* – saying that she could recommend *The Three Hostages* as 'a young friend of mine' had enjoyed it very much! I think I was 11!

In April 2005 the *Manchester Evening News* reported that Rose Hill, which had been a nursing home for two decades after Olive Shapley sold it in 1981, had become the first Didsbury property offered for sale for one million pounds.

Lawnhurst, Didsbury, Manchester

Henry Simon and family outside Lawnhurst, 1898

Lawnhurst is one of several mansions in Didsbury, built as family homes by wealthy industrialists and businessmen in the second half of the nineteenth century. Ernest Simon, later Lord Simon of Wythenshawe, was thirteen years old in 1892 when he moved with his parents and seven siblings to Lawnhurst. The house had been built for his father, Henry Simon, and the family moved that year from a smaller, but still very large, house on Palatine Road, about a mile away. Ernest was the oldest of Henry Simon's seven children by his second wife, Emily; there was also an older brother, Ingo, son of Henry's first wife, Mary Jane who had died in 1876. Ernest Simon's biographer gives an idea of life at Lawnhurst in those years:

> At Lawnhurst the young Simons led country lives, kept animals, made hay, and played games. It was a happy home, with money to spare for education, travel, hospitality, and philanthropy. It was an intellectually alert home, in which books were read and discussed, and in which the humanist agnosticism of Henry Simon was, during his life, and remained after his death, the dominant Simon philosophy.

There's a wonderful photograph, reproduced in a short biography of Henry Simon by his grandson Brian Simon, of the entire family posing outside Lawnhurst in 1898.

Ingo, third from the left and about twenty-three years old when the photo was taken, already looks the part of the aesthete. Not remotely interested in going into the family business, he devoted his life to singing lessons and recitals, foreign travel and, later in life when married to his third wife, archery, at which they both excelled. His impressive collection of bows, arrows, guns and other weapons is now in the University of Manchester Museum. His special expertise was in Turkish and other oriental bows, and it seems that in 1913 he achieved a world record of 462 yards 9 inches for 'flight shooting', reported (in *The Field*) as 'the longest recorded shot since 1794', with a Turkish bow over two hundred years old pulling 80 lb weight. His wife, Erna, had become Lady Champion archer of the world at meetings held in Paris. Having travelled widely, to Switzerland, Italy, Germany and the United States, Ingo returned to England to live near Sidmouth in Devon. He died in 1964, having outlived all seven of his younger half-siblings.

In fact the three youngest sons had died long before that – all killed in the First World War. Eric, the youngest, had married a Jewish woman, Winifred Levy, and converted to Judaism – once, several generations earlier, the religion of his father's family. Pacifist by strong inclination, he had started a farming life in Surrey and went reluctantly to fight for his country. He was killed in action in France in August 1915 at the age of twenty-seven. His older brother, Victor, was a professional soldier. He won the Military Cross in September 1915 at the battle of Loos and was promoted to Major. He was killed in June 1917, aged thirty-one – shot while inspecting some recently installed wire. And Henry, known as Harry, who after school and university had joined Ernest working in the family firm in Manchester, died later the same year, in September 1917, also in France. He was thirty-six. All three sons were married; Harry had four children and Eric two. The names of the brothers are on the cenotaph in the centre of Didsbury Village, as well as on the family memorial at the Manchester Crematorium (a crematorium Henry Simon had been instrumental in establishing in 1892, and only the second in the country).

Their father, Henry Simon, was no longer alive to suffer this terrible loss. He had died in 1899, the year after the family photograph was taken. His widow Emily, more than twenty years his junior, continued to live at Lawnhurst until her own death in 1920. During the war Lawnhurst was taken over by the Red Cross as a military hospital, which Emily was actively involved in running. She was sixty-two when she died two years after the war ended. Since then, Lawnhurst has had many incarnations – as a private school, a nursing home, a sound studio, and now, since 2011, as an apartment building.

Ernest Simon was in fact away from Lawnhurst much of the time after the family first took up residence in 1892, at least during term time. He was sent off to Rugby public school the following year, and in 1898 went up to Pembroke College in Cambridge, where he studied engineering. By the time he graduated in 1901 his father had died, and he was in line to take over at Henry Simon Ltd and Simon-Carves Ltd, the two companies established by Henry. He gave his own account of the firms and his accession in an introduction to a 1953 book about the Simon Engineering Group:

> My father, Henry Simon, introduced into Britain two new industrial processes of considerable importance. Starting without capital or influence he built the first complete roller flour milling plant in Britain in 1878 and the first by-product coke oven installation in 1881 ... In twenty years Henry Simon built up two highly technical businesses, developing them entirely out of profits and leaving them in so strong a position that Henry Simon Ltd has ever since remained the leading British firm of milling engineers and Simon-Carves Ltd one of the two British leaders in the building of coke ovens ...

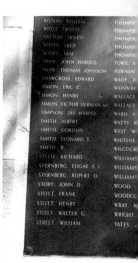

War memorial outside Didsbury library

Simon family memorial, Manchester Crematorium

I was twenty when my father died; I joined Henry Simon Ltd in 1901, and after an interval during which the businesses were carried on by members of his staff the shareholders of both companies increasingly gave me their confidence. I have been Chairman or Governing Director of both companies since 1910, and as such have been ultimately responsible for everything, good and bad, that has happened.

Despite – or perhaps because of – Ingo Simon's abandonment of industry for the arts, there seems never to have been any question about what Henry's next son would do in life. In 1890 Henry had written a note for his sons, urging them, according to Ernest, 'to acquire a sound technical education, to avoid the well-trodden arts and professions in their choice of a career, to keep in close touch with scientific development throughout the world, and to search for engineering specialities and patents which could be used to improve the efficiency of large-scale industrial processes in Britain and elsewhere'. While Ernest was still at school, both his parents were intervening with his house-master, putting pressure on him and the school to steer their son in the direction of science and mathematics and away from the traditional Classics education. It seems this was – or became – Ernest's own desire too. About his father's note he comments: 'Rarely has paternal advice and example been more wholeheartedly accepted.'

There is something rather melancholy in reading about the life of Ernest Simon. He succeeded in everything he did, from running the family businesses to political activities and important social projects later on. He had an exceptionally happy marriage to a woman – Shena Potter – with her own strong social and political commitments. And he had time, in a busy and fulfilling professional life, for foreign travel, friendships and many visits to the place he adored in the Lake District, a cottage in Langdale called Hellsgarth. Somehow, though, there is a sense that responsibility was at the expense of pleasure and enjoyment. His relationship with his father was not close, though it is not recorded whether he ever resented Henry's more affectionate relationship with his next son, Harry – or, indeed, the way his older half-brother, Ingo, had simply ignored any expectations of a business career. His biographer, Mary Stocks, who knew him quite well, describes him as quite shy and rather formal, always fairly serious and not at all good at the small talk which is essential on some occasions. When he was at Cambridge, his father wrote to him, urging him to make friends:

You scarcely ever mention the names of comrades with whom you go out, play, or ride. You style them 'another fellow'. We would like you to become acquainted with their names, and take an interest in those names which occur oftenest. We are, you must remember, not jelly-fish, but so called human beings – with proper hearts and affections ready for use.

About his early involvement with the social reformers Sidney and Beatrice Webb, which was to prove crucial in his developing political views, Mary Stocks comments on why they might have taken an interest in him:

He was intelligent, public-spirited, hard-working and rich. He was, incidentally, a most engaging personality. So young, in some respects so unsophisticated, in others so mature; so ardent and withal so good looking. That he lacked a sense of humour would not have troubled Mrs Webb, since she had none herself.

His relationship with his own two sons perhaps reproduced the formalities of period and wealth that had characterised his own childhood. His son Brian Simon writes that 'The upbringing of children was also efficiently organised, with the due provision of nurses and nurseries characteristic of the time', and that the children 'were welcome in the sitting room at suitable moments'. There was also a younger daughter, Antonia, adored by Ernest, who died of cancer in 1929 at the age of twelve, a great sadness in his life. But more than anything, I think, it's the sense of duty that pervades the accounts of Ernest's life from early on, including in some of the extracts from his own letters and diaries quoted by Mary Stocks, that makes me feel a little sad for him. This is from a letter to his mother, which he describes as part of his diary, from April 1911:

It is the old question: what are my ideals? And what sort of an attempt am I making to live up to them? It is all very complex and difficult, and takes a good deal of persistence and energy to think out at all ... I am quite content to assume that one has to try to make the world a happier place to live in ... I work pretty hard at business and I think fairly efficiently. But I do not feel content to make that my life. I believe I can do more good in public work than in business. I must devote myself to the latter almost exclusively for at least five years.

In his diary the same year he records being 'hopelessly ragged' by the boys at school, and says he 'never had the courage to LAUGH till I was 28!!'. But I am quite aware that I may be over-identifying, from the point of view of another 'good' child, and that the sympathy is probably misplaced.

Ernest Simon was an important figure in Manchester and nationally in the first half of the twentieth century. His political career, inspired by the Webbs and by the example of his own wife Shena, began seriously when he was elected as a Liberal to Manchester City Council in 1912, representing Didsbury. By 1921 he was Lord Mayor of the city for that year. He stood for Parliament for the first time in 1922, and the following year won a seat, representing the Withington constituency of south Manchester. He lost that seat in the general election of the following year, and gained it again in 1929, holding it until 1931. He was never elected to the House of Commons again but, after getting a knighthood in 1932, he accepted a peerage in 1947, after which he was an active member of the House of Lords. His main areas of concern and expertise, on several of which he also wrote articles and books, were smoke abatement, housing, higher education and, later, nuclear disarmament. Amongst other things he served as Chairman of the BBC from 1947 to 1952, and as Chair of the Council of the University of Manchester from 1941 to 1957. He was involved with the Webbs in the establishment of the *New Statesman* in 1913. One of his most important political acts was in buying Wythenshawe Hall and park in 1926 and donating it to the city. The adjacent area was developed as a housing estate as part of the project of slum clearance. He was given the freedom of the City of Manchester in 1959, the year before his death. Shena, for her part, was also involved in planning the Wythenshawe estate, as well as in various campaigns for education and for women. As a member of the City Council, she served as Chair of the Education Committee in 1932–33, and as Chair of the Education Advisory Committee of the Workers Educational Association.

Although Ernest was not elected to Parliament again after 1931, he did stand for election one more time, in a 1946 by-election. This was the Combined English Universities seat, which had become vacant on the death of Eleanor Rathbone. Ernest stood as an independent candidate this time, after decades in the Liberal Party. The independent vote was split, however – the competing candidate being his friend, and later biographer, Mary Stocks – and the Tory candidate won. Soon after that, Ernest switched his allegiance to the Labour Party, joining his wife Shena, who had been a member since 1935. This connection with Eleanor Rathbone was more than a belated opportunity for Ernest; they had been allies in Parliament in earlier years, and by all accounts got on very well. This, of course, is a very nice coincidence for me, given Eleanor Rathbone's place in my own family history. Simon supported her work in relation to family allowances and for rent rebate for children. Their shared interest in questions of housing brought them together, and Rathbone's biographer Susan Pedersen also describes them as personal friends.

And Mary Stocks points out Rathbone's collaboration with Simon in connection with the Greenwood housing bill during his 1929–31 stint as an MP:

In this, as in other matters, Ernest worked in contact with Eleanor Rathbone, Independent M.P. for the Combined English Universities and at that time in the full tide of her campaign for a national system of children's allowances. Here, then, was a colleague who knew almost as much and cared quite as much about municipal housing as Ernest did. It is recorded that after listening to her speech in the House on differential rents, Ernest remarked to a friend that it was the only parliamentary utterance on housing from which he felt that he had something to learn.

They were connected, too, through two women, both involved with each of them in different ways. The first was Mary Stocks herself, later Baroness Stocks, an economist and academic who had worked with Rathbone in her early years in politics, on the campaign for women's suffrage, and then on other issues connected with women and the welfare state. She wrote biographies both of Rathbone and of Ernest Simon. The second was Eva Hubback, who had also worked closely with Eleanor Rathbone on many feminist issues, from suffrage to legal reform, later in her role as President of the National Union for Equal Citizenship. She was also an associate of Ernest and Shena Simon – indeed, according to Stocks it was Eva Hubback who brought Shena Potter, her college friend from Cambridge and now a postgraduate student at the London School of Economics, to Manchester in 1911 and introduced her to Ernest Simon at a dinner party. They married the following year. Later, in the 1930s, Ernest was to work with Eva, by then Principal of Morley College for Working Men and Women, on the question of education for citizenship, on which they published a book together in 1935. Although my own link to Eleanor Rathbone and Ernest Simon is perhaps rather tenuous, I find it very gratifying that they were friends and allies.

Ernest and Shena Simon retained their left-liberal beliefs throughout their lives, and their two sons continued in the tradition, both taking up public service careers. Ernest's siblings moved to the right as adults. His sister Eleanor married George Hamilton, who became a Tory MP, opposed to women's suffrage and conservative in ways that Ernest could not abide. In his diary he wrote: 'I simply can't stand having him in the house … I MUST SEE LESS OF HIM.' In a later entry, in October 1918, he mentions the 'lure of politics' and the hope of doing something on behalf of the family and his father's memory 'to combat George's reactionary influence in the world'. He also records in 1913 that his brother Harry preferred the *Spectator* to the *New Statesman* and had voted Tory. Margaret, another sister, also married a conservative, and there is no evidence that the sisters opposed their husbands' views. Brian Simon, younger son of Ernest and Shena, records the 'evident move from the quite radical liberalism of Henry and Emily Simon towards a more general quietism or conservatism on the part of most (but not all) of his descendants', adding that this liberalism 'was passed on only to Ernest'.

In Henry Simon himself, the liberal principles were strong, right to the end. On 24 January 1899, in the last year of his life, he wrote to the Committee of the Schiller Institute in Manchester (on notepaper headed, to my delight, 'Lawnhurst, Didsbury'), resigning as President of the Institute. The reason was the decision of the Institute to celebrate the German Kaiser's birthday. He writes:

> I do not understand why the Committee has chosen to celebrate the Kaiser's birthday this year. The political and social circumstances in the heart of Germany ... are such, that one feels compelled to cover one's head in shame ... Does the Schiller Institute wish to celebrate things such as the expulsion of Danish milk-maids or the sudden removal of three reliable and highly-respected Jewish lady teachers from their posts in Berlin which they had held for years and where they had worked hard and honourably, or is it the now highly favoured and numerous governmental careerist and informer excesses which have led to the countless defamation trials and which recently culminated in the sentencing of an editor ...? Is it the Kaiser's and the Kaiserin's arm-in-arm friendship with the Sultan ... or is it the hand shakes which the Kaiser offers to over-zealous, naive sentinels, who, in a state of total peace, shoot down, without hesitation, a drunken citizen, which should be celebrated by the Schiller Institute?

In a short follow-up letter, in response to the Institute's urging that he reconsider, he says this: 'I do not fit in with the new German political spirit. I am the oldest descendant of a family which was heavily involved in the 1848 uprising, and I cannot renounce the idealistic aspirations of those times.' It was Henry's uncle, Heinrich Simon, who was actively involved in the 1848 revolutions, serving as a deputy in the Frankfurt Parliament, convened to present demands for a democratic constitution. The following year, as members of the assembly gradually left, or were recalled by their states, Heinrich remained as a member of the smaller but more radical Rump Parliament, which met in Stuttgart. In June 1849, military force was employed to prevent a meeting; the ninety-nine remaining members, including Heinrich Simon, faced serious charges. Simon went into exile in Switzerland, where he lived for the rest of his life. He took with him the Seal of the Reich Regency (the Rump Parliament).

Henry Simon, born in Prussia in 1835, studied mechanical engineering at the Zurich Polytechnic from 1855 to 1858, during which time he lived with his uncle Heinrich. It was Heinrich, in fact, who first arranged for Henry to visit Manchester. Heinrich's contacts were with the German community in Manchester, including others who had been involved in the 1848 events. In 1860 Henry moved to England, bringing with him the Seal which Heinrich had left to him. Many years later, the Seal was returned to the German government at a ceremony at the Ruhr University in Bochum in June 1990, a few months before the official reunification of Germany. Dr Rita Süssmuth, then President of the Bundestag, who was there to accept an honorary degree, was handed the Seal by Brian Simon, son of Ernest and grandson of Henry. It is possible Henry kept in a bank vault during the forty years in which he owned it. But of course I like to think that for at least some of the time it was kept here, at Lawnhurst.

Clara von Rappard,
*Portrait of Henry
Simon*, 1885

In Lysaker, Norway, just outside Oslo, there is another mansion house, called Polhøgda, which is very like Lawnhurst. Especially if you compare the interior grand hall and atrium, you see the similarities. The upper floor of the atrium shows this too. The exterior is in a rather different style – inspired by Italian Renaissance architecture – but the hall, staircase and interior gallery are more or less identical to those at Lawnhurst. It is no coincidence. The house was built in 1901 for the Norwegian explorer Fridtjof Nansen, who then lived there until his death in 1930. It was inspired by Lawnhurst: Nansen had borrowed the plans from Henry Simon, after staying there as Henry's guest in 1897. Nansen had recently returned from his successful three-year expedition to the Arctic, and on this occasion Simon delivered an address at a reception he held for Nansen to celebrate the success of the exploration, which had established a new Furthest North of 86°13.6'N. The speech praises Nansen's scientific work (he was also a pioneering neurologist and oceanographer) as well as his journey towards the North Pole and his difficult and hazardous return, concluding his comments on 'this worthy descendant of the Vikings' with an evocative passage about the homeward journey:

But even this homeward journey – fancy what it meant. Until they found land, for month after month on ice or mixtures of ice and

Interior, Polhøgda (left)
Interior, Lawnhurst (right)

Upstairs interior, Polhøgda (top)
Upstairs interior, Lawnhurst (bottom)
Polhøgda, Lysaker, Norway (right)

Houses and barns

water, in pitiless temperatures of cold and storm, sometimes near
starvation, the narrow escapes through which they passed are
enough to make any sensitive soul shudder at the possibilities
involved, *and that after all this we should have the great pleasure
of seeing our friend here before us is verging more nearly on the
miraculous than anything I have ever before come across in my life.*
[Italics in original]

For Henry Simon, the return of Nansen to Manchester must have been
particularly gratifying. He had been for many years a generous
supporter of scientific and educational activities in Manchester. With
C.P. Scott, editor of the *Manchester Guardian* newspaper, he founded
Withington Girls School, so that his own daughters and other girls
might have a good education. With two other Manchester men he
guaranteed the continuation of the Hallé Orchestra after the death of
Charles Hallé in 1895, and was prominent in the appointment of Hans
Richter as the new conductor. He took an active interest in Owens
College, precursor of Manchester University, endowing a chair in
German literature, and in 1898 laying the foundation stone for the
new physics laboratory. (His devotion to science was so passionate
that he had named his earlier house on Palatine Road 'Darwin
House', and given Ernest the middle name Darwin.) Simon had first
met Nansen in February 1892, at a dinner at Owens College, when
he decided to contribute funds to the forthcoming expedition. Later
the same year, he visited Nansen in Norway, taking his son Ingo with
him, to observe the construction of the new ship, the *Fram*, which
was to take the team north. He sent a donation of £100, which was
the only donation from outside Norway apart from that of the Royal
Geographical Society. Nansen, for his part, described Simon as 'the
only reasonable man I have met in England'. It is not recorded what
he thought of Henry Simon's contribution of books of philosophy
for the library of the *Fram*, notably works by Schopenhauer. Henry
wrote: 'They are for me ... what to a fervent Christian ... the Bible is
said to be ... I have no doubt that you and the friends that go with
you will find many a sentence for pleasurable discussion during the
possibly long hours of confinement.'

As it turned out, Nansen's record of Furthest North was overtaken
only five years later, in September 1899, by Luigi Amadeo, Duke of
the Abruzzi. Nansen undertook no further exploration, abandoning
an earlier hope of attempting a South Pole expedition. But because
of his reputation, and his innovations in equipment and strategy,
he remained a central figure in polar exploration, advising both

Scott and Amundsen (to whom he gave the *Fram* for his South Pole expedition) and many others. He also kept up his scientific research and publication into the first decades of the twentieth century.

But he is best known, in his post-adventurer life, as a diplomat and human rights worker. He helped negotiate Norway's independence from Sweden in 1905, and served as his country's representative in London in the following three years. In 1920, he was appointed by the Council of the League of Nations to investigate the plight of remaining prisoners of war after the 1914–18 war, many of them in Russia. By the summer of 1922, about 430,000 prisoners had been repatriated. That same year, Nansen was awarded the Nobel Peace Prize for his work. The citation also refers to his work with refugees – in 1921, he had also been appointed High Commissioner for Refugees for the League of Nations:

> The Peace Prize has been awarded to ... Nansen for [his] international work during the past few years. Especially his work for the repatriation of the prisoners of war, his work for the Russian refugees, his work to bring succour to the millions of Russians afflicted by famine, and finally his present work for the refugees in Asia Minor and Thrace.

Although some critics thought his intense focus on the question of prisoners of war was at the expense of the refugee problem, Nansen – or his office – produced an important and lasting aid to refugees then and since in what became known as the 'Nansen Passport'. Established in July 1922, originally developed for Russian refugees whose nationality had been revoked, the passport was to be issued by the country of residence, providing the crucial certificate of identity and the right to travel to stateless persons. Among holders of the passport were Marc Chagall, Igor Stravinsky, Vladimir Nabokov and Anna Pavlova. Eventually fifty-four countries recognised this arrangement. As Nansen's biographer notes, this was the first time that the position of the refugee was regularised. After his death in 1930, the Nansen International Office for Refugees was set up. In 1938, this Office was itself awarded the Nobel Peace Prize. Nansen aid was not available for refugees from the Third Reich – the League established a separate High Commission for Refugees from Germany in 1933 – though the fact that among the beneficiaries of Nansen aid were Saar refugees settled in Paraguay after 1935 is of personal interest to me. In February 1943, Eleanor Rathbone, in the middle of her exhaustive efforts on behalf of refugees from Nazi Germany, proposed (unsuccessfully) to the Foreign Office the adoption of a 'new Nansen', providing British visas to help save Jewish lives in Europe.

Nansen passport

In his second incarnation, as international statesman, Nansen narrowly
missed a meeting with Henry Simon's son. On a visit to Manchester
in February 1922, on a lecture tour to raise money for victims of the
famine in Russia, Nansen spoke at the Free Trade Hall. Ernest Simon,
at the time Lord Mayor of Manchester, was meant to preside at the
meeting, but was recovering from double pneumonia, and Shena
Simon took his place.

Fridtjof Nansen died three years before the accession of the National
Socialist regime in Germany created new kinds of refugee problems.
There is no question that his work on behalf of twentieth-century
displaced populations laid some of the groundwork for the political
and organisational efforts of the 1930s and 1940s. (I say this despite
some rather disconcerting things learned from his biography, including
his involvement very late in life with a Norwegian nationalist party,
and his friendly working association on the Russian famine problem
with Vidkun Quisling, later to become the collaborationist Minister-
President of Norway during the Nazi occupation.) But it was Nansen's
son, Odd Nansen, architect and writer, who took up the humanitarian
challenge in the new context. In 1936, he founded Nansenhjelpen,
to assist Jewish refugees from Central Europe escape to Norway.
After the invasion and occupation of Norway in 1940, he was active
in the resistance movement. He was arrested by the Gestapo in
January 1942, and spent three years in concentration camps, including
Sachsenhausen near Berlin. After his release at the end of the war, he
returned to Norway and resumed his career as an architect. Amongst
other projects, he led restoration work on Polhøgda, the Norwegian
Lawnhurst.

On 8 June 1940 the artist Kurt Schwitters and sixteen other refugees
left Norway on the icebreaker the *Fridtjof Nansen*. It was the last ship
to leave Norway before, two days later, the whole of Norway was
occupied by the German army. As a 'degenerate artist' (included in
the National Socialist anti-modernist exhibition of that title in Munich
in 1937), with an additional reason to fear Nazi policies because of
his tendency to epilepsy, Schwitters had reluctantly left Hanover on
2 January 1937. He and his wife Helma had spent enjoyable summers
in Norway since their first visit in 1929, in particular on an island in
the Moldefiord, Hjertoya, where he had taken a ninety-nine-year
rental on a tiny, primitive hut. It seemed the best place to go at

fairly short notice – the Gestapo were already taking an interest in his movements. He found an apartment in Lysaker, near Oslo. In his three years in Norway, he made a living teaching art and selling portraits and landscapes. There was no interest at all there, or later in England, in the avant-garde Dada-ist work for which he had been famous in Europe, and for which he was already known in the United States. Nevertheless, he started work on a new 'Merzbau' in his garden – like the original in Hanover, though on a far smaller scale, a three-dimensional, eclectic (and eccentric) collage of found materials on to an architectural frame. (The Hanover Merzbau eventually took over three storeys of a house, including the balcony and the top landing. It was destroyed in Allied bombing in 1943.)

When the Germans invaded Norway in April 1940, it was time for another hasty escape, this time with his son and daughter-in-law. Encumbered as always with many suitcases carrying his artist's materials, Schwitters also insisted on taking two white mice on the journey. The route was difficult and hazardous – a train ride north, a fishing boat in an area beset with mines. They found Trondheim already under German control, so had to continue up the coast. After a short internment in a school in the Lofoten Islands, which were still in Allied hands, they took another boat to Tromsö, where along with other refugees they boarded the *Fridtjof Nansen* and sailed to Scotland. After detention in a series of camps he was put on another boat, from Liverpool to the Isle of Man, where he was interned with other 'enemy aliens' for over a year and a half. Hutchinson Camp, where Schwitters was held, is on a hill in Douglas, overlooking the sea. (Onchan Camp, where my father spent a year at the same time, is a short distance along the coast, on the outskirts of Douglas.) Rather ironically, these months were the best of times for Schwitters in the eleven years between his departure from Germany in 1937 and his death in January 1948. In Norway he had financial troubles; his collage work and avant-garde sculpture were not understood; and he was often under suspicion as a German. After his release from the internment camp in November 1941, his health was very poor and his financial circumstances dire. In England too he failed to get recognition for his Dada (Merz) work, relying on support from old colleagues in Europe, supporters in the United States and the occasional critic or gallery owner in London. (The critic Herbert Read was highly complimentary in an essay for the catalogue of an exhibition of his work in 1944.) In Hutchinson Camp, though, he was surrounded by other Central European artists, writers and musicians. Famously, this camp quickly established a 'university', of lectures, performances, concerts and

172P

ISLE OF MAN

KURT SCHWITTERS
Portrait of Klaus E Hinrichsen 1941

Kcreative   2010   Lowe-M

Kurt Schwitters, *Portrait of Fred Uhlman*, 1940

Isle of Man Stamp, based on Kurt Schwitters's portrait of Klaus Hinrichsen

Austerity baby

debates. Best of all, Schwitters was able to get art supplies, especially for painting. As in Norway, he took commissions for portraits, charging £5 a piece for most. His co-internees record a likeable if very strange person, who chose to sleep under his bed, and had the habit of opening his window and barking like a dog in the evening. Still committed to his dual-aesthetic practices, he tried his best to continue to make Merz sculptures from whatever he could scavenge, most notoriously left-over porridge. The art historian Klaus Hinrichsen describes the scene: 'There, in the middle of the room stood, or rather shook, three pyramid-like sculptures, studded with stamps, cigarette boxes, nails, pebbles and shells and covered with mould – the world's first abstract porridge sculptures!' Another account from the artist Fred Ulhman:

At the time when I first met him he was living in a garret in our camp. On the walls hung his collages, made of cigarette packets, seaweed, shells, pieces of cork, string, wire, glass, and nails. A few statues made of porridge stood about, a material more impermanent than any other known to mankind, and it emitted a faint but sickly smell ... On the floor were plates, bits of stale bread, cheese and other remnants of food, and among them some larger pieces of wood, mostly table and chair legs stolen from our boarding-houses, which he used for the construction of a grotto round a small window.

Since that time Schwitters has been best known for his wonderful collage pieces, and his late small sculptures. These were featured in a major retrospective of his work at Tate Britain in 2013. But he was a brilliant portraitist too, reverting to skills he learned early at Dresden School of Art. Both Uhlman and Hinrichsen were among those who sat for him in the internment months. The Hinrichsen portrait was used in a special series of stamps, issued in the Isle of Man in 2010 to mark the seventieth anniversary of the internment of aliens.

Schwitters left Hutchinson Camp in December 1941. After three and half years in London, he moved in June 1945 to the Lake District with his new companion, Edith Thomas. They lived in Ambleside, and again he made a meagre living from portrait commissions, now asking £30 or 30 guineas rather than £5. In very poor health and increasingly weak, he was inspired in his final year by work on a new Merzbau. This was in a barn near Elterwater, at Cylinders Farm (called, of course, the Merzbarn). He managed to acquire funding from the Museum of Modern Art in New York (the gallery owned several of his works), and worked on the barn as much as his health would allow. It doesn't quite

Kurt Schwitters, *'Merzbarn' Wall Relief*

Merz Barn, Elterwater, Langdale Valley

Austerity baby

make sense to say that he left it unfinished on his death – the case of the Hanover Merzbau shows that such a work was never finished for Schwitters, since even after writing to a friend in 1934 that it was complete, he couldn't resist expanding and adding to it. But he was still working on the Merzbarn until his final short illness. He described it as the greatest sculpture of his life.

In 1965, the wall that is the central part of the Merzbarn was transported to Newcastle University, where it can today be seen in the Hatton Gallery. Conditions in the Cylinders barn were deteriorating, and the artist Richard Hamilton was instrumental in rescuing the work and taking it to Newcastle. In the past few years, Littoral Arts Trust has been awarded a grant to restore the Merz Barn, following two conferences near the site focusing on Kurt Schwitters's life and work, and his Lake District connections. Arts Council funding was cut off in 2011, and another one-off grant was acquired to deal with urgent structural repairs. The future of the barn is uncertain, but it can be visited today. It is in the Langdale valley, not far from Ernest Simon's Lake District cottage, Hellsgarth.

ISLE OF MAN

ERNST EISENMAYER
Violinist at Onchan Camp 1941

132P

Kcreative   2010   Lowe-Martin

Isle of Man stamp, 2010, based on Ernst Eisenmayer's
drawing of a violinist

8: **Philately and chemistry**

The Schwitters portrait of Klaus Hinrichsen was one of six 2010 special issue stamps in the Isle of Man. Among the others are paintings by other internees – Herbert Kaden, Herman Fechenbach, Imre Goth and an artist known as Bertram.

The stamp with a cover value of 132p is a 1940 drawing of a violinist in Onchan camp, by the Austrian artist Ernst Eisenmayer. I first saw the drawing at the Sayle Gallery in Douglas, Isle of Man, in April 2010. The exhibition, a version of which had originated at the Ben Uri Gallery in London the previous year, was 'Forced Journeys: Artists in Exile in Britain c. 1933–45'. For the Douglas show, I had loaned two works on paper, which had been my father's and which he had saved from his year in internment. One was a woodcut by the artist Paul Humpoletz – an image of a Jewish New Year service held in the Palace Theatre, Central Promenade Camp, on 3 October 1940.

Paul Humpoletz, New Year card, Isle of Man internment camp. 1940

Paul Humpoletz cartoon, Isle of Man internment camp, 1940

Later I found another print by Humpoletz in my father's papers – a cartoon about life in the internment camp.

We – my sisters and I – also loaned a drawing of my father, made in Onchan camp in 1940 by an unknown artist. The signature is not legible, and even the expert on Jewish artists in exile, Jutta Vinzent, who has written a book on the subject, could not recognise it. It is a beautiful drawing which I think really captures my father's character. The work itself is very large, and also unframed. I had had smaller copies made, so we could each have one, and it was one of the copies that was on display at the Sayle Gallery. It was also included – as was the Humpoletz New Year woodcut – when the exhibition transferred in June 2010 to the Williamson Art Gallery & Museum in Birkenhead. (Another lovely anonymous cartoon from Onchan – a tribute to my father, the camp's postmaster, on his thirty-seventh birthday – is also in our family album.)

At the opening of the exhibition in Douglas I was captivated by three drawings by Ernst Eisenmayer, including the violinist. They hadn't been in the original Ben Uri exhibition, which I'd seen the year before, and which showed six linocuts and three oil paintings of his. I learned from the curators of the exhibition that Eisenmayer was still alive, and that he would probably be delighted to hear from me. Through his

ZUM 27. NOVEMBER 1940.

Portrait of Arthur Wolff, Isle of Man internment camp, 1940

Birthday drawing for Arthur Wolff, Isle of Man internment camp,
27 November 1940

Ernst Eisenmayer violinist drawing, in Lawnhurst apartment

Austerity baby

daughter in London I got his email address, and we began an online correspondence. My first email from him is dated 15 April 2010. At the time, he was living in Israel with his other daughter; a year later he moved back to Vienna. I got used to finding an email from him in my inbox first thing in the morning – often several times a week. I think he read *The Guardian* online as soon as he got up. Many of his emails were about the (in his view) deplorable state of contemporary art.

I saw the report and photos on the Turner Prize shortlist. Can it get any worse?

What a lot of pretentious mediocrity!

The art-scene; the most promising young artists for 2011 had one with three balloons on separate thin rods in a small room. The others I can't even recollect. Three cheers for next one that features crap. And today a painter (!?) in Israel with abominations of figurative pictures. Anything you can do they can do worse.

I tend to get tired these days, so my correspondence has suffered a bit.

But today's modern 'art' on the guardian has given me a kick.

what price art!? Wei Wei and all. To me it is either laughable or very sad.

And so boringly dull. Piles of this, piles of that and piles of something else.

Ernst Eisenmayer

And, when I happened to mention that I was writing a catalogue essay for an exhibition of the feminist artist Mary Kelly's work: 'I find Mary Kelly boring, pretentious and sentimental. Even Germaine Greer has admitted that she went well over the top.' Never mind. The correspondence was very enjoyable, and I am pretty sure, anyway, that Ernst was trying to provoke half the time. In any case, he had agreed to sell me the Onchan violinist, and I was delighted about that. I took possession when it came off tour, after Birkenhead. Now it's on my wall, near the piano and next to my Harold Riley print of the Hallé conductor, John Barbirolli, whom I remember so clearly from my teenage years in Manchester.

With a friend, I visited Ernst Eisenmayer in Vienna in September 2011 – a memorable few hours of conversation and looking through art books in his little apartment. He took us for lunch in the apartment complex, a Jewish retirement home, where we were interrupted several times by elegant ladies of various ages coming up to greet and kiss Ernst, in one case with a gift of some delicacies brought back specially from a trip. In the past couple of years the email has gradually tailed off. Eisenmayer was already nearly ninety when we first began to correspond, and now, some years later, he has less energy for writing. Though I doubt that the passionate opinions about art and artists have abated.

The Isle of Man stamps commemorate an important moment in the island's history – one which was so little acknowledged even a few years earlier that when, in 2006, I asked staff in the main hotel in Douglas, which had been requisitioned as a camp prison during the war, what they knew about those years it was the first they had heard about it. The Sayle Gallery exhibition, articles about it in the local press, and the stamp issue seem to have changed that to some extent. As for the stamps themselves – I have never particularly taken an interest in stamps, but I have recently come to see how fascinating they can be and what stories they can tell. William Kaczynski, another refugee to Britain from Nazi Germany, interned at the age of four with his parents on the Isle of Man, has put together over many years a unique collection of postal history artefacts, all relating to the lives of refugees in the 1930s and 1940s. With Charmian Brinson, a scholar of the German exile experience in Britain, Kaczynski published a large selection of the letters, postcards and stamps in a beautiful book in 2011. These include letters from concentration camps and internment camps, postcards sent from boats en route to emigration, identity cards of refugees, wartime letters (sometimes with the stamp of the censor) to and from family members interned in camps, and letters and other documents from the organisations that assisted refugees in various countries. To see the facsimile documents – the handwriting, the old-fashioned type, the multiple stamps, recording journeys and, often, failed deliveries – is to understand somehow in a more immediate way the familiar and generic stories of persecution and exile.

Another story about stamps:

'What is that?' he said and extracted a stamp with his pincers. I bent down over the table to see what stamp he had fished out, but I had known immediately and was momentarily struck dumb ...

'What a queer affair,' he said, 'it's an overprint, I didn't know these existed. All the ones I know look different.'

'Every stamp looks different,' I said. 'Let me have a look.'

Cover of Charmian Brinson and William Kaczynksi, *Fleeing from the Führer: A Postal History of Refugees from the Nazis*, 2011

Philately and chemistry

'S-a-r-r-e,' he spelt out, 'Sarre? I know there are specimens with this overprint,' he continued, 'but this one looks queer, don't you think?'
'I've never seen any others,' I replied, tense and attentive.

'It's a genuine stamp all right,' he said, held it up in his pincers and looked at it against the light. 'It's been post-marked.'

In fact, it is not genuine. The narrator of Hans Keilson's 1959 novel *The Death of the Adversary* (described as a 'lost classic' on its reissue in 2010), is here a young boy, swapping stamps with his friend Fabian. The time is soon after the First World War, the place is Germany. The book records the narrator's experience of the rise to power of an unnamed 'adversary' through the 1930s until he (like the author himself, a German Jew) is obliged to flee to the Netherlands. In this early episode, he had been given a children's printing outfit for his birthday, and was trying his hand at overprinting on certain stamps. This, as he points out, was itself an interesting exercise in the postwar years:

> At that time, stamps with overprints were the great fashion. It was some time after the end of the first world war, and the general uncertainty showed itself in the field of stamps by overprints of every kind. Overprints have a curious fascination for collectors. The postal administrations everywhere seem to know it and ceaselessly fan this desire.

As it happens, this is something I know about – and very specifically in relation to those 'Sarre' stamps.

My own family's history can be read through stamps. In this case, it appears in the complex and fascinating philatelic transformations in the Saar area of Germany, which borders on north-eastern France. My father had a Saarland stamp collection, which at a certain point he handed over to my brother-in-law, a keen and knowledgeable stamp collector and dealer. From him I learned how the twentieth-century history of the Saar is legible in its stamps. As the territory changed hands, language, currency and denomination were all transformed, with overprinting sometimes registering recent or immediate shifts, and special issues recording particular events and appeals. And what was manifest in the stamps was, certainly for a few years in the 1930s, radically disrupting the lives of my grandparents and my father.

My father was born in 1903 in Fraulautern, a small town in the Saar region, not far from Saarbrücken, capital city of the region. The town was incorporated into the city of Saarlouis (renamed Saarlautern from 1936 to 1945), across the river Saar, in 1936. My father had left the Saar in 1923 to go to university, first in Freiburg and then in Berlin, but his parents remained there until 1939. Here is an early photograph of

Map showing Saarland

Family wedding group, Germany, c. 1906

Bertha and Arthur Wolff, Fraulautern

Philately and chemistry

Austerity baby

the family, taken somewhere in the region – the Saar or its adjoining territories. My father is the little boy at the front, in a sailor suit, so I suppose it dates from around 1906. His parents are at the top right, just below the man in a top hat. The other photo is of my grandparents' house in Fraulautern.

Like its neighbours in France, Alsace and Lorraine, the Saarland has had a complicated history of national affiliation, before and during the twentieth century. Through the nineteenth century the region was divided between France, Bavaria and Prussia, before being incorporated into the German empire in 1871. After the First World War French troops occupied the Saar. From an online encyclopaedia:

> The Saar Territory came into existence as a political unit when the Treaty of Versailles (1919) made it an autonomous territory, administered by France under League of Nations supervision, pending a plebiscite to be held in 1935 to determine its final status. France also received the right to exploit its coal fields until that time. When more than 90% of the votes cast in the plebiscite favored its reunion with Germany, the Saar was restored (Mar., 1935) to German control and constituted the Saarland prov.

The first new stamps, on sale on 30 January 1920, were contemporary German stamps, overprinted with 'Sarre', and with a heavy solid bar striking out the 'Deutsches Reich' at the bottom. A couple of months later, more German overprints were issued, reading 'Saargebiet', but not striking out the name of the Reich. The first definitive series for the Saar was issued in early 1921, showing local scenes.

Saarlouis is depicted in a new series of 1927, which borrowed designs from the earlier series, but in different shapes (and photogravure replacing roughly letterpress printed stamps).

In advance of the plebiscite (*Volksabstimmung*) of 1935, the Saar came under the German postal system, and four stamps were issued, perhaps to encourage voting.

Given the outcome of the vote, and the consequences for my grandparents, it is difficult not to regard this philatelic invitation with (if there can be such a thing) retrospective foreboding. Just as anti-Nazi Germans had left Germany for the Saar in 1933, inhabitants of the Saar now began to leave. But of course crossing the border into Alsace would not necessarily have done much more for enemies of the Third Reich than give them another five years of safety. And for those, like Leonie and her husband, who remained in that area of Germany – the Saar and its neighbouring regions, Baden and the

Palatinate – forced expulsion to France in October 1940 was the beginning of a new nightmare.

After the Second World War, with the Saar under French administration again, the complicated sequence of stamp issues reflects the political changes ('Saarpost', 'Saar', German currency then French currency), ending with the return of the region to Germany in January 1957, and special stamps inscribed 'Saarland' and 'Deutsche Bundespost'.

⟳⟲

The Holocaust memorial in Saarbrücken, capital city of Saarland, is an example of what James Young has called a 'counter-monument'. Designed by Jochen Gerz in 1991, it can be found in front of the palace in Saarbrücken, a former Gestapo headquarters. It is, however, invisible. The monument, entitled *2,146 Stones – Monument against Racism*, consists of cobblestones, each inscribed with the name of a German Jewish cemetery, placed into the ground with the inscribed side face down. A kind of conceptual art, the project has the very serious purpose of refusing viewers easy assimilation – or avoidance – of the history told. It is one of a number of such memorials and monuments which engage the viewer in a more active kind of contemplation.

James Young describes the characteristics of this kind of work:

> As the antimonument-makers show so well, by themselves memorials remain inert and amnesiac, mere stones in the landscape without life or meaning. For their memory, these memorials depend completely on the visitor. Only we can animate the stone figures and fill the empty spaces of the memorial, and only then can monuments be said to remember anything at all. In this way, we recognize the essentially dialogical character of Holocaust memorials, the changing faces of memory different visitors bring to them.

Another memorial by Jochen Gerz, in collaboration with Esther Shalev-Gerz, is the *Monument against Fascism* in Harburg in Germany (1986–93), a twelve-metre-tall, lead-covered steel column, on which visitors were invited to inscribe their names, and which – with seventy thousand signatures – gradually vanished into the ground, finally disappearing on 10 November 1993. As Young says: 'In effect, the vanishing monument will have returned the burden of memory to visitors: one day, the only thing left standing here will be the memory-tourist, forced to rise and remember for himself.' Its creators describe this as a *Gegen-Denkmal* – a 'counter-monument'. In the

Saarland stamps

Jochen Gerz,
*2,146 Stones
– Monument
against Racism*,
Saarbrücken,
1991 (right)

Philately and chemistry

square in Saarbrücken, though there is of course nothing to see, the street plaques reading 'Place of the Invisible Monument' ('Platz des unsichtbaren Mahnmals') indicate, albeit obliquely, the hidden presence.

Ernst Eisenmayer, attempting to leave Austria for France after the Anschluss of 1938, was arrested trying to cross the border near Saarbrücken, and taken to the city's prison. In his memoir, *A Strange Haircut*, he tells the story in comedic form, though he was kept there for weeks, and eventually sent to Dachau. He was released when his brother got him a visa to emigrate to England. His account of the prison, and of his two cell-mates, is cheerful throughout.

Sunday night was very much the same. It had been an uneventful day.

Bill and Bob had enjoyed their three after-meal-smokes. They had declared lunch, with the small piece of boiled beef next to the pell-potatoes and cabbage, a major feast truly worthy of a cigarette.

We had had a half hour's exercise, walking round the confined yard. We had played a few games of 'mills' on the bench. The pattern had been scratched into the wood, and the 18 pieces were made of kneaded bread. An awareness, that another week had passed without any news from outside, or what may or might not be in store for us made us both drowsy and restless. We had spent a good deal of time lying on our backs, heads on folded arms, occasionally dozing off.

'Till tomorrow, my lads!' said Bill at lights out.

'Another day, another week!' said Bob.

'Good night!' said, I watching the bright strips on the ceiling.

After finishing high school in Saarlouis in 1923, my father went to the University of Freiburg to study chemistry. His first semester's course registration list includes, rather surprisingly, an introduction to contemporary painting, with the famous art historian Walter Friedländer – scholar of the Baroque, teacher of Panofsky and later dismissed from his post by the Nazis. In the same semester, my father also registered for a class on 'selected phenomenological problems' with the founder of phenomenology himself, Edmund Husserl (also dismissed by the Nazis some years later). Disappointingly, neither professor has signed the Anmeldungs-Buch.

Freiburg, 1922 print

Arthur Wolff registration book, University of Freiburg

Arthur Wolff class register, University of Freiburg, Summer 1923

Anmeldungsbuch für stud. *chem. arthur wolff*

Sommer ~~Winter~~ Semester 192 3

a) Vorlesungen und Übungen — Die Titel derselben sind tunlichst vollständig einzutragen.	b) Namen der Lehrer	Vermerk der Quästur betr. Honorar (M. | ₰)	Prakt.-Beitrag (M.)	Eintrag der Lehrer über die Abmeldung
Einführung in die Malerei der neueren Zeit.	Friedländer	4.00		
Bildende Kunst Ostasiens	Grosse	6.00		
Übungen im Betrachten und Beurteilen ostasiat. Kunstwerke	Grosse	6.00		
Differential- u. Integralrechnung (mit Übungen)	Heffter	10.00		Heffter 28.7.23.
Experimentalphysik	Himstedt	*Na*		*Himstedt*
Die Religion Zarathustras	Lehmann	—		*Edv. Leh.*
Analyt. Geometrie d. Ebene (mit Übungen)	Loewy	10.00		*Loewy 25.7.2*
Weltwirtschaft u. Aussenpolitik	v. Schulze-Gaevernitz	4.00		Sch. G.
Experimentalchemie	Wieland	15.00		*H. Wieland* 26. JUL 1923
Ausgewählte phänomenologische Probleme	Husserl	8.00		
Teilnahme an Leibesübungen?				

Regelm. Teilnahme wird bescheinigt.
Das A. f. L.
i. V. Buchgeister

	M.	₰
Honorare	76.00	
Ersatzgelder (Praktikantenbeiträge)	2.00	
Auditoriengeld und Institutsgebühr		
Seminargebühr	4.00	
Bibliothekgebühr	1.00	
Lesehallegebühr	2.00	
Studenten-Krankenkasse	1.00	
Studentenausschuß und akadem. Hilfsbund . .		
Diebstahl- und Unfallversicherung	1	
Beitrag für „mensa academica" und Wohlfahrtsbeitrag	1.00	
„ „ Leibesübungen	1.00	
Summe		

Erhalten

Freiburg i. B., den 14 VI. 192 3

Akad. Quästur:

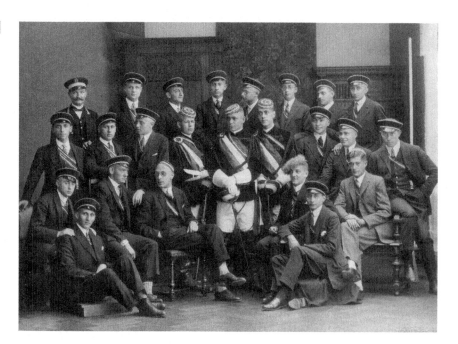

Jewish student fraternity, University of Freiburg,
c. 1923-26

Arthur Wolff in fraternity uniform

Austerity baby

Later, pursuing his studies for the PhD in chemistry at Friedrich-
Wilhelms-Universität in Berlin, my father also took a philosophy class
with the illustrious Professor Wolfgang Köhler (another academic who
would be gone ten years later, emigrating to the United States in 1935).
In Freiburg, my father joined the Jewish student fraternity, Ghibellinia.
Membership of a duelling fraternity always seemed a most unlikely
thing for him, but I learn now that it was more or less a requirement.
Miriam Rürup, scholar of German Jewish fraternities, has shown how
student fraternities were an integral part of student life. Banned from
membership of other fraternities, some of them explicitly antisemitic,
Jewish students established their own societies from the late 1880s.

But chemistry was the main thing, the subject for which his wealthy
American uncle Max was sponsoring him. He got his PhD in 1930,
the year he started his first job at the Oranienburg chemical firm in
Berlin, with a thesis on 'parawolframate'. I wish I could say I know what
that is, or what it was that he discovered. I also wish I could find his
chemical element in Primo Levi's 'periodic table'. From the internet,
I learn that 'wolframite' is an iron manganese tungstate mineral; and
that 'tungsten' is also known as 'wolfram', an element with the symbol
W. Wolframite has the composite formula $(Fe,Mn)WO_4$. The nearest
to it in Levi's classic chemistry-themed memoir is iron, though actually
I can't find any Fe in the many formulas and equations in my copy of
the thesis, so there is little profit in pursuing this connection. In fact
it is in Primo Levi's other writing that I discover suggestive links and
associations, though in *The Periodic Table* we find a very beautiful
formulation of what chemistry meant to him. It comes in the early
chapter on hydrogen, and recounts a time, when he was sixteen,
when he and his friend Enrico gained rather unauthorised access to
the laboratory, where their experiment ends with the lab 'filled with a
choking fog'.

> We had no doubts: we would be chemists, but our expectations
> and hopes were quite different. Enrico asked chemistry, quite
> reasonably, for the tools to earn his living and have a secure life. I
> asked for something entirely different; for me chemistry represented
> an indefinite cloud of future potentialities which enveloped my life
> to come in black volutes torn by fiery flashes, like those which had
> hidden Mount Sinai. Like Moses, from that cloud I expected my law,
> the principle of order in me, around me, and in the world.

By 1941, by now at university, and in the context of the new political
realities, he lost faith in chemistry as the source of certainty:

> Chemistry, for me, had stopped being such a source. It led to the
> heart of Matter, and Matter was our ally precisely because the Spirit,

dear to Fascism, was our enemy; but, having reached the fourth year
of Pure Chemistry, I could no longer ignore the fact that chemistry
itself, or at least that which we were being administered, did not
answer my questions.

Later, as is well known from his memoir *Survival in Auschwitz* (also
translated as *If This Is a Man*), being a chemist saved his life, when he
was employed in the Buna chemical plant at Auschwitz.

I am really no more interested in chemistry than I am in philately. And
yet the subject keeps drawing me in. It isn't just that it was my father's
profession, I think. In some research I did recently on the history of
Manchester, specifically the involvement of cotton manufacturers
and calico printers in the development of art education, I learned
fascinating things about the German dye industry, and the centrality of
immigrant German dye-experts in both manufacture and the nascent
university education in the city. And then my interest in colour – blue
and otherwise – led me to read about the history of synthetic dye.
Which turned out to link back to my father's job in Oranienburg in the
1930s, through the figure of Friedlieb Runge. Once you start reading
about chemistry in Germany, it also becomes unavoidable to confront
the implication of the profession with the politics of the Third Reich.
In *The Alchemy of Air*, Thomas Hager follows the doomed trajectories
of the brilliant chemists, Fritz Haber and Carl Bosch, whose careers
began with distinction (including, as it happens, discoveries relating to
synthetic dyes). In the early twentieth century, they both worked for
BASF, which had started as a dye company in the 1860s. In 1925, BASF
merged with two other companies to found IG Farben.

It became official in the fall of 1925 under the name of
Interessengemeinschaft Farbenindustrie Aktiengesellschaft (literally
the Interest Community of the Dye Industry, Inc.), an unwieldy name
that the public quickly shortened to IG Farben, or, simply, Farben.
Farben was, at the moment of its birth, the largest business in
Europe, the largest chemical company in the world, and the third-
largest business organization of any sort, measured by the number
of employees, on the globe (bested by only U.S. Steel and General
Motors).

IG Farben's part in the Nazi regime, and in the concentration camps,
has long been known. The company was 'Nazified' in 1937, and all
Jewish directors removed. It conducted chemical research in the
concentration camps, as Esther Leslie and others have recorded. And
IG Farben owned more than forty per cent of the company, Degesch,
which produced Zyklon B, the prussic acid mix used in the gas
chambers. Neither Haber nor Bosch was involved directly in any of this

work – in fact Haber resigned as head of his research institute in 1933, rather than obeying the directive to dismiss all his Jewish staff. And yet the perversion of his work could not be prevented. In the First World War, Haber's research had been essential for the development of gas attacks and chemical warfare, and for this collaboration he was briefly cited as a war criminal, moving temporarily to Switzerland in 1919 to avoid prosecution. But the fact that his research on insecticides had [179] some role in the development of Zyklon B cannot be laid at his door. He died in 1934, Bosch in 1940. Both had been awarded the Nobel Prize, Haber in 1919, the very year he expected prosecution, and Bosch in 1931.

In 1942, IG Farben built a factory to produce Buna substitute rubber, needed to help the war effort. Esther Leslie describes it:

> The SS supplied the bunks. The SS also supplied the guards. IG Farben contributed factory police. The SS took on the surveillance, discipline and supplies of inmates. Auschwitz IV had all the features of other concentration camps: watchtowers, barbed wire, sirens, armed guards ... Thirty-five thousand prisoners were deployed in the Buna plant of IG Farben in Auschwitz-Monowitz.

Primo Levi spent nearly a year in Monowitz, from arrival in February 1944 until the liberation of Auschwitz in January 1945.

> Every morning we leave the camp in squads for the Buna; every evening, in squads, we return. As regards the work, we are divided into about two hundred *Kommandos*, each of which consists of between fifteen and one hundred and fifty men and is commanded by a Kapo. There are good and bad Kommandos; for the most part they are used as transport and the work is quite hard, especially in the winter, if for no other reason merely because it always takes place in the open. There are also skilled *Kommandos* (electricians, smiths, brick-layers, welders, mechanics, concrete-layers, etc.), each attached to a certain workshop or department of the Buna.

When, after a few months, a Chemical Kommando was formed, Primo Levi was transferred to that. Managing to avoid a major 'selection' (that is, for the gas chamber) in October, he was saved again by fortune in January, when he escaped the 'death march' because he was ill with scarlet fever. After his return to Italy – itself a difficult journey taking another eleven months and related in his second book, *The Truce* – he resumed work as a chemist. He returned to the house – number 75 Corso Re Umberto in Turin – where he had been born, where he had lived most of his life, and where he remained until his death in 1987. From 1948 he worked at a chemical business specialising in varnishes and paints, retiring in 1977 to devote himself full-time to writing. In one of the last essays he wrote before his death, 'The spider's secret', he reflects on his professional life:

It seems strange to many people, and it is beginning to seem strange to me as well: for thirty years, that is, for the entire active center of my life, I've worked at producing varnishes – liquid substances that, when spread in a thin layer, after a certain period of time, become solid, either spontaneously or when heated. It seems to me just as strange that varnishes are displacing Auschwitz in the 'ground floor' of my memory: I realise this from my dreams, from which the *Lager* has by now disappeared and in which, with increasing frequency, I am faced with a varnish maker's problem that I cannot solve.

As for writing and chemistry – in an interview with Philip Roth that same year, 1986, he says: 'I worked in a factory for almost thirty years, and I must admit that there is no incompatibility between being a chemist and being a writer: in fact, there is a mutual reinforcement.'

Corso Re Umberto, 75, Turin

In 1937, realising he needed to leave Germany, my father began to apply for jobs abroad, writing to chemical companies with which his employer, ORACEFA, had connections. Amongst these were two in Italy – one in Milan and one in Pisa. In his letters, he gives his qualifications and describes his expertise. To Dr Sessa, at Industria Applicazioni Chimiche in Milan, he says only that he wants to leave his job 'for personal reasons'. A reference from ORACEFA on his behalf is a little more specific, though peculiarly (if understandably) bland in giving the real reason: 'Our chemist, Dr. Wolff in Oranienburg, who has been with us since February 1930 and whom you perhaps remember from your visits to Oranienburg, intends, as a non-Aryan, to leave Germany and start a life abroad. He has decided on Italy.'

Clearly it didn't work out for this particular move, but it's an interesting thought that my father might have continued his own work as a chemist in Italy instead of England.

In September 1994 I was in Berlin for a conference on art education, and took the opportunity to visit Oranienburg – the last stop on the S-Bahn north of the city. From my father's short memoir I knew that he had lived at Königsallee 22 – later, as he explains, to save his landlady embarrassment at having a non-Aryan in her house, he moved in with a Dr Baerwald and his wife at Markgrafenstrasse 2. Having these addresses proved not to be much help in the new Oranienburg.

Job reference for
Arthur Wolff,
10 June 1937

Oranienburg

,10.6.1937.

U/We.

Herrn

Dr. L. S e s s a ,

m.Br. S.A.Industrie Applicazioni Chimiche,

16, Via Ariosto,

Mailand (1/40) / Italien.

Sehr geehrter Herr Doktor !

Betr.:Dr.Arthur Wolff.

Unser Chemiker, Herr Dr. Wolff in Oranienburg,der
seit Februar 1930 bei uns ist und dessen Sie sich vielleicht
aus Ihren Besuchen in Oranienburg erinnern, beabsichtigt,
als Nichtarier Deutschland zu verlassen und sich im Ausland
eine Existenz zu gründen ; seine Wahl ist auf Italien gefallen. Herr Dr. Wolff kennt unseren Betrieb in Oranienburg

Oranienburg Chemical Factory (Oracefa), 1930

Austerity baby

When I got home (Rochester, New York), I wrote a long letter to my sisters to tell about my search:

> Neither of his streets was in the map. So I first assumed that the town had been bombed in the war and totally rebuilt ...

> Before I got there, I'd realised something else – that of course the street names wouldn't be there any more because they were both royalist names. So the East German city government would have given them new names. There were plenty to choose from on the map I'd bought – Leninallee, August Bebel Strasse, Strasse des Friedens. (Anyway, re-reading Dad's book on the train, I remembered that Königsallee had been re-named Adolf Hitler Allee – which I assume had been changed since the war.) So then I thought perhaps everything was still there, but with new names.

> I'd been told to find the Kulturamt at Schlossplatz 2, which didn't exist either on my map. So in Oranienburg I asked and got directions, and realised that (of course) the names had all changed again after reunification. So I bought another map. (I ended up with 3 Oranienburg maps.) Schlossplatz had been Platz des Friedens. I found it – the office was in the castle itself (which Dad talks about, and which seems to be pretty much as it was in his day) ... The castle was mostly derelict and empty, with signs of some redecoration in a few rooms. I eventually found Frau Herzberg, who was sitting down having coffee and cakes with a woman in an overall, who looked like the cleaner ... Didn't speak English, of course (being east not west German), so I had to mobilize my German, which seemed to work OK. The cleaner turned out to be (I think) another employee of the Kulturamt, because they both started rushing around looking for old maps and information – so did another woman (with heavy makeup and a beehive hairdo) who came in and immediately ran out again in search of other information for me. Eventually they told me that Königsallee is now Bernauerstrasse – the main road through the town, which I'd walked along from the station to the castle; that Markgrafenstrasse is Freiburgerstrasse, near the station on the other side; that ORACEFA is now a Dutch chemical factory called Byk; and that Runge's house is no longer there, but that there is a memorial to him on a nearby street ... However, I also found out (realised in walking through the town anyway) that Oranienburg *had* been heavily bombed in 1945, and that both dad's original addresses had gone. That's why I'm sending you photos of unattractive housing and shopping developments.

From one of the books they gave me – a photo of ORACEFA in 1930.

I was right about the bombing. There were three American bomber raids, in March 1944, and March and April 1945, in which hundreds were killed and much of the town destroyed. According to *Spiegel* magazine, on 15 March 1945, 612 aircraft flew on a mission against Oranienburg, which was an important SS command centre; in forty-five minutes, a total of 4,977 explosive bombs and 713 incendiary bombs were dropped. A few postcards I bought there, and the photographs in the books given to me at the Kulturamt, are all I have to give me an idea of what it was like when my father lived there from 1930 to 1938.

Odd Nansen also experienced the bombing of Oranienburg, described in his wartime diary, *Day after Day*. Arrested by the Gestapo in January 1942 as member of the resistance in Norway, he was held first in the Grini prison camp and then transferred in October 1943 to Sachsenhausen concentration camp, where he remained until March 1945. I knew the camp was near Oranienburg but, as I wrote in my letter to my sisters, I was shocked to find it was only a fifteen-minute walk from where my father lived. Nansen records the raid of 15 March 1945:

Then came the alert, and one of the heaviest raids we have ever witnessed. It was on Oranienburg, and the camps and buildings in the immediate neighbourhood of Sachsenhausen were levelled with the ground.

From the moment the first bombs dropped, we realised that this was more our concern than usual. For in general we've got used to taking very little notice. But the bomb-thuds this time were not to be stifled. At every deafening crash, and one had the impression that whole showers of bombs were coming down, the huts shook so that everything hanging on the walls or standing loose on shelves fell to the floor, and every moment we were expecting that the roof would lift in the blast and the walls collapse on us. But they stood up, for a wonder. The raid lasted two hours – that is, it didn't leave off, only quietened down a bit, and the planes stopped coming; otherwise it's still on, twenty-four hours later, and has been all the time, with an unbroken series of exploding time-bombs. During the raid the whole of Oranienburg and district, up to this camp, was larded with bombs, a large proportion of them time-bombs. All night long colossal explosions have been shaking the huts in all their joints.

On 18 March, three days after the raid, Nansen writes that time-bombs were still exploding:

The condition of Oranienburg is said to be indescribable. Thousands of people were killed. Dead men are lying in the ruins, and bits of people lying everywhere. They have no water or electricity. We are without them in camp as well, and the lavatories can no longer be used.

Earlier in the diary he records his arrival at the camp, which has echoes of the accounts of arrival at Gurs camp, where Leonie arrived three years earlier:

We were in cattle trucks, tired and stiff after a night and a day without sleep or rest. The train stopped at a station with a jerk. A board said: *Oranienburg* ... Then suddenly the whole train moved on again. It didn't stop till we reached another station, which said Sachsenhausen and was some distance from Oranienburg. There we were ordered out ...

We were lined upon the platform in three ranks and counted ... It was a country station with an elderly station-master, whose entire family was assembled at the door of the station building looking curiously at these prisoners from Norway. Up in the garret rooms on the first floor a married couple sat gazing on us. He in shirt sleeves, with a cutty pipe in his mouth, and she gaping eagerly, no doubt at the queerest of us, wanting to make out what kind of people these were. I don't suppose it was the first prison transport she had gazed on from that window.

In his memoir, my father writes that his Works Director, Dr Kurt Lindner, was arrested soon after the National Socialists took power in January 1933, and sent to Sachenhausen, though soon released. In fact the camp at Sachsenhausen was established only in 1936, so it is more likely that Dr Lindner was sent to a camp set up in 1933 in an old brewery in Oranienburg, which was used for political prisoners in the first years of the regime. This closed the following year. Sachsenhausen too was for political prisoners, but also for 'racially or biologically inferior' people. Over two hundred thousand prisoners were held there between 1936 and 1945, and one hundred thousand of them died. From an online summary:

The camp was established in 1936. It was located 35 kilometres (22 mi) north of Berlin, which gave it a primary position among the German concentration camps: the administrative centre of all concentration camps was located in Oranienburg, and Sachsenhausen became a training centre for *Schutzstaffel* (SS) officers (who would often be sent to oversee other camps afterwards). Executions took place at Sachsenhausen, especially of Soviet prisoners of war. Among the prisoners, there was a 'hierarchy': at the top, criminals (rapists, murderers), then Communists (red triangles), then homosexuals (pink triangles), Jehovah's Witnesses (purple triangles), and Jews (yellow triangles). During the earlier stages of the camp's existence the executions were done in a trench, either by shooting or by hanging. A large task force of prisoners was used from the camp to work in nearby

Sachsenhausen Tower A

Sachsenhausen monument

Austerity baby

brickworks to meet Albert Speer's vision of rebuilding Berlin. Sachsenhausen was originally not intended as an extermination camp – instead, the systematic murder was conducted in camps to the east. In 1942 large numbers of Jewish inmates were relocated to Auschwitz. However the construction of a gas chamber and ovens by camp-commandant Anton Kaindl in March 1943 facilitated the means to kill larger numbers of prisoners.

The camp was liberated in April 1945 by Soviet and Polish units of the Red Army, and for the next five years it served as a Soviet Special Camp, soon holding twelve thousand prisoners; in all, sixty thousand were detained over the five years before the camp was disbanded in 1950. The prisoners were mainly German officers, Nazi collaborators and anti-Soviet activists. At least twelve thousand of them died of malnutrition and disease during that period.

When I visited Sachsenhausen in 1994, it was only a few years after the reunification of Germany. I was struck by a prominent notice there (German only), which I copied down carefully:

Sehr geehrte Besucher,

Diese Ausstellung wurde 1961 eröffnet. Sie entspricht den Intentionen der damaligen Partei- und Staatsführung der DDR. Eine völlige Neugestaltung der Ausstellungen ist in Vorbereitung.

Die Leitung der Gedenkstätte

My translation:

Dear visitors,

This exhibition was opened in 1961. It represents the views of the previous party and state leadership of the DDR. A completely new configuration of the exhibits is in preparation.

The management of the memorial

And, indeed, the later display, which I saw on another visit in June 2007, is radically different. For one thing, the fate of the Jews was no longer marginalised. The story the regime of the DDR wanted to tell was centrally one of the anti-fascist struggle and the heroism of the Soviet fighters. As Caroline Wiedmer says, 'This ideal fighter was in no way related to the masses who had been persecuted for racial reasons, i.e., the Jews and the Sinti and Roma, nor indeed did it include women'. Moreover, the insistence on interpreting National Socialism 'through the lens of a Marxist theory of fascism' also obviated any focus on the primary victims of the regime.

The ramifications of this economic interpretation of fascism were that those aspects of mass killing that could not be perceived as having been economically motivated – in other words, the genocide of the Jews and the Sinti and Roma – were naturally threatening to the self-understanding and legitimization of the new state … Since anti-Semitism and racism, according to the GDR paradigm, were at most lesser symptoms of class struggle, the destruction of the Jews was hardly mentioned in the exhibit.

The primary monument erected on the site, called the Monument of Nations, 20 metres tall, is intended to recall the heroic resistance of the prisoners of the camp, and the triumph of anti-fascism. In its focus, and in its aesthetic and political strategies, it could not be more different from the Saarbrücken memorial.

As for the observers at Oranienburg station, watching the Norwegian prisoners arrive, the evidence of local knowledge is elsewhere very clear. Another Sachsenhausen inmate, Jerzy Pindera, records an episode in the summer of 1941, when – rather incredibly – the concentration camp inmates were sent to work on a job in the middle of the town itself:

The whole day was an unusual one – for the first time since I had arrived at Sachsenhausen, I was assigned to a Kommando that was working in Oranienburg, a small city not far from the camp and not far from Berlin. We were building a sewer system in a residential area of the city. I was in shock, just from seeing the city. It was a typical residential neighbourhood, of single-family homes with neat lawns, small flower gardens, and with normal, properly dressed men and women walking along the sidewalks, and children playing in the yards. It was like a fairy tale, so far removed was it from what had become my reality … I could sense that these people, the residents, were very uncomfortable around us. We did not belong, we felt that as well. We were intruding and not welcome, our presence was dangerous and only just tolerated. Some viewed us with contempt, some with open hostility. I also saw embarrassment and confusion in the faces of some who passed by. I suppose we did not look like the hardened criminals they have been told we were.

A melancholy afterthought on the question of stamps in the period of exile. Or rather, here, a question of lack of stamps. Among the papers kept by Leonie's daughter, Eri, in New York – mostly letters from Leonie in Gurs and Marseilles – is this much-travelled envelope.

Envelope for 13 October 1941 letter

Brooklyn, October 13 1941

Meine liebe Mutti!

Ich komme gerade aus einer Stelle, die nur ein Tag gedauert
denn es hat mir nicht gefallen. Ich konnte kaum los kommen, denn sie wollten
mich kaum gehen lassen, & musste allerlei Ausreden benützen, um wegzukommen. Ich
warte nun auf Willy, der natürlich nochmkeine Ahnung hat, dass ich schon wieder
zu Hause bin. Nun es findet sich schon wieder was anderes. Jedenfalls habe ich
in diesem einen Tag nahezu verdient, um dafür ein Paket an Dich zu bestellen.
Ich habe nämlich gestern noch ehe ich zu arbeiten anfing ein Paket ab Lissabonn
für Dich bestellt mit allerlei guten Sachen, wenn es nur auch ankommt. Eine
Frau Dr. Ebert, die früher Euch auch beraten hat in Auswanderungsfragen, nahm die
Bestellung hier an, & bestellt es per Kabel durch das Rote Kreuz in Portugal.
Sie sagte, dass es etwa in 4 Wochen bis 2 Monaten dort ankommen sollte. Sie selbst
erinnert sich Deiner, & hat auch selbst noch Verwandte dort. Wenn es klappt, sen-
de Dir öfters durch sie was. Es soll enthalten: 450 Gramm Kuchen, 360 Gramm Kakao,
580 Gramm Ölsardinen, 750 Gramm Schokoladerippen, 400 Gramm Tunafisch, 900 Gramm

Extract from letter, 13 October 1941

Austerity baby

It is pretty difficult to read all the stamps and the handwritten addresses (and readdresses). As far as I can see, it is an air mail letter from Eri Kahn (by then Mrs William Cohen) in New York to her mother, Leonie Kahn, in France. It is sent from New York to the Gurs camp in October 1941. Someone has forwarded it to Leonie at the Hotel du Levant in Marseilles (where we know she went in December 1941), so the letter perhaps arrived too late in Gurs. But it seems Leonie never got it – it was returned to Eri in New York, with a flurry of stamps and dates – right up to one of 2 September 1949! At the top right, on the front of the envelope, it says 'Parvenu Oloron sans timbres'. Oloron is the small town near Gurs, probably the access point for mail to the camp in Gurs. The letter is still inside the envelope, at least the first page. Eri tells her mother she has just sent her a package via Lisbon, 'mit allerlei guten Sachen' (with all kinds of good things) – 450 grams of cake, 360 grams of cocoa, 58 grams of sardines in oil, 750 grams of chocolate, 400 grams of tuna, 900 grams of marmalade, 450 grams of honey. She tells her mother the packet is for her alone, and not to share. She speaks about trying to get the requisite papers for Leonie, about her husband Willy's plans to go to Washington on her behalf. A year after her father's death in Gurs, she says how sad it is that he can't be there to share Leonie's difficulties with her. And offers a sad reflection: 'It is often like a dream for me when I look at the picture of you both in front of me on my writing desk, only four short years before my departure.'

I don't know whether the non-delivery was because it arrived too late to catch Leonie in Gurs or – perhaps more likely – because the letter arrived 'sans timbres' – without stamps.

George Romney, *The Spinstress: Lady Emma Hamilton at the Spinning Wheel*, 1782-86

9: Spinster

George Romney's portrait of a 'spinstress' in Kenwood House is a bit misleading. The subject, Romney's muse Emma Hart, later Lady Hamilton, was not actually a spinner – this was just one of many romantic and theatrical poses she held for the painter. Nor was she a spinster. By the time she sat for Romney for this painting in 1784–85, she had already been employed in a 'temple of health' (possibly a brothel), become pregnant at the age of sixteen and been for a few years the mistress of the Hon. Charles Greville, second son of the Earl of Warwick. Greville brought Emma to Romney in 1782; the artist was very taken with her, and in the next four years she sat for him over a hundred times. In 1786, Greville needed to find a bride with a substantial income, and he offered Emma to his uncle, Sir William Hamilton, British Envoy in Naples. Hamilton had already commissioned her portrait from Sir Joshua Reynolds, and in Naples he arranged for other artists to paint her, including Elisabeth Vigée le Brun. Rather sadly, it seems that Emma did not quite understand the new arrangement, and hoped that Greville would join her. In 1791, she and Hamilton were married, at the respective ages of twenty-six and sixty-one, putting an end to any chance of claiming her for what, fifty years later and in another country (America) was called 'the maiden sisterhood', with its associated state of 'single blessedness'.

In thinking about the single women in the recent history of my family, a tradition I continue, I have become interested in the changing discourses about spinsters and unmarried women. The usual definition of a spinster is on the lines of 'an unmarried, childless woman of middle age or older'; you can't be called a spinster if you have children or if you are divorced or widowed, and you are not a spinster if you are only twenty-five (although of course there was a time when that was on the edge of becoming an old maid). It's not clear whether single women who have had sexual relationships are spinsters – perhaps only if the relationships have been relatively short-lived? More complex still, with regard to terminology, is the case of women living with women, which many single women have done, particularly in the late nineteenth and early twentieth centuries. Eleanor Rathbone made that comment about not wanting her portrait painted because 'a spinster does not want to gaze on her own portrait in her own home'.

But by then (1932) she had been in a decades-long relationship with Elizabeth Macadam, and, although Rathbone's biographer concludes that it was very unlikely that it was a sexual relationship, there is no doubt that it was a committed and loving life-partnership. So not really single, then. But spinster in the sense of being unmarried and childless. In any case, more interesting than establishing definitions is to trace the ways in which single women have been regarded in Western culture, specifically Britain and America, over the past two centuries. I feel myself on some kind of mission to reclaim the word 'spinster' as, if not positive, at least neutral, though I think this may be doomed. Most dictionaries have a note that the term is usually derogatory. Even the lovely sounding Italian name for spinster – Zitella – has 'pej.' in brackets after the word in the dictionary.

In my father's family, there have been women who never married, and whose lives I'd love to know more about. His father's cousin Emma (sister of Julie, the mother of Marcel who died in the French Resistance) was single, and lived with her widowed sister, and *her* sister-in-law in her later years. It was with them that my cousin Marlyse lived, in France, as a young girl in the 1930s.

Emma is on the right in this photograph from 1953 (and I am in front, with Julie's hand on my shoulder). More mysterious, and a generation earlier, is Emma's aunt Minette Levy (1845–1919), my father's great-aunt, oldest of nine siblings, whose grave I first saw in the Jewish cemetery in Saarlouis in June 1993 (and then on a later visit in September 2014). The familiar story of the oldest daughter looking after the elderly parents? I have really no idea – I know nothing at all about her.

On my mother's side, though, I had more direct knowledge of spinsters. Cousin Bessie for instance, who was often at my grandparents' house, a few doors from ours in north Manchester. She lived with her brother, Joe, in a small terraced house in Cheetham Hill. I think her blonde hair must have been peroxided. I recall her as sweet and kind, perhaps a bit simple. Certainly she remained placid and smiling in the face of the bossiness of my grandmother, her cousin, including one particular recurring put-down. My grandmother, Becky Noar (née Gertler) was determined that her granddaughters wouldn't become old maids. This meant we were never to have the last biscuit or cake from a plate (a superstition which shows up quickly in a google search). She would say to her cousin 'Bessie, you have the last cake. You're an old maid anyway.' And Bessie would laugh (and perhaps take the cake – I can't remember that part). The other important

Detail of family photograph Thionville, 1953

Grave of Minette Levy,
Saarlouis Jewish cemetery

Spinster

Author as bridesmaid

Author as bridesmaid
(standing second
from left)

Author as maid of
honour

Austerity baby

Noar family photograph, north Manchester, 4 March 1964

superstition, still circulating now, was 'three times a bridesmaid, never a bride'. A mistake I did make.

This is my grandparents' golden wedding anniversary party. Bessie is to the right of grandma in the main picture, linking her arm. And next to her are two other spinsters, my grandmother's sisters, Rosie and behind her to her left Mary Gertler. 'The aunties', as we all referred to them, played an important role in my childhood. They lived together, and for many years had their home in Blackpool – 17 Peel Avenue. My parents used to send me and my sister Veronica to stay with them in the holidays.

My grandfather came sometimes. On 5 June 1952 he wrote to my mother, enclosing letters from Veronica and me, from which I discover how we spent the time there. (Ever the good girl – age nine and only one spelling mistake in my letter.)

Dear mummy, daddy and granny [my father's mother].

We are enjoying ourselves here very much. We will send you a postcard soon, but now we want to write quite a lot to tell you what we're doing. Yesterday we went on the sands with Grandpa and Auntie Rosy. Grandpa took us in the morning and bought us ice-cream. Then after dinner Auntie Rosy took us and we had fairy-floss and a donkey-ride. Veronica didn't have one though because she was frightened that she'd fall off. Of corse she had the fairy-floss. Today, in the morning, uncle Michael [mother's youngest brother] took us to the pictures to see Laurel and Hardy. First he took Grandpa to the Ritz to book for to-night. We left him there and went to the pictures. But we didn't see the picture because it is Sunday. We went to the Jewish Men's Club to look for him but he wasn't there, so we went on the pier for a bit. We went on the penny-in-the-slot machines and uncle Michael spent a shilling, Veronica spent a shilling and I spent a shilling. Uncle Michael spent three whole shillings. (But Grandpa said it didn't matter because if boys take girls out the boys should pay for the girls.) After that we went back to the club to see if Grandpa was there yet. He wasn't so we went home.

In another letter in the same envelope, I report that we went on the motor launch on the lake in Stanley Park with Veronica and Auntie Bessie (so apparently she visited there too), and that the lake is three times bigger than the one in Heaton Park, which our grandfather used to take us on in north Manchester. The next day was pretty active:

This afternoon Pat, Margaret, Paddy and I made up a concert of acrobats. It was quite good. Pat's mother and Grandma watched. I did cartwheels on both hands, cartwheels on one hand, walking on my

Letter from Blackpool by author (aged 9)

Spinster

hands, standing on my hands, standing on my head, tossing over, and standing in crab, and standing on my hands and putting my feet up to the wall at the same time. I wish you could have seen the concert.

Auntie Mary isn't mentioned in the letters, and it may be that she was working. She was a dressmaker and seamstress, while her younger sister Rosie kept the house. Many of our dresses were made by Auntie Mary, including the frocks for my second bridesmaid appearance with my sister and cousin and a fourth young girl. According to family lore, Mary had a fiancé, or a beau, who was killed in the First World War. It was never discussed, though, and the only remaining (possible) evidence is a few postcards from France and Belgium among her possessions when she died. There is nothing written on the back, and no address or stamp, so they must have been enclosed in an envelope, or perhaps even brought back at some point.

Where studio portraits of Mary and Rosie Gertler don't give much away (we were always so impressed by Rosie's waist-length hair though), a few other photos of Mary as a young woman suggest a real sense of style and a certain liveliness which she retained throughout her life, and which the more down-to-earth, imperturbable, prosaic Rosie didn't share.

Souvenir cards from Belgium and France

Whether or not Mary Gertler lost someone in the First World War, the aunties were among the one and three-quarter million 'surplus women' in Britain in the 1920s. This figure meant, as Virginia Nicholson has said, that one in four British women remained single. But although her book, *Singled Out*, is subtitled 'How Two Million Women Survived Without Men after the First World War', it is more about thriving than about just surviving. Nor does she assume that all – or even most – of the women were reluctant spinsters. Rather, in this period of expanding opportunities for women, and in the context of continuing constraints for married women, remaining single was often a positive choice. One of the women she interviewed told her 'Once you get over the disgrace, it's the best life!' I assume the reference to disgrace is intended humorously – in many ways, earlier negative stereotypes of the spinster had disappeared in the postwar years, as women increasingly took up professions and other kinds of work, and expanded the travel adventures embarked on earlier by a few intrepid 'Victorian lady travellers'. Nicholson quotes the writer Cicely Hamilton, from 1940:

Time was – and not so very long ago – when the middle-aged English woman who had not found a husband was considered fair game for the jester; by the humorists of the Victorian age she was always depicted

Studio photograph of Mary Gertler (top)

Studio photograph of Rosie Gertler (left)

Spinster

Mary Gertler

Studio photograph of Mary Gertler in gypsy costume

Austerity baby

Studio portrait of Mary Gertler

Spinster

as a figure of fun – an unattractive creature who, in spite of all her efforts, had failed to induce a man to marry her. That was the old maid as a past generation saw her – and as we do not see her today; we have too many unmarried women successful in business or professional life, distinguished in literature, science, and art, to be able to keep up that joke.

In other ways, though, the negative image persisted, as Nicholson says:

[204]

Twenty years into the twentieth century an unmarried woman had possibilities undreamed-of by her spinster aunts. But the aunts, with their wispy buns and ruined hopes, were still there to haunt her. The contempt and humiliation suffered by maiden ladies were an ever-present reminder of the spinster's predicament.

Even the feminist writer Winifred Holtby confronted the assumed fate of the unmarried woman, in an essay in 1934:

What am I missing? What experience is this without which I must – for I am told so – walk frustrated? ... Shall I suffer horribly in middle age? At the moment, life seems very pleasant; but I am an uncomplete frustrated virgin woman. Therefore some time, somewhere, pain and regret will overwhelm me. The psychologists, lecturers and journalists all tell me so. I live under the shadow of a curse.

A peculiar aspect of the changing discourse of the spinster is the collusion of feminism with her demonisation in the early twentieth century. Or rather, the spinster is once again negated, but this time by the (apparently) forward-thinking work of feminists and sexologists. Eleanor Rathbone, champion of women's rights throughout her life, is berated by Sheila Jeffreys for her long campaign for the endowment of motherhood, in the form of family allowances. In this privileging of marriage, and of married women, Rathbone 'betrayed the cause of spinsterhood and the independent woman' – even though, as Jeffreys points out, Rathbone was herself a 'lifelong spinster'. Even worse was the consequence of new theories of sexuality and post-Freudian psychology, whose emphasis on the importance of sexual fulfilment pathologised those who were not sexually active (as well as those of 'non-normal' – that is, non-heterosexual – sexuality). Jeffreys quotes an article in the first issue of the feminist magazine *Freewoman* in November 1911, entitled 'The spinster':

I write of the High Priestess of Society. Not of the mother of sons, but of her barren sister, the withered tree, the acidulous vessel under whose pale shadow we chill and whiten, of the Spinster I write ... In the auditorium of every theatre she sits, the pale guardian ... She haunts every library ... In our schools she takes the little children, and day by day they breathe in the atmosphere of her violated spirit.

And Alison Oram quotes Stella Browne, a feminist sex reformer writing in 1917:

> I would even say that after twenty-five, the woman who has neither husband nor lover and is not under-vitalised and sexually deficient, is suffering mentally and bodily – often without knowing why she suffers; nervous, irritated, anaemic, always tired, or ruthlessly and feverishly fussing over trifles.

Oram shows that there were other voices in the interwar period, rejecting this view of the single woman. But the fact is that once again the spinster – the idea of the spinster – was the receptacle of the negative imagery that was the incidental product of contemporary thought. The irony in this early twentieth-century historical moment is that it was progressive, even feminist, discourses which pathologised singleness.

The postwar period was not the first time that the problem of 'surplus women' had come up in Britain. According to the 1851 census, there were 405,000 more women than men in the population at that time. In 1862 the essayist W.R. Greg suggested enforced colonial emigration, though he did foresee a few practical problems:

> The first difficulty is chiefly mechanical. It is not easy to convey a multitude of women across the Atlantic, or to the Antipodes by any ordinary means or transit. To transport the half million from where they are redundant to where they are wanted, at an average of fifty passengers to each ship, would require 10,000 vessels, or at least 10,000 voyages.

In post-revolutionary America too there were growing numbers of single women. Lee Virginia Chambers-Schiller records the percentage of spinsters rising gradually through the nineteenth century, to about eleven per cent among those born between 1865 and 1875. This wasn't necessarily the result of a gender imbalance in the population – she does not give those figures (or the numbers of unmarried men). But the fact (or choice) of singleness for women is significant in the period. And especially interesting, in the light of the changing idea of the spinster over two centuries, is the high esteem in which single women were held, and the great value placed on singleness by many women themselves. In the seventeenth century, spinsters were seen as sinful, 'an evil to be exorcised from community life because solitary women menaced the social order'. By the eighteenth century the judgement was less severe: 'To be unmarried was disgraceful, a reproach rather than a sin. Society regarded the spinster with more scorn than fear.' But in the years after the revolution all this was replaced by a benign, even adulatory, attitude. The Cult of Single Blessedness affirmed the vocational life of unmarried women. Celibacy was perceived by some as a healthy choice, as well as, in religious discourses, a moral one. In particular, the good works done by single women, free from the demands of marriage and motherhood, contributed to their promotion as admirable beings:

> Antebellum culture correlated goodness with usefulness, and usefulness with happiness ... Noble work of high purpose provided the only meaningful satisfaction in life ... Single blessedness, then, assured unmarried women eternal grace and social approval if they assumed a noble work in a good cause at the inspiration and command of their God.

At the same time, many women were vocal in their criticisms of the institution of marriage, and the greatly circumscribed role for women who married. Chambers-Schiller even quotes a (male) Unitarian clergyman on woman's prospects as a wife, writing in 1841:

> Perhaps if she knew what life has in store for her, she would shrink back. The marriage festivity would not be without its fears ... so many whom I have united for life have I seen overtaken by calamity ... that to me there is ever an undertone of sadness in the wedding's mirth.

The feminist Susan B. Anthony wrote to a friend in 1859: 'In the depths of my soul there is continual denial of the self-annihilating spiritual or legal union of two human beings.' But of course unmarried women were themselves, in this period, very much constrained in social and legal terms; and in many cases were expected to fulfil family responsibilities. And negative stereotypes never entirely disappeared. By the late nineteenth century, the view of the spinster had shifted again. The expansion of opportunities in education and work increased women's autonomy and independence, and single women began to be seen as more of a threat. Accordingly, the derogatory discourses emerged again, here too compounded in the early twentieth century by sexological theories which proposed the harm of celibacy, at the same time proclaiming the dangers of non-married sexual practices.

Leonora Carrington, *Old Maids*, 1947

In Britain, probably the spinster's best moment was in the last years of the nineteenth century and the very early twentieth century – the time of the 'new woman'. Judy Little traces what she refers to as 'the spinster code' up to the 1930s, a period in which, as we have seen, opinion turned away from single women, a real contrast with the situation a few decades earlier:

> With the pioneering example of Florence Nightingale behind them, unmarried women were by the 1880s actively defining a positive image of themselves in occupations outside the family and outside the traditional work of governess and companion. These spinsters did not perceive themselves as burdens on family or society; they saw their new roles as nurses, settlement administrators and workers, or college teachers as vocational choices which allowed them independence and yet gave them an opportunity to serve others ... The spinster of the late nineteenth and early twentieth century could choose the unmarried state and know that this implied a positive vocation.

This essay, about spinsters in the novels of Muriel Spark, appears in a collection about unmarried women in the twentieth-century novel, tracing the journey from 'old maid' to 'excellent women' to 'radical spinster'. It is interesting that often when we try to think about unmarried women we turn to literature – Miss Matty in Elizabeth Gaskell's *Cranford*, certain figures in Dickens (Miss Haversham), the 'new women' in novels by George Gissing (Rhoda Nunn) and H.G. Wells (Ann Veronica). Even in the modern novels, like Gissing's *The Odd Women*, the heroine may be shadowed by the other kind of spinster – haunted by the 'aunts, with their wispy buns and ruined hopes', as Nicholson puts it. For Rhoda Nunn, it is the Madden sisters, a kind of relic of the Victorian unmarried lady, with no profession (though in the end they plan to start a little school) and a modest, circumscribed existence. The essays in Laura Doan's *Old Maids to Radical Spinsters* show this tension between the two images of single women: limited, conservative, timid, constrained, and adventurous, outgoing, even transgressive. In novels by E.M. Forster, Virginia Woolf, Barbara Pym, Dorothy L. Sayers and others, these types and trajectories are explored. In the end, in fiction and in life, the spinster never quite shakes off the residue of the aura of loneliness and unfulfilment.

From *Cranford*:

> Miss Pole began a long congratulation to Miss Matty that, so far they had escaped marriage, which she noticed always made people credulous to the last degree; indeed she thought it argued great natural credulity in a woman if she could not keep herself from being married ...

> I don't know if it is a fancy of mine, or a real fact, but I have noticed that, just after the announcement of an engagement in any set, the

unmarried ladies in that set flutter out in an unusual gaiety and
newness of dress, as much as to say, in a tacit and unconscious
manner, 'We are also spinsters'.

From *The Odd Women*:

> 'We differ a good deal, Rhoda, on certain points which as a rule
> would never come up to interfere with our working in harmony. You
> have come to dislike the very thought of marriage – and everything
> of the kind. I think it's a danger you ought to have avoided. True
> we wish to prevent girls from marrying just for the sake of being
> supported, and from degrading themselves ...; but surely between
> ourselves we can admit that the vast majority of women would lead
> a wasted life if they did not marry.'

> 'I maintain that the vast majority of women lead a vain and miserable
> life because they do marry.'

Sylvia Townsend Warner's much-admired novel *Lolly Willowes*
is sometimes cited as an excellent model for the spinster. The
protagonist, Laura (Lolly) Willowes, decides at the age of forty to go
beyond the roles of daughter and then sister and aunt, and to live
alone in a village. Eventually, in a strangely supernatural turn in what
had seemed a traditionally realist novel, she communes with witches
and with Satan before claiming her own absolute independence:

> The night was at her disposal. She might walk back to Great Mop and
> arrive very late: or she might sleep out and not trouble to arrive till
> to-morrow. Whichever she did Mrs. Leak would not mind. That was one
> of the advantages of dealing with witches; they do not mind if you are
> a little odd in your ways, frown if you are late for meals, fret if you are
> out all night, pry and commiserate when at length you return. Lovely to
> be with people who prefer their thoughts to yours, lovely to live at your
> own sweet will, lovely to sleep out all night!

I have never particularly liked the novel – and this idea of the spinster,
reminiscent of the equally unappealing 'crone' once advocated by
Germaine Greer as women's best feminist guise, is too eccentric
and anti-social for my taste. (I do realise it's a kind of fantasy, not a
programme for action.) But a strange coincidence has brought me to
a keen interest in Warner's life, and to the story of her partnership
with the writer Valentine Ackland (called Molly until the late 1920s). In
the late 1930s, their relationship was shaken by Valentine's affair with
another woman, which for a few years caused Sylvia great pain, and at
times threatened to destroy their partnership. For me, the story starts
in Rochester, New York.

When I interviewed Elizabeth Holahan in Rochester in 2002, she told me that Kathleen McEnery had made small portraits of her and of her sister Margaret. She told me a little about her sister, who died quite young and who, she said, had had a warm friendship with McEnery's husband, Francis Cunningham. Margaret is the rather frail-looking young woman in a checked dress.

I didn't know – there was no reason for her to mention it – that she had two other sisters (and, I think, a brother). Annie Holahan was living in New York City in the 1930s, trying to establish herself as an actress. After a brief affair with the English writer Llewellyn Powys, she followed him – apparently without his invitation or consent – to his home in Chaldon, Dorset, in 1935. Another sister, Evelyn Holahan, born in Rochester, was also living in New York, working for the Benton and Bowles advertising agency in Manhattan. She travelled to England to rescue Annie and bring her home, and during her stay in Dorset she met Sylvia Townsend Warner and Valentine Ackland. The three got on well, and stayed in touch after Evelyn's return to America. (At one point, in May 1936, Sylvia wrote to Evelyn to ask her to bring her a copy of Havelock Ellis's *The Psychology of Sex* if she came to England – probably one of those texts to blame for the denigration of the single woman.) It seems likely that Evelyn and Valentine had a brief affair during the Dorset visit, and although this was never pursued, another of Valentine's romantic entanglements, three years later, had long-lasting consequences for all three women.

In May 1939, Evelyn Holahan went to meet Sylvia and Valentine and to welcome them to New York when their boat docked at the quayside. With them was an American woman, Elizabeth Wade White, who had first met Sylvia at a literary event in New York in 1929, and who was now in a difficult triangular relationship with her after starting a passionate affair with Valentine Ackland in late 1938. It was an affair that was to continue, on and off, for several years after the war. On this occasion in 1939 she had been staying with them and then in a nearby cottage in Dorset for several months, and was accompanying them to the United States. Sylvia had been invited to the Third American Writers' Conference in New York in June. For Elizabeth Wade White and Evelyn Holahan the quayside encounter was their first meeting. Within a year they were partners, sharing an apartment in New York City. They were together until Evelyn's death.

Although when I met her in Rochester in 2002 Elizabeth Holahan did not mention her sister Evelyn, she herself is mentioned twice in

Kathleen McEnery, *Portrait of Margaret Holahan*

Austerity baby

Kathleen McEnery, *Portrait of Elizabeth Holahan*

Spinster

Peter Haring Judd's book about the Warner/White/Ackland triangle. Soon after a visit to Dorset by Elizabeth White in 1950, Evelyn was in Rochester, looking after her sister Betty, who was recovering from an operation. In a letter to Elizabeth she declares again her love for her, referring to 'whatever sorrow and unhappiness we have had between us' and offering her hope and belief that they 'will know a good life always'. She adds:

[212]

> I am distressed about my situation here for I so want to go home & yet I cannot bring myself to leave Betty at this moment for she is as weak as a kitten. Her arm is getting better but she still cannot completely dress herself. I know I am a comfort to her & she has begged me to stay but I told her today that I have a home & obligations and that I cannot & do not wish to remain away indefinitely.

Judd's second reference to Betty (Elizabeth) Holahan causes me to wonder whether there might have been another reason she wanted her sister to stay longer. He recalls talking to her at a memorial service shortly after Evelyn's death in 1985, when the subject of Evelyn's relationship with Elizabeth White came up:

> With no preliminaries, Evelyn's sister came in with what she, I suspect, had been holding back for years. Coming directly to the point, she told me that Elizabeth had 'killed' her sister, turning Evelyn into 'a housewife'. So, she became an alcoholic and victim of its antecedent ills. I was not surprised. For at least the previous twenty years on social occasions and at home in the evenings, Evelyn became unsteady, her slurred speech leading to bickering and arguments ... In Oxford ... I heard Helen Gardner warn Elizabeth not to do so much entertaining, 'remember Evelyn, Elizabeth'. Evelyn told me more than once how she enjoyed 'following this one' who brought her to friendships and experiences that she enjoyed. But she did not have the same level of physical and psychic stamina ... Evelyn was also aware, as her letters showed, that Elizabeth had been more deeply attracted to Valentine than to her; after the 'end of the affair' she saw the frequent letters come in from Valentine and forced herself to accept the periodic meetings, not secret but excluding her ... Elizabeth's break with Valentine in 1950 was a clear choice in Evelyn's favor, but over the ensuing years the continuation of relations with Valentine seemed to have had a subtly corrosive effect.

Evelyn had long ago given up professional life, and apart from a three-year period in Oxford in the early 1950s, when Elizabeth resumed her long-postponed research on her distant ancestor, the seventeenth-century poet Anne Bradstreet (receiving a B.Litt in 1953), the couple lived from 1943 in the house in Connecticut that

Elizabeth had inherited. They gave up their New York apartment on East 19th Street in October 1945. For a time, they ran a small business in old books, 'White & Holahan Books', from their home; Judd doesn't record how this fared, or how long the project lasted. It does seem that for the most part Evelyn, whose letters indicate a rather sad acceptance of an inequality of love, lived much of her life in Elizabeth's shadow. Though Judd records that when she died Elizabeth was 'for a time almost speechless with grief'.

Among the 'surplus women' of the interwar years in England, teaching was the most likely career. Katherine Holden reports that in 1931 over half of single professional women aged thirty-five to forty-four were teachers – one in eleven of all single women of comparable age in employment. Virginia Nicholson provides the detail – 180,000 women teachers in 1911, another 13,000 during the First World War, and a total of 210,000 by 1931. As for the continuing ambivalence about the unmarried woman in the period:

> Schoolmistresses had been long defined by their spinsterhood ... teaching remained, par excellence, the profession for middle-class single women – 85 per cent of women teachers in the 1920s and 1930s were unmarried. Servants, typists, mill-girls and shop-assistants might view their employment as a way of marking time till they married, but teaching carried the heavy stigma of spinsterhood.

> So, if you hoped for a man, you would go to great lengths to avoid admitting you were a teacher. 'That would put off every man in sight,' lamented one of them, '... so young teachers ... said they were secretaries or something like that.'

Nicholson quotes a young woman from the early 1920s:

> So what did the world have to offer a surplus young woman in the aftermath of the First World War? For Winifred Haward, now twenty-three, the answer was staring her in the face. It was the job that any educated woman like her would qualify for: teaching. As many as 80 per cent of female graduates from Oxford and Cambridge colleges in the 1920s got jobs in the classroom. But Winifred was determined not to become a teacher:

> 'All our mistresses at the High School were spinsters and that seemed the predestined fate of anyone who entered the profession. I like men's company. I wanted to marry, and had romantic ideas of love.'

I don't have statistics for women teachers in the period after the Second World War, and have not read similar studies of the lives of – and attitudes to – single women in that period. But I find myself recognising (and now feeling rather ashamed of) that somewhat disdainful attitude to the spinster teachers. I can't remember much about primary school, but certainly at my single-sex secondary school, especially during the years, perhaps from the age of fifteen, when I had a pretty active social life outside school, I had the view that these teachers had somehow missed out on what was important.

Looking, at random, at the records for Manchester High School for Girls for the year 1956 (I was thirteen), I count thirty-seven 'Misses' (and two 'Mademoiselles' – French *assistantes*) and seven 'Mrs'. Sometimes teachers got married and left (or stayed on in their new names). The same record states:

Miss Butterworth married and became Mrs Stevens.

Miss Gilmartin married and became Mrs Walker.

Miss Anne James married and became Mrs Sharples. She left to move to Canada.

But most of the teachers (mistresses) were older and single. The school's most famous headmistress, Sara Annie Burstall (head from 1898 to 1924) had nothing against marriage. In her autobiography, she recalls the famous Miss Buss, head of North London Collegiate School where Miss Burstall taught from 1882 (on £120 per annum), speaking on the subject: 'We were encouraged to go on, to remember that we might be called to another "state of life" and be ready for it. She rejoiced for her mistresses to get married, and promoted more than one engagement.' What strikes me most now, though, is the richness and fulfilment of the lives of the single teachers. They were highly educated, cultured women – especially impressive in the late nineteenth and early twentieth century. Miss Burstall studied mathematics at Girton College, Cambridge, from 1878 to 1881, at a time when women could not graduate with a degree. Later, in 1884, she was able to take a BA at the University of London. At MHSG she took over from the first headmistress, Elizabeth Day, who had held the position since the foundation of the school in 1874. About this important step in her life she writes: 'On the 18th of May, 1898, after buying a new hat to give me confidence, I went down to Manchester summoned to meet the Governors of the High School ... And so began the real work of my life, for which all the rest had been a preparation.'

Sara Burstall

In a history of the school which she wrote in 1911, she describes Miss Day's appointment in 1874: 'The Head Mistress is Miss Day, a lady who holds a first-class Cambridge certificate, and who has distinguished herself highly in divinity, English literature, French, Italian, and Greek.' She quotes a contemporary source:

> Miss Day, the young Head Mistress of the new School, was a very attractive and interesting personality. Although small and slight and girlish in appearance, she gave the impression of forcefulness and power. Her keen and eager face expressed strong determination and decision as well as kindliness and goodwill. It was set off by crisp, black, wavy hair turned back very simply over a fine and shapely head. Her piercing, brown eyes looking out from under rather heavy black eyebrows, seemed to take in everything at a glance.

A pupil remembers her, at a later date, sometimes sitting in a classroom at a lesson 'knitting quickly all the time'. 'She was fond of green, a dark hunter's green, and usually dressed in green cashmere.' Another teacher in the 1890s, Miss Agnes Simons, student of Newnham, taught history until she left in July 1898 to go to Italy to study art. Another pupil praises her:

> She was one of the most stimulating teachers I have ever known. When we girls first saw her, we wondered whether we should like her, for she looked very erect, very grave and statuesque, and almost austere. But when she began to teach us History we saw that we had fallen into master-hands ... She vivified each person she named, and as she described in glowing words the personalities of those stirring times, we almost felt we were back among them ...

> Tall and slim, clad in soft shades of blue or green or terra-cotta, she was a pleasure to watch, her head so finely poised, the brown hair parted down the middle, the oval face alight with interest, the brown eyes, rich colour of cheeks and lips, and the delicacy and strength of the lines of the mouth, forming a whole which we girls found very attractive.

By the time I was at MHSG, the Head Mistress was Miss Agnes Mary Bozman, head from 1945 to 1959. Educated in Scotland, with an MA with honours in maths and natural philosophy from St Andrew's University, she had been headmistress of Dame Alice Owen School for Girls in London.

Agnes Bozman

To us she always seemed a rather distant and forbidding, though elegant, presence, but eulogies on her retirement in 1959 and her death the following year describe her as someone who took a personal interest in everyone – girls, teachers, groundsmen, caretaker. Her professional life was full – president of the Association of Headmistresses, serving on the Joint Matriculation Board, the Court of Manchester University and the National Committee of Vice-Chancellors and Principals. Her Presidential address at a conference of the Headmistresses' Association indicates a nice sense of humour:

> The ideal headmistress should possess the physical vigour, enthusiasm and optimism of a healthy woman of thirty. This should be combined with experience, caution and the staying power of Methusaleh. She should show tenderness, sensitive awareness of the problems of others and an imperturbable calm in facing her own. She should love children and adults as well, of course, as her car and probably her dog.

Miss D.L. Pilkington, chairman of the governors of the school, spoke warmly of Miss Bozman on her death, recalling her great success in rebuilding the school, destroyed in the bombing of December 1940, on her arrival after the war:

> It was in no small measure due to her enthusiasm and imaginative resource that this was successfully accomplished so soon. Her mature and purposeful intelligence, her zest and her gracious charm brought her ready allegiance from her staff and pupils. Her quick and tender sympathy was the great support to many and notably to less successful colleagues.

A tribute in the school magazine describes her as a 'truly wise person' with 'dignity and grace, energy and gaiety, wit and deep humanity'. My regret at not having had any sense of this – of barely having her in my vision – is only partly alleviated by another comment:

> Girls in Junior forms, who probably felt that a Head Mistress was someone rather remote and awe-inspiring, would have been surprised at just how well they were known. If they fell ill, they never failed to receive a message and the gift of a book or jigsaw puzzle from Miss Bozman.

The school dedicated a new rose garden to her in 1962, with a plaque reading 'We recall the pleasure which Miss Agnes Bozman found in roses, especially in yellow roses'.

Miss Annie Ellis taught physics at Manchester High School for Girls from 1917 to 1959. (I am surprised to see, when I look up old school reports, that I got A for physics with her in three terms in the Fifth and the Upper Fifth forms in 1958 and 1959.) It was always said she had an important past – that she had helped Rutherford split the atom. Of course this meant nothing to us, though we knew it was somehow a major scientific advance. We just couldn't imagine how she could have helped

– she was a tiny woman, and we (at least I) had some vague vision of her wielding a huge hammer as she attacked the thing, trying to split it. It seems to have been true. Miss Ellis took the Maths Tripos at Girton College in Cambridge from 1911 to 1914, followed by a first-class physics degree at Manchester in 1917. On 30 June 1919, Ernest Rutherford (the 'father of nuclear physics') wrote a short reference for her:

She proved herself an unusually able student and her work both theoretical and practical was very well done. In her final year she did a number of advanced experiments in Optics and commenced an investigation in that subject. In recognition of her ability she was awarded the Hatfield Scholarship. I consider Miss Ellis to be an unusually well qualified physicist as she is strong both in the mathematical and the experimental side.

Her final year as a student, 1917, was the year in which Rutherford and his colleagues succeeded in splitting the atom; it's not clear what role Miss Ellis had in that particular project. She continued to work with him at the university on a part-time basis, while teaching at the high school, until his departure for Cambridge in 1919. At the Rutherford Jubilee International Conference in Manchester on 5 September 1961, she received an honorary M.Sc in recognition of her work with him.

An interviewer for the *Manchester Guardian* in June of that year, two years after her retirement, captures a still lively and happy woman. She says she spends her leisure time walking in the hills ('wherever they are, but particularly in Scotland, the Shetlands and the Outer Hebrides'), and reading – mystery novels and historical fiction. A boy calls at her door regularly on Tuesday and Thursday evenings for help with his maths or physics homework.

If there is a single striking fact about this little woman – she is barely 5ft high – it is her jolliness. She is the living rejection of all the unkind things ever said about schoolmistresses, yet she is immensely proud of having been one.

Her hair is silver and swept back to an academic bun, but it caps a pink and round face that breaks into creases and smiles at the slightest provocation.

I don't think I read that piece at the time. As it happens, it was the summer I left high school, at the age of eighteen. Painful though it now is to acknowledge it, I probably wouldn't have believed then that a single woman of a certain age could really have been happy.

Child's coloured drawing

Austerity baby

10: **Annunciation**

When I was living in California in the late 1980s and early 1990s, for those years in the role of quasi-stepmother, there was one day a moment of revelation. At the kitchen table in our El Cerrito apartment, Jamie, aged about four, was working on a picture in his crayoning book. It was one of those line drawings, of the sort I had taken such pride in doing neatly when I was a child.

Instead of carefully keeping within the lines, he was happily scribbling his colours down, only vaguely respecting the outlines of the shapes. I found this quite stunning – as if it had never occurred to me that you were allowed to do that. I think I envied the freedom he felt, to do exactly what he wanted without caring about rules, and without an idea of what was 'right'. In a way, in that moment I understood how early the good-girl imprint had solidified for me, and how such training in children then tends to block any real possibility of creativity and imagination. There are plenty of psychoanalytic accounts of this kind of blockage. And the particular obstacles produced in the context of parental damage or trauma were something I began to read about a few years later: Anne Karpf's book about growing up as the child of Holocaust survivors was published in 1996. But in that moment I wasn't thinking about explanations. I was simply struck by seeing an image of what an unobstructed expression might look like.

I am surprised now to see in my old school reports that my teachers sometimes referred to my 'originality' and 'imagination'. I am almost certain that I never exhibited much of either, at primary or at secondary school. A report when I was seven says 'Her work is neat, and shows originality' (which somehow sounds quite contradictory to me). The year before, at six: 'Much neat careful work done – shows imagination'. Perhaps teachers in 1949 and 1950 equated neatness with imagination. At secondary school I appear to have got B+ and even A marks for Art and Music, and even more strangely, given my physical timidity, one report for Gymnastics says 'Janet has imaginative and original ideas, particularly in group work'. I have no idea at all what kind of ideas these might have been. I am quite convinced that my route, through school and since, has been the dutiful one of study, a good facility for quickly grasping information and rules (I excelled in Latin and Maths especially), and a constant eye on what was required for approval and for getting things right. In a way, I also think this explains the choice, eventually, of an academic career, and before that the decision to work for several years as a secretary. (There is still a real pleasure in filing, putting things in alphabetical order, getting beautiful stationery, attending to all the necessary administrative aspects of life and work. And in those days too, there were the joys of the elegant Pittman's shorthand, with its own compensatory aesthetic rewards.) And yet this life of efficiency has been paralleled – or perhaps it's better to say occasionally interrupted – by repeated attempts at creativity. Over the years, I have from time to time taken piano and classical guitar lessons; enrolled in drawing classes; studied ballet and contemporary dance; joined creative writing groups and workshops. Nearly always, and even when my attempts were good enough, I managed to undermine this, finding a reason to give up or drop out. I recently came across a little sketch I did in my early twenties, of my friend Linda, sitting on a windowsill and writing to her boyfriend. I don't remember why I was inspired to do it, but now I think it's really not bad.

Sketch of a girl

I think I would like to have taken art more seriously – perhaps even studied it. Somehow there was never any question of it. Recently I've gone back to occasional life-drawing sessions and am happy enough with some of my attempts.

The most unlikely example of my on-off half-hearted relationship to artistic work was the offer in 1971 of a place to study contemporary dance full-time at London School of Contemporary Dance. After starting ballet again at the age of twenty, while I was working as a secretary in Manchester, I discovered Martha Graham and contemporary dance when I was a student at Birmingham University, and moved to London half-way through my PhD studies to take classes at LSCD. For reasons I still don't understand, as I never had the slightest intention of taking dance seriously, I signed up one day for an audition for the School. And was accepted.

At the age of twenty-eight, and with students about ten years younger, I spent another year taking classes there, working part-time as a secretary in the Anthropology Department of University College. Within a couple of years, I'd abandoned this, finished my PhD, and moved to Leeds for an academic job. It isn't that I see this as a missed opportunity, or that I wish I'd become a dancer. It just makes me wonder what was behind that decision to audition. A desire for a sign that a different version of myself might have been creative-artistic, rather than practical-analytic? Maybe that's it.

Line drawing of a woman and charcoal drawing of a man from life-drawing classes

Patrons of the School: Dame Ninette de Valois D.B.E.
Miss Martha Graham
Sir John Gielgud
The Rt. Honourable the Earl of Harewood
Henry Moore O.M., C.H.
Dame Marie Rambert D.B.E.

London School of Contemporary Dance

The Place,
17 Duke's Road,
London, W.C.1.
Telephone: 01-387 0151/2/3

Miss Janet Wolff,   3rd June, 1971.
41 Pine Road,
Didsbury,
MANCHESTER.

Dear Miss Wolff,

As a result of the audition you attended on Friday, 28th May,
I have pleasure in offering you a place at this school as a Full
Time student from 14th September, 1971.

I understand that it will be necessary for you to work during
next year and I wonder if you would like to come and discuss this
with me.   Perhaps you would like to telephone and make an appointment.

I shall look forward to hearing whether you will be able to
accept.

Yours sincerely,

Pat Hutchinson Mackenzie

Pat Hutchinson Mackenzie
Principal

General Director : Robin Howard   Principal: Pat Hutchinson Mackenzie

Annunciation

With writing it has been something similar. At moments alongside a
university career I have considered, sometimes attempted, so-called
creative writing. The first time was when I worked at the South Bank
Centre in London, before moving to the United States in 1988. In our
small writing group, which met once a week at lunch time, I wrote a
version of the piece that now starts the third chapter of this book. On
one occasion our exercise for the week was to produce a response to
the meal vouchers we had – as usual, a task at first I thought would
be impossible but one which, when I sat down to it, turned out to be
unexpectedly easy. With this little piece, though, what emerged quite
surprised me and I think rather shocked my three writing colleagues.

23.2.88

SBC meal voucher – Nightmare version.

Pastel colours, pleasant shapes, neat typography disguise the
hideous intent of this document. Innocent repetition in three
sections calms the recipient while obscuring its true meaning. The
visual imbalance, overweighted to the left, should have warned of
its other purpose. The haphazard mix of lettering was a clue to the
unbalanced mind of its designer.

Meal voucher, South Bank
Centre, London, 1988

Eighteen pale blue images of the river threaten death by drowning.
To reinforce the point, a darker identical image dominates the top
right of the document; it is impossible to escape. The progression
of primary numbers gives the illusion of progress, perhaps of
development. But there is no difference between the three, and we
are trapped in a static, enclosed world.

Unassuming red letters, which appear to promise sustenance, in fact
represent the anorexic's worst fears. Here, we will be forced to eat:
red for danger.

At the bottom, the concentration camp number is stamped three
times.

Later that year I left London to live in Berkeley, California. There I took
a couple of informal writing workshops, too 'alternative' to inspire
me to write anything interesting (instructions to intuit our feelings –
that sort of thing, which others did seem to find useful). Teaching for
a term at the University of Minnesota a couple of years later, I was
accepted into an MA memoir-writing class, for which I wrote a couple
of rather mediocre longer pieces. And that was it, until January 2006,
when, having decided to move back to England from New York that
coming summer, I wrote the first three chapters of this book within a
few weeks.

I had decided to major in sociology. It was a safe subject and would not interfere with my painting. (Chaim Potok, *My Name Is Asher Lev*)

Meal
voucher

In early May 1990, still in California, I was ambushed by another surprising thought. When a routine medical exam at Kaiser Permanente Hospital disclosed a lump on my thyroid gland, the nurse-practitioner sent me for a follow-up check. The oncologist called to say that a fine-needle biopsy showed a malignancy. After meetings with her and with the surgeon, it was agreed that I could postpone surgery for a few weeks so that I could keep a commitment to a three-week visiting appointment at the University of California in Davis, and eventually I was operated on on 13 June that year. Thyroid cancer has an excellent prognosis and survival rate, and compared with other cancers its treatment is not usually very debilitating. There was the surgery to remove the gland, and (as it turned out) an adjacent lymph node which was affected; and then doses of radioactive iodine, taken by mouth. And that was it. The weeks without thyroid replacement did leave me weak and rather ill, as did the regular follow-up checks for a few years, when each time I had to come off the thyroid replacement medication for several weeks. But no radiation sessions, and no chemotherapy. And since then, now a quarter of a century ago, no recurrence. The thing that took me by surprise, though, was my intuitive image of the tumour, and my relationship to it during those weeks of waiting. My reaction wasn't in fact very different to my reaction to Jamie's picture. I was in awe of the cancer, and full of admiration for its boldness, its brave venture and, most of all, its flaunting of the rules. It was as if, at last, some part of me was daring to be independent, even bad. I felt proud of it, and also very protective of it – a small thing, trying to grow, which needed encouragement and preservation. At some level I was sad that the surgeon was planning to foil its efforts and cut it out.

A number of writers, including cancer survivors, have written about the way in which cancer and its treatment have been conceptualised in military terms: invasion, attack, destruction and so on. Most famously, Susan Sontag's *Illness as Metaphor* explores this language of war, premised as it is on the idea of colonisation of the body by something quite alien. 'In cancer, non-intelligent ("primitive", "embryonic", "atavistic") cells are multiplying, and you are being replaced by the non-you. Immunologists class the body's cancer cells a "nonself"'. The visualisation techniques often recommended to cancer patients, especially by practitioners of alternative medicine, generally involve imagining the chemotherapy as an ally, a kind of avenging army, attacking the evil tumour so that it shrinks and disappears, though as Jackie Stacey says, in her reflections on the narratives of cancer and its cure, there are 'plenty of images in the alternative medical literature: from the aggressive ones, hungry sharks eating a cauliflower, to the gentler ones, a block of ice melting in the sun'. Stacey, motivated by the need to understand her own cancer and the discourses she encounters in its diagnosis and treatment, also considers the pervasive rhetorics of self-blame – the idea that there is a 'cancer personality', whose disease is the result of repressed emotion, suppressed anger and stress. Interestingly, despite my own self-image as unexpressive and very self-contained (I almost recognise Anne Karpf's early question to her therapist: 'What is a feeling?'), I never once had this conception of my cancer, as a punishment for years of inhibition. But nor was I able to think of it as my enemy. Possibly if I had gone through chemotherapy I would have had to imagine the toxic doses as the good guys. Jackie Stacey records this moment:

I am now required to embrace the treatment I have been struggling to avoid. Chemotherapy must be visualised as a positive intervention. Not poison, but pink champagne, they suggest in Bristol [the Bristol Cancer Help Clinic]. The more I can think of it as an ally, the less it will harm me.

But I was fortunate enough not to have to embark on those most difficult and incapacitating treatments, and so there was no need to mobilise imaginary weaponry to destroy the invader. My totally benign view of my malignancy therefore persisted, though, needless to say, not to the extent of telling my doctor that I didn't want surgery.

I find, in fact, that I am not unique in harbouring a kind of affection or respect for my cancer. Catherine Arthur, diagnosed with the breast cancer from which she eventually died, produced a series of 'cancer drawings' as a response to the disease and its progress. Her partner, Dale Gunthorp, describes the first drawing, 'The Egg', about the discovery of the lump, as something 'which glows with the dawning life within it'. Debbie Dickinson, a survivor of bladder cancer, records an occasional friendly relationship with her illness:

Sometimes, I feel like it is my secret lover, my bottle of gin, my comforter, my way out … Cancer as an addiction – what a thought. Yet – it offers me the comfort of the secret affair, the means to escape, an excuse for only dealing with what is real and immediate in life.

For Barbara Rosenblum, cancer itself did not particularly take on a positive aspect, but she drew something positive from it: 'I have cancer but it is not consuming me. Rather, I am as alive as I can be; my creative juices have never been as electric; my thoughts have never been as clear.' It seems clear that despite the dominant – and recommended – narratives of cancer, sometimes metaphors and images suggest themselves, emerging unexpectedly and perversely from deeper senses of the self. In my own case, although I must have been shocked at the diagnosis and at times afraid of my scan results (typically, I can't really recall those feelings), what I still vividly remember is something like an epiphany – a real sense of something new and exciting trying to emerge.

Visions of a cancer tumour as an egg, as something 'glowing with dawning life', of course evoke an analogy with birth, and as Jackie Stacey writes, it isn't too difficult to draw parallels. 'In threatening death, cancer echoes the beginnings of life, for the malignant cells resemble those of embryonic development.'

> Cancer and pregnancy have both been described as abject conditions ... As such they are both 'borderline states in which there is confusion and lack of distinction between subject and object' ... More than one, but less than two, the reassuring boundaries of self and other are lost in an unsettling haze. The malignant cells which belong to the self and yet are other to it, and indeed threaten its existence, disturb the subject's space. Pregnancy, too, shows the body hosting another that parasitically grows from the maternal body's apparently endless generative source.

Again, not necessarily every cancer patient's visualisation; certainly it wasn't mine. But this gets confused for me with another such common analogy: between childbirth and creativity. Here too, is something embryonic, developing internally, waiting to be born. This is an analogy I really hate, and it is certainly one that in the past has been employed in the most androcentric discourses of the arts, to privilege men's creativity and to deny women's. Roszika Parker and Griselda Pollock quote the sculptor Reg Butler, from a notorious lecture in 1962:

> I am quite sure that the vitality of many female students derives from frustrated maternity, and most of these, on finding the opportunity to settle down and produce children, will no longer experience the passionate discontent sufficient to drive them constantly towards the labours of creation in other ways.

Other such sentiments, compiled by Christine Battersby:

I believe that artistic creativity is a male surrogate for biological creativity. (Anthony Burgess, 1986)

[Women's] chief destination [is the] perpetuation of the human species ... the true woman, the true mother has a mentality incompatible with such kind of creative activity. (Andrew Gemant, 1961)

The creative act is a kind of giving birth, and it is noteworthy that as an historical fact intellectual creativity has been conspicuously lacking in women, whose products are their children ... Men bring forth ideas, paintings, literary and musical compositions ... and the like, while women bring forth the next generation. (Frank Barron, 1968)

For rather different reasons, feminists have pointed out the incompatibility for women of having babies and producing art or literature, particularly in earlier periods when domestic labour and ideas of women's proper role conspired against it. It is not surprising that Lee Virginia Chambers-Schiller, in her study of single women in ante-bellum America, can quote the writer Louisa May Alcott and the sculptor Harriet Hosmer, both proposing singlehood as essential for women artists.

Such material constraints may be of the past, and the patriarchal views of male artists may date from half a century ago now. But if maternity and creativity are no longer seen as incompatible, and if these days it may be only an antiquated and eccentric view that asserts that women cannot be real artists, the childbirth analogy persists. Susan Stanford Friedman suggests that even though it often retains its older divisive ideas about gender when applied to male artists and writers, and despite the risks of essentialising women's 'true' attributes, it may have a positive value in validating women's artistic work 'by unifying their mental and physical labor into (pro)creativity'. I cannot see this myself, and I would be very happy to ban any further discussion of creativity that links it, in any way, with pregnancy and childbirth. I don't think it's because I happen not to have children myself that I find the analogy objectionable and ridiculous. I think it's partly because it can never really get away from the gendering of artistic work; but mainly because it inevitably carries with it a certain mystification and worship of procreation which surely cannot be useful or relevant in thinking about art work (or, for that matter, about childbirth itself).

Giovanni Bellini, *Angel of the Annunciation and Virgin Annunciate*, c. 1500

Annunciation

Artist unknown
(Bruges),
Annunciation, c. 1520

Francesco
Pesellino, *Diptych –
Annunciation*
(detail), *c.* 1450–55

Austerity baby

Petrus Christus, *Die Verkündigung an Maria*, 1452

Rogier van der Weyden, *The Annunciation*, c. 1455

Annunciation

Perhaps as perverse as my positive imagining of the malignant tumour, and especially given my aversion to displaced conversations about childbirth, is my long-standing attraction to the scene of the Annunciation in Western art. The appeal is, I'm sure, connected with the fact that the Feast of the Annunciation – Lady Day – is my birthday, 25 March. But still, given the alienness of Christian doctrine and imagery for me, and my especial distaste for representations of the madonna and child (all those grotesque fat babies, often weirdly and horribly adult in their features), it's a strange affinity. It is only possible because, against all the biblical, theological and iconological evidence, I have never really believed that Gabriel was announcing the Incarnation to the Virgin. Rather it seemed that he was suggesting something more mysterious and more exciting. I like the fact that the Virgin is often shown interrupted while reading a book (the scriptures, possibly the passage in Isaiah 7:14, prophesying the birth of Jesus). And of course there is the appeal for me of the fact that her robe is dark blue, particularly in paintings after 1400.

The convention of depicting the scene in an enclosed space – a walled garden (*hortus conclusus*) or bedchamber – provides the additional pleasures of contemplating the domestic scene, with beautiful interior detail, which draw me to the genre, in paintings from Vermeer to Hammershøi. Beautiful too are the dove and the ray of light, symbolising the conception, and the lily – attribute of Mary, symbolising purity – which is sometimes held by Gabriel, at other times placed to the side.

None of this is in the original text, Luke 1:26–38, which recounts the annunciation as a brief exchange: arrival of Gabriel, his greeting and Mary's response, Gabriel's announcement, Mary's question, Gabriel's answer, Mary's acceptance, and Gabriel's departure. The fifteenth-century Florentine friar Roberto Caracciolo identifies three aspects of the Annunciation: the Angelic Mission, the Angelic Salutation and the Angelic Colloquy, and others have followed him in discussing the five successive 'laudable conditions of the virgin', stages of the event depicted in pre-Renaissance and Renaissance art. According to Michael Baxandall, the first two stages – disquiet (*conturbio*) and reflection (*cogitatio*) – are the most frequently depicted, in which Mary is shown at first alarmed by the appearance of Gabriel and then considering his greeting and announcement.

The fourth stage, humility or submission (*humiliatio*) is also common; the third and fifth stages, inquiry (*interrogatio*) and merit (*meritatio*) appear less frequently. Baxandall quotes an amusing warning by Leonardo da Vinci on how not to paint the moment of disquiet:

Paolo Veronese, *The Annunciation*, 1578

Dante Gabriel Rossetti, *Ecce Ancilla Domini! (The Annunciation)*, 1849-50

Dante Gabriel Rossetti, *Found*, begun 1859

some days ago I saw the picture of an angel who, in making the Annunciation, seemed to be trying to chase Mary out of her room, with movements showing the sort of attack one might make on some hated enemy; and Mary, as if desperate, seemed to be trying to throw herself out of the window. Do not fall into errors like these.

But my own readings of Annunciation paintings have nothing to do with the biblical story or with later religious commentaries and interpretations. The seductions of the painted scene are primarily aesthetic – the rooms, the robes, the figures, the detail and also, importantly, the tendency towards, but resistance of, symmetry. In the context of the beautiful setting, I always see a more secular announcement – vague and unspecified, but hinting at new possibilities and the fulfilment of an unrecognised yearning.

At the same time, I cannot resist Linda Nochlin's suggestion – a throwaway comment in her essay on Rossetti – that, after all, the Annunciate can say 'No thanks'. In her discussion of Rossetti's *Found* – my Rosabell(e) painting – she suggests we see it as 'a sort of dark Annunciation, a perverse revision of *Ecce Ancilla Domini*', Rossetti's own Annunciation.

As she says, 'there also a cowering female is set in opposition to a towering male figure – but here, the fallen woman refuses to "know" the messenger and sends him away instead of receiving glad tidings'. It's a nice thought. I suppose it really depends on what it is that's on offer.

11 Granville Avenue,
Broughton Park,
Manchester

The letter from London School of Contemporary Dance offering me a place to study was addressed to me at my parents' house in Didsbury. Now, more than forty years later, I live about five minutes' walk from that address, in Henry Simon's house. It's not quite full circle. For that I would have had to return to the streets of Cheetham Hill, now inhabited by ultra-Orthodox Jews and a variety of other ethnic groups. In the 1980s it had a reputation for drug trafficking and gang warfare. As so often with inner-city residential areas, different immigrant populations arrived there, later moving out to somewhat more affluent areas, confirming the classic geographical pattern identified by W.I. Thomas and others at the Chicago School of sociology in the 1920s. Before the Jews, who arrived in the early twentieth century, the Irish lived there. From the mid-twentieth century the majority of immigrants were Indian, Pakistani and Caribbean. Adjacent to Cheetham Hill, just west of Cheetham Hill Road (and technically in Salford rather than Manchester) is Broughton Park, which has a large Jewish population, primarily Orthodox and Hasidic. The street my

parents lived in when I was born and until my second year, Granville Avenue, is now central to that community, as I discovered on a visit there with a friend recently.

The other house of my black-and-white years, which is just north of Cheetham Hill in Higher Crumpsall, further along Bury Old Road, is also currently the home of orthodox Jews. But I left there at the age of thirteen, and throughout my forty-one years of travel I associated the idea of home with the place in south Manchester where I lived in my teens and early twenties, and where my parents lived for the last thirty years of their lives. And so my return there a few years ago is in the most fundamental way a return to the past, and to my past self. It took a long time for this to become both possible and necessary.

In the introductory essay to my book *Resident Alien*, written in the mid-1990s, I wrote about the connections between travel and writing, exile and the sense of self. At the time, I very much identified with others who had spoken about the liberating effect of distance from home, and the possibilities for a different, more 'authentic', self to emerge at a physical remove from the place of its suppression. In my case the fantasy of 'America' played the role of the desired other place, specifically the America of the 1950s (Hollywood and especially rock 'n' roll). Others have attached themselves to different fantasy places (the places were real, of course – the fantasy lay in their imagined magical qualities). Some discovered that learning and speaking a new language enabled the new self. Alice Kaplan, as an American student in Paris, found that 'in a new language, you are unbuttoned, opened up'. Finally succeeding in articulating the French 'r', she exults in her new freedom:

Learning French and learning to think, learning to desire, is all mixed up in my head, until I can't tell the difference. French is what released me from the cool complacency of the R Resisters, made me want, and like wanting, unbuttoned me and sent me packing.

She concludes that 'speaking a foreign language is ... a chance for growth, for freedom, a liberation from the ugliness of our received ideas and mentalities'. For Eva Hoffman, a writer and psychoanalyst, it was learning English that coincided with her self-discovery, after arriving as a thirteen-year-old Polish girl in Canada and later living in the United States. In her case, her exile was involuntary, and her account of being 'lost in translation' is coloured by nostalgia for home. But she too understands in retrospect that her entry into adulthood, her emergence as a writer, must be seen as the product of her switch to a new language, in the context of a different culture. I recognised these stories, which at the time I felt expressed my own strong sense that something quite unconnected with academic job possibilities, and even unconnected with the relationship that first took me to California, was the real reason for my transatlantic move. And so the moment of getting a green card, of becoming a 'resident alien', in 1992 was a significant one.

But, as it turns out, I was wrong. Or perhaps not entirely wrong. I think the eighteen years in the United States were transformative in many ways. But in fact it was only on the point of return that I began to write differently. I also began to write about Manchester, my home town, co-editing a collection of essays on the city's cultural history and writing essays on calico printers in the nineteenth century, on Manchester's claim to be the 'capital of the nineteenth century', and on the writer W.G. Sebald and his relationship to the city. In this last essay, acknowledging my apparent need to defend Manchester against the negative image of the city in his work (just as I did with Henry Norr's critical comments in his 1909 diary), I quoted Ibsen's character in *Enemy of the People*, Dr Stockmann, who explains his love for his home town as the passion of someone who has been away from it for a long time.

I've loved my native town as deeply as any man can love the home of his childhood. I was still young when I went away, and separation, memories, and homesickness cast a kind of enchantment over the town and its people ... And when, at long last, fate granted me the great happiness of coming home again, it seemed to me, my friends, that there was nothing else I wanted in the whole world! At least, there was just one thing: I had an urgent, tireless, burning desire to work for the good of my native town and its people.

For me, Manchester was always 'home'. I am fortunate that I came back to a place where I still have close family members, old friends as well as new ones. During the years after I left, in 1965, I came home frequently – during my time at university in Birmingham, the dance study/secretarial period in London, and then more than a decade teaching in Leeds, and nearly twenty years in the United States. After that, though the strong connections never faltered, each move was weirdly shadowed by an external drama or catastrophe, each one only affecting me marginally and minimally, but in some way symbolising – I'm not even sure what – a warning? a punishment? I am well aware that even to link these events and tragedies to my small local world sounds at best narcissistic and at worst psychotic. And of course I don't actually think the universe had me in mind. But I was, despite myself, able to read each moment, which coincided with a transfer to a new city, as meaning something rather particular for myself. The last of these, five weeks after I moved from Rochester to New York City in 2001, was the catastrophe of 9/11 and its continuing consequences for those living in Manhattan. The first event was on 9 July 1984, when York Minster was struck by lightning, a year after I moved there (for another relationship) and was living a few streets away in King's Manor. The roof in the south transept was destroyed, and repairs took four years and cost £2.5 million. On the night of 15 October 1987, a few months after I moved to London, there was a major hurricane in the south of England. From Wikipedia, on 'The Great Storm of 1987':

> The strongest gusts, of up to 100 knots (190 km/h; 120 mph), were recorded along the south-eastern edge of the storm, hitting mainly Hampshire, Sussex, Essex and Kent. The Royal Sovereign lighthouse 6 miles (9.7 km) off Eastbourne recorded wind speeds on their instruments pegged at 110 mph offscale high, i.e. could read no higher … The storm caused substantial damage over much of England, downing an estimated 15 million trees … Fallen trees blocked roads and railways and left widespread structural damage primarily to windows and roofs. Several hundred thousand people were left without power, not fully restored until more than two weeks later. Local electric utility officials later said they lost more wires in the storm than in the preceding decade.

More than twenty people were killed. A month later, on 18 November 1987, a terrible fire broke out at King's Cross Tube station in London, in which thirty-one people died. It happened that I was changing trains at that station at exactly that time (7.30 pm), in a separate interchange of train lines, though I didn't hear the news until I got home. On 17 October 1989, a year after I moved to northern California, I was ten miles from the epicentre of a major (7.1) earthquake near Santa Cruz, where I was teaching at the time. And then, on 3 March 1991, a few weeks after I moved to Rochester, the city suffered the 'ice storm of the century', bringing down trees and power lines, and putting phones and electricity supplies out of action for days and costing an estimated $500 million in damage. Five years after 9/11 I left New York to return home, a transfer unaccompanied by any disaster.

I was surprised to find that the word 'exile' came to mind, around the time I began to think about coming home. I had never considered my time away from Manchester, or even my years in the United States, as an exile, a term which implies an enforced and reluctant departure. Unlike my Russian and Romanian grandparents over a century ago, and my German father and grandparents in the 1930s, I was not obliged to leave home. My status was more of an expat, a visitor, an immigrant than that of a refugee. The travel was entirely voluntary. So I had to consider why such a word would occur to me. I think it has to do with another kind of expulsion, not politically but internally motivated. Despite the unwavering attachment to my city, somehow I had to leave, and even eventually travel quite far, to the fantasised place. There is nothing very surprising about this, after all. In California I met several people who told me they simply had to get away from the east coast – even from New York – to feel able to thrive and be(come) themselves. In New York, there were friends who felt they could not have survived (psychically, not materially) if they had remained in their small town communities or their mid-West cities. I don't even think it has anything to do with the (real or fantasised) characteristics of the destination. More important is the drive, even against a residual and strong 'pull' back, to leave, to find another place and allow the emergence of another aspect of the self. I suppose many people who act on this impulse for one reason or another never go home again: because they start a new life, perhaps with a family and children, because their work then ties them to the new location, because there is nobody and nothing left in the place of origin to which they want to return. It has been my own very good fortune that somehow everything conspired to allow my homecoming.

Gino Severini, *Blue Dancer*, 1912

Annunciation

Family photograph, Wissembourg, France, 1953

Austerity baby

Postscript

On that visit to France in 1953, when the family photograph with Julie and Emma was taken in Thionville, we met other members of the family, these on my grandmother's side. This photo was taken in Wissembourg, also in Alsace. (Matching dresses again for me and my sister Veronica, my mother standing behind us.) Julius, one of the brothers of my grandmother Bertha, and of Leonie and Rosa, is at the back on the left.

For many years I had the idea that the tall young man at the back was someone called Claude. I couldn't remember why I thought that, and I didn't know who he was. When I started my research into Leonie's story, I went back to the family tree, and found that there was a Claude Levy – grandson of Rosa, and son of Leo and Meta Levy, who were on the same transport to Auschwitz as Leonie on 16 September 1942. Paulette and I found the Stolpersteine for Leo and Meta in Busenberg, outside what must have been their house. Leo's brother Siegfried, like Leonie's daughter Eri, had emigrated to New York in the 1930s. And, as I eventually found out, Rosa herself survived a series of camps in France and also ended up in New York. If this was the Claude from that part of the family, I didn't know why he would be in Wissembourg in 1953.

On Sunday 29 November 2015, the German television channel OKTV Südwestpfalz livestreamed a documentary by the American film-maker Peter Blystone, called *The Jewish Cemetery – the Last Jews of Wasgau*. Wasgau is a five-hundred-square-mile area of the Palatinate (Pfalz) in south-west Germany, also including the French departments of Bas-Rhin and Moselle. The film focuses on four small German towns, including Busenberg, and gives an account of what happened to the Jews there after the Nazi accession to power in January 1933. Those Jews who had not already left were, as I already knew from Leonie's story, expelled into France on 22 October 1940, together with Jews from the Saar and from Baden. Many did not survive the war. The film focuses on particular families, including Leo and Meta Levy. And then their son, Claude Levy, appears on camera, arriving to meet the film's presenter, Otmar Weber, at Strasbourg station. In his early eighties, he is instantly recognisable as the twenty-three-year-old young man in my photograph from 1953.

As he and the presenter meet and go to eat together at a restaurant, his story is told in voiceover, both by Otmar Weber and by Claude himself.

In 1939 he was sent to Wissembourg in France, to stay with his (and my) great-uncle Julius. Originally called Kurt Levy, he was renamed Claude by a cousin. He survived the war and the occupation, sometimes in hiding. He has spent the rest of his life in Alsace. Widowed in 1994, he seems to be very close to his daughter and his granddaughter. In 1957 he met his sister Hannah in Paris for the first time for nearly twenty years. She had, like Leonie and other relatives, been in Gurs camp, and then been hidden with other children in a convent, eventually being transported through Spain and to Palestine. She grew up there, and remained in Israel until her death in 1997. When she and Claude met in 1957 they no longer had a language in common – she knew only Hebrew.

On Sunday 5 June 2016 a ceremony took place in Busenberg to unveil three large information and memorial boards near the Jewish cemetery. They record the earlier Jewish community, and they honour those who died in the Holocaust. Speakers recalled a time when Jews and Christians had lived together in peaceful and mutually enriching relations. The afternoon started out sunny, but a storm broke in the middle of the proceedings, and the speeches continued under heavy rain. Among those attending – about fifty people – was Claude Levy.

The local paper, the *Pirmasenser Zeitung*, notes his presence:

> Berührend war die Anwesenheit des ältesten Teilnehmers, Claude Levy, der einst als Kurt Levy in Busenberg das Licht der Welt erblickte. Aufrecht stehend wohnte der weit über 80-Jährige in strömenden Regen der Veranstaltung bis zum Schluss bei.

> The presence of the oldest participant, Claude Levy, was moving; he first saw the light of day as Kurt Levy in Busenberg. Well over 80 years old, he remained standing upright in the pouring rain until the end of the event.

From his own narrative in the film, and from an article about him in another German newspaper, *Die Rheinpfalz*, I learned a few new things about the family. It seems that Claude visited his parents twice in Gurs internment camp in late 1940 and 1941. He and his great-uncle Julius were about to visit them in the Rivesaltes camp in September 1942, but learned that they had just been deported. I already knew that Leo and Meta were deported from Drancy camp to Auschwitz on 16 September 1942 – from the transport list available online through the Mémorial de la Shoah in Paris, and from the Stolpersteine in Busenberg. I assumed both were murdered immediately on arrival. Claude's mother Meta

Claude Levy (film stills)

Memorial boards, Jewish cemetery in Busenberg, Germany

Jewish cemetery, Busenberg

Austerity baby

was killed, presumably gassed, right away. But Leo survived for two years, working as a slave labourer in Auschwitz III (also known as Monowitz, or Monowitz-Buna). Amazingly, several postcards arrived from Leo during that time, sent to neighbours in Schifferstadt. They asked for food and money. The last card, dated June 1944, came from Heydebreck in Oberschlesien. This is where prisoners worked for IG-Farben's Badische Anilin & Sodafabrik (BASF) production centres. It is not really a circumstance in which one can take any pleasure in learning that Leo Levy had an extra two years of life. And of course – chillingly – this belated information brings the story back again to chemistry. To Primo Levi, also enslaved there, and to my father's own connections with the German chemical industry.

Article 116 (2) of the German Basic Law concerns the rights of descendants of those deprived of German citizenship on political, racial or religious grounds to apply for naturalisation. Now, writing in the immediate aftermath of the Brexit vote, I am compiling the documents I need to demonstrate my eligibility for this. Some of my American cousins – the daughters and the granddaughter of Albert Schwarz – took out Germany citizenship some time ago on the same grounds, in order to acquire European passports. My father's birth certificate has arrived from Saarlouis, and I have found the name of a notary in my neighbourhood, who can validate the copies of papers I would send to the German Embassy with my application. As one of 'the 48 per cent' (those who voted not to leave the EU), I was shocked and depressed by the outcome, and within a day was – perhaps only therapeutically – planning to retain my own EU membership by becoming German as well as British. Within a week, I saw in the press that there was already a notable trend of people cashing in on their eligibility for Irish, Italian, German and other nationalities. As I write, only a month after the referendum, things are far from clear, and I suppose I won't do anything apart from assemble my documents at least until Article 50 is triggered, beginning the formal process of separation. In the meantime, having completed this extended meditation on my family's history, including the traumas of its relationship to an earlier Germany, and reflected too on Henry Simon's connection to German politics and culture, there is a certain strangeness – but also satisfaction – in contemplating a belated and renewed connection to that country. It is also, perhaps, an appropriate way to end a story about travel, exile and belonging.

Austerity baby

Acknowledgements

Although I wrote the earliest chapters of this book in 2006, it has 245 a prehistory in my first writing group, and two fragments from that time appear here. So my first thanks are to my friends in that group, colleagues at the South Bank Centre in London in 1987 and 1988: Nick Napier, Jo Shapcott and Antony Smith. More recently, members of my 'writing otherwise' group in Manchester gave me invaluable help and feedback as I worked on the book, and I am very grateful for their support and their reliably perceptive comments: Margaret Beetham, Brenda Cooper, Viv Gardner, Ursula Hurley and Judy Kendall. Thanks also to those who attended a meeting of the Manchester Feminist Theory Network in June 2010, where I presented a version of the first chapter of this book, who responded with interesting thoughts and ideas.

Many of my friends and colleagues from my years in the United States have made contributions, in some cases with detailed comments on sections of the book, and otherwise by their enthusiasm and support for the project. Members of my Columbia University feminist reading group were among the first to read the early chapters in 2006, in the weeks before I left New York to return to England; many thanks to them for their very helpful feedback. In particular my thanks to Marianne Hirsch, a member of the group, who contributed both to the Writing Otherwise conference in Manchester arranged on my retirement in 2010, and to the book of that title which I co-edited with Jackie Stacey. Marianne also supported my application for a writing residency at the Bogliasco Foundation in Italy, where I worked on completing the book. Thanks too to Nancy Miller and Janet Berlo for comments on the manuscript; to Julie Diamond and Phyllis Trager, from my apartment building on West 92nd Street, for their continuing interest in the book; and to my Rochester colleagues and now long-term good friends, Michael Holly and Douglas Crimp, as well as Keith Moxey, an honorary Rochester friend, and later a Columbia colleague. My friend Tony Platt, in Berkeley, read most of the book chapter by chapter as I wrote it, and gave me excellent critical comments. Tony and I were at primary school together in north Manchester, and have been close friends since I lived in Berkeley in the late 1980s. We also share an interest in memoir (and in memories of Manchester in the 1950s), and in bridging the divide between academic and other non-fiction writing. Another friend from primary school, Linda Langton, now a literary agent living in New York, gave me excellent advice and encouragement about publication. My last – and saddest – acknowledgement to my friends in the United States is to Andrew Goodwin, whose early and tragic death on 10 September 2013 shocked so many of us on both sides of the Atlantic. He is not named in the book, but he was the father of Jamie (the uninhibited young colourer of drawings), and the person I lived with in California. A brilliant writer and critic himself, he was a strong supporter of my turn to new forms of writing. He read what is now the first chapter of this book, first published in an edited collection just before he died, and his approval meant a great deal to me. I wish I had been able to continue sending him my writing.

There are many people to thank in Britain. Returning to England in 2006, I found very soon that I had wonderful colleagues at the University of Manchester. They, and in some cases their partners, have provided the supportive, stimulating and witty social and intellectual life which was the context for my writing this book. In particular (though the circle is much larger) I thank Ursula Tidd, Monica Pearl, Hal Gladfelder, Manu Basile and Jeff Geiger for their friendship. Ursula also helped me with various French aspects of my book. Laura Doan gave me helpful comments on parts of the book. I also have to thank her for being instrumental, albeit indirectly, for getting me back to the UK and to Manchester – in fact I followed her (and, as it happens, Hal) from Rochester. Mar Mussell kindly agreed to let me use her gorgeous blue photo from the Aeolian Island of Panarea. Dani Caselli was one of the first to read the entire manuscript, and I thank her for her warm and generous encouragement, as well as for a little help with chasing image-reproduction permissions in Italian museums. Cathy Gelbin had good advice on German aspects of my story, and was helpful with translation of one or two of the German letters. She also put me in touch with Eva-Maria Broomer, who has done a fantastic job of transcribing from difficult archaic German script the letters of Leonie and others. Without Jean-Marc Dreyfus I would not have been able to tell Leonie's story. He explained to me how it came about that my German family ended up in France in October 1940, and he showed me the key websites and links I needed to trace their fate after that. And when I finally found my cousin Claude Levy, it was Jean-Marc who telephoned him from Paris to make contact. Many thanks, too, to John McAuliffe – first for publishing what is now Chapter 4 in the journal he co-edits, *The Manchester Review*, and then for his strong support for the publication of the book. Jackie Stacey has been a colleague and friend for nearly ten years now, and very much involved in many ways in the book, including with excellent feedback and advice on final editing. She arranged the Writing Otherwise conference in 2010, and worked with me on editing the volume we published three years later – a very enjoyable process. It was Jackie who persuaded me to go public for the first time with this writing, and because I couldn't really think of a good reason to encourage others to publish while refusing myself, 'Atlantic moves', now the first chapter of this book, appeared in print in our book. And thank you to Matthew Frost, editor at Manchester University Press, for working with us on *Writing Otherwise* and for encouragement and enthusiasm over the past months for *Austerity Baby*.

My old high-school friend Charlotte Gringras, and my newer friend Philippa Comber, share my interest in forms of writing, and have given me helpful feedback on parts of this book. Patrick Joyce – another academic colleague working on memoir – read a couple of chapters and sent me his thoughtful reflections on them. Another British-American transplant who returned home is my long-term friend Tony King, now living in Bristol. We knew one another for a number of years in Leeds; later we lived in fairly close proximity in western New York State for ten years. Over many meetings and days out together in the Finger Lakes region of New York, we discussed shared interests in memoir, social history and – not least – our origins in Lancashire. He has taken an interest in this book since its early stages, and I thank him for his encouragement.

Griselda Pollock, an old friend from my Leeds days, contributed to the *Writing Otherwise* collection, and supported my application to Bogliasco for the writing residency. Anna Lee came with me to Vienna, and took the photo of Ernst Eisenmayer I have included in the book. And another friend from high school, Jen Coates, whose memory of those years is far better than mine, sent me a wonderful email about Didsbury in the 1950s, and particularly about Olive Shapley; with her permission, I've included some of it in the book, under Jen's name at that time.

Other people to thank: Dr Christine Joy, archivist at Manchester High School for Girls, for sending me documents about the school in my time and, together with Mrs Claire Hewitt, MHSG headmistress, giving me permission to reproduce sections, as well as the photographs of Sara Burstall and Agnes Bozman. Diana Leitch, historian of south Manchester, for information about the Simon family. Margaret Simon, for permission to visit Helsgarth, her grandfather's cottage, and also to reproduce the portrait of Henry Simon and the photograph of Henry and his family.

Melanie Garner, Keeper of Fine and Decorative Arts at Tullie House Museum and Art Gallery, Carlisle, for helpful information in a phone call in October 2012 about Rossetti's *Found*. Hans Peter Klauck, historian of the Jews of the Saar area of Germany, for filling in a lot of gaps in my knowledge of my grandfather's family. Marcel Wainstock of Saarbrücken showed me around Saarbrücken and Saarlouis, including the Jewish

cemeteries where my grandfather's family members are buried, and later put me in touch with Hans Peter Klauck. Ernst Eisenmayer, who was willing to let me buy his beautiful little drawing from the Onchan camp in the Isle of Man, and who entertained me for months with his witty and contrary emails, and then entertained me and a friend in person in his residence in Vienna in September 2011. Alessandra Comini, for giving me access to the papers of Eleanor Tufts in connection with my work on Kathleen McEnery. Ivor Nicholas, for allowing me to reproduce his amazing – and historic – photograph of Windscale on that fateful day in October 1957. Peter Blystone, for providing film stills of Claude Levy from his film about the Jews of Wasgau, and for his permission to include them in this book. Dr Horst Seferens of the Brandenburg Memorials Foundation in Oranienburg, for providing photographs of Sachsenhausen, and for permission to reproduce them. Thank you to Manuela Vehma, at the Kreismuseum Oberhavel in Oranienburg, for permission to reproduce the photographs of Orianienburg. Finally, to the Mémorial de la Shoah in Paris, and the Conseil Général des Pyrénées-Atlantiques for permission to reproduce documents about Leonie's time in France, and her eventual fate.

When I still lived in Rochester, New York, I spent a couple of years doing research on the artist Kathleen McEnery. During that period – 2000–1 – I interviewed many people who had known her. The chapter in this book about Rochester in the 1920s returns to my notes on those interviews. Inevitably in the intervening fifteen years some of my informants, already elderly then (and recalling life decades earlier), have died, including Nancy Watson Dean and Elizabeth Holahan. Sam Spanier, who kindly agreed to a phone interview about Nina Balaban, also died a few years ago. Here I record my thanks, belatedly, to these people. Other Rochesterians who gave me useful information and helped in other ways were Betsy Brayer, biographer of George Eastman; Margie Searl, at the Memorial Art Gallery; Doug Howard, local art dealer as well as academic, and endlessly knowledgeable about the history of the Rochester art scene. Bruce Kellner of Pennsylvania, found via internet research, was kind enough to talk to me on the phone about Nina Balaban. Most of all, I record my thanks and gratitude to the family of Kathleen McEnery – the Cunningham and Williams families – who give me a great deal of assistance when I was doing research on the artist and curating an exhibition of her work in 2003, and with many of whom I continue to have warm friendships: especially Anne Subercaseaux, Mary Cunningham, James Cunningham (who also toured Marseilles with me in November 2013, following in Leonie's footsteps), Louisa Cunningham, Kitty Williams and Brigid Williams. And I will always be grateful to the late Peter Cunningham and the late Joan Carey Cunningham, each of whom gave me a painting by Kathleen McEnery.

The last group of acknowledgements is of members of my family, in England and the United States. My sisters, Veronica Kaiserman and Eleanor Wolff, though I think slightly bemused by my intense interest in our family history, and my habit of collecting more and more American cousins, were very supportive. Veronica undertook to visit the French camp at Gurs, where Leonie had been interned, during a holiday in France, and sent me photos of the place and of the grave of Sigmund Kahn, Leonie's husband. Eleanor went to the offices of the Mémorial de la Shoah when she was in Paris with her son Sam, and picked up some documents for me and took photos. (That's a photograph of her near Leonie's wall towards the end of Chapter 6.) My brother-in-law, David Kaiserman, told me everything I now know about Saar stamps, and patiently took me through the stamp collection that he inherited from my father, explaining history, iconography, currency and many other things; he also gave me helpful comments on some of the chapters, and did expert Photoshop work for me on a couple of images. My cousins Diane and Mike Smith have always asked to read my writing – way beyond the expectations of cousinhood – and have been generous and encouraging as I worked on this. (Diane is in fact a real cousin – her father and my mother were brother and sister. But she is the only one in this book. Everywhere else I use the word 'cousin' for a range of cousinly connections, in France, Germany and the United States, to keep things simple: second cousin, second cousin once removed, third cousin.) My great-nephew Oscar Walmsley eagerly took up the challenge of showing me how you can colour in a drawing without staying within the lines; the drawing in chapter 10 is his, done in the spirit of Jamie Foley. And the late Rita Greenburgh, my mother's cousin (also my mother's bridesmaid, in February 1940), was the one to introduce me to David Norr in New York, and to give me the history of the Noar/Norr family she had compiled with another cousin, Ernest Moritz.

Three other cousins I am indebted to have also died in the past few years. David Norr, whose father's diary opens my first chapter, died on 19 August 2012 at the age of eighty-nine. I met him only twice, at his home in Scarsdale, but have him to thank for the way in which the diary inspired my first reflections on family in a transatlantic context. My cousin Marthe Hanau, on my father's side of the family, was someone I had known from childhood. (She is in the 1953 photograph with me and others, in Chapter 3.) After my father died I visited her in Metz in France, where she cooked the most elaborate and delicious meals for me and my sister and brother-in-law. She was my best informant on my German family, and put together the main outlines of the family tree for me. Through her I met another cousin of that generation, Gerda Feldman, who had left Germany for France in 1935, and emigrating to Cuba in 1942. She arrived in New York in 1946. We met many times after I moved to the United States, and until her death. She too filled in gaps for me in the family tree, and introduced me to yet more cousins.

Like Marthe and Gerda, Marlyse Kennedy was related to my father on his father's side (Josef Wolff). I met her about twenty years ago, also introduced by Marthe, and throughout my years in the United States and in the ten years since, we have been in very close contact, with many visits, at least one a year. Now in her early nineties, Marlyse has had two careers since leaving Germany and France for the United States, where she has lived in Washington, DC, for more than half a century. After retiring as a doctor and hospital anaesthetist, she spent twenty years as a highly active docent (gallery guide) at the Freer and Sackler Galleries of Asian Art in Washington. For years now we have exchanged old photographs of the family, copies of letters, documents. She too has recently completed a book about her family during and after the war, based on photographs and an amazing trove of letters. My thanks to her for friendship and shared obsessions with family history, and for hospitality over a long period.

One cousin I want to thank is someone I have never actually met – the artist Temma Bell, who lives in upstate New York and in Iceland. She (like David Norr – who first told me about that branch of the family) is related to me on my mother's side. We spoke on the phone, and she arranged for me to get permission to reproduce a work by her father, the artist Leland Bell. The remaining American cousins are on my paternal grandmother's side – that is, related to Bertha, Leonie, Rosa in one way or another. Paulette Johnson is Leonie's granddaughter. Thanks to her we have the letters Leonie wrote to Eri, Paulette's mother. Paulette and her husband Dean came with me to Busenberg, Offenburg and Saarbrücken on the family research trip in September 2014. Emily Kaufman, granddaughter of Albert Schwarz of New York, has provided invaluable information to me over the past few years. She is at least as involved in family research as me, and her German is a lot better than mine! Through her Busenberg connections I learned about the plan to erect memorial boards at the Jewish cemetery, which were eventually installed in June 2016. She also found out about Peter Blystone's television film about the Jews of Busenberg, and sent me details so that I could watch online on German TV on 29 November 2015. And through this I found out that Claude Levy was still alive, and – thanks to Emily's persistence – finally got contact information for him. Steve Robbins, a cousin-in-law, told me about Thomas Hager's book about Haber, Bosch and chemistry in twentieth-century Germany.

Finally – in the hope of putting together Rosa's incredible story, of survival of expulsion from Germany, internment in several French camps, and eventual arrival in New York at about the age of seventy – I tried to find her great-granddaughter. I knew she was called Judy and was a lawyer, and hoping against hope that she had kept her maiden name, I looked up Judy Fensterman in the phone book for New York City. I found someone who looked possible – with phone number and even home address. There was no email address, which I would have preferred to use. Instead, I called the number listed as her office, assuming I would get someone on reception and I would leave a message, or ask for an email address. Judy picked up the phone herself. She was admirably calm in the face of an unknown Englishwoman claiming to be a cousin, and within a few months we had met at a family reunion in New York. She gave me a copy of a photo of Rosa in very old age, with Judy and her sister as small children. Though I am still waiting for her to find time to go through her own family papers and letters.

I record my gratitude to the Bogliasco Foundation in Italy for a writing fellowship and for hosting me for five weeks in late 2014, when I completed the first full draft of this manuscript, as well as to my co-fellows there who discussed my work with me. A beautiful place, with kind and lovely staff, and a fabulous location in which to write.

A version of Chapter 1 of this book was published in Jackie Stacey and Janet Wolff, eds, *Writing Otherwise: Experiments in Cultural Criticism* (Manchester: Manchester University Press, 2013)

A version of Chapter 2 was published in the online journal *In[]Visible Culture*, no. 21, October 2014. Thanks to the editor for permission to publish here.

A version of Chapter 4 was published in the online journal *The Manchester Review*, No. 10, April 2013. Thanks to the editors for permission to publish here.

Family trees

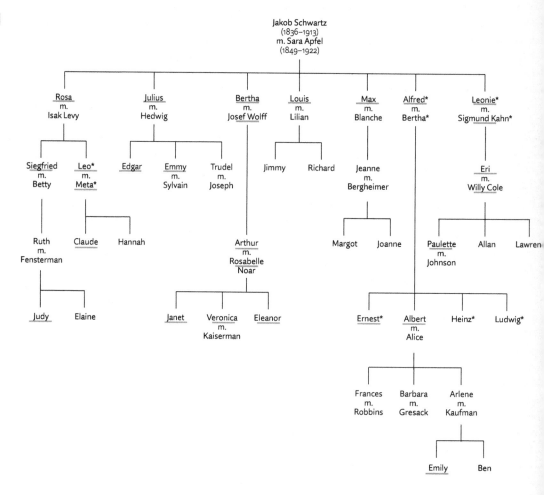

* Victim of the Holocaust

——— Denotes being referred to in *Austerity baby*

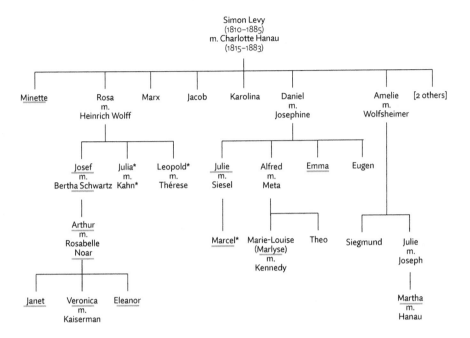

* Victim of the Holocaust

——— Denotes being referred to in *Austerity baby*

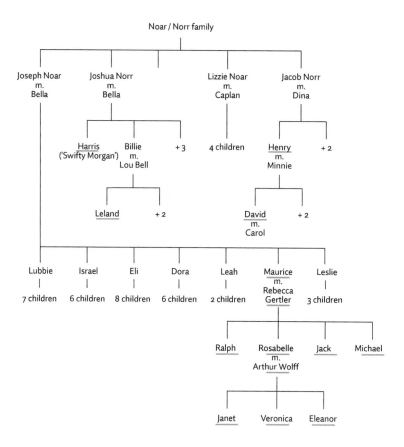

Noar / Norr family

Joseph Noar
m.
Bella

Joshua Norr
m.
Bella

Lizzie Noar
m.
Caplan

Jacob Norr
m.
Dina

Harris
('Swifty Morgan')

Billie
m.
Lou Bell

+ 3

4 children

Henry
m.
Minnie

+ 2

Leland + 2

David
m.
Carol

+ 2

Lubbie

Israel

Eli

Dora

Leah

Maurice
m.
Rebecca
Gertler

Leslie

7 children 6 children 8 children 6 children 2 children

3 children

Ralph

Rosabelle
m.
Arthur Wolff

Jack

Michael

Janet

Veronica

Eleanor

——— Denotes being referred to in *Austerity baby*

When the family began to leave Russia, where the father of the four siblings had been a tailor to the Tzar in St. Petersburg (and hence granted a residence permit to live in the city), the spelling of the name became variously 'Noar' (in England) and 'Norr' (in the United States). Joseph Norr arrived in England in 1886, his wife and children following a year later. His brother Joshua arrived at about the same time, but continued to the U.S., as did their younger brother Jacob in 1891. Their sister Lizzie first went to Manchester, where she married; in 1910, they and their children emigrated to the U.S.

Image credits

Chapter 1

p. 5   Lady Ottoline Morrell, *Mark Gertler*, vintage snapshot print, 1918. © National Portrait Gallery, London.

p. 5   Leland Bell, *Standing Self-Portrait*, 1979. Private collection, courtesy of Steven Harvey Fine Art Projects (and with the permission of Temma Bell).

p. 9   Windscale, 10 October 1957, photograph by Ivor Nicholas.

p. 12   Cover of Richard Hoggart, *The Uses of Literacy*. © Penguin Books, 1958.

p. 13   Map of New York State. US Department of the Interior / US Geological Survey.

Chapter 2

p. 18   Photograph of Kathleen McEnery. Courtesy of the Cunningham and Williams families.

p. 19   Nahum Ellan Luboshez, *George Eastman*, 1921. Digital positive from an original gelatin nitrate roll film negative. Courtesy of the George Eastman Museum.

p. 21   Kathleen McEnery, *Eugene Goossens*, c. 1927. Courtesy of the Sibley Music Library, Eastman School of Music, University of Rochester (and with the permission of the Cunningham and Williams families).

p. 23   Kathleen McEnery, *Woman Seated (Charlotte Whitney Allen)*, n.d.. Courtesy of Rochester Institute of Technology.

p. 28   Kathleen McEnery, *Portrait of Nina Balaban*, n.d.. Courtesy of Anne Subercaseaux, San Francisco.

Chapter 3

p. 60   Kathleen McEnery, *Fritz Trautmann*, 1927. Memorial Art Gallery, Rochester, New York (http://mag.rochester.edu): Anonymous gift, 71.82.

Chapter 4

p. 62   Anna Atkins, *Cyanotype of British fern*, 1853. © National Media Museum / Science & Society Picture Library.

p. 69   Cover of Tim Guest, *My Life in Orange*, 2004. Courtesy of Granta Books, London.

p. 72   Vincent van Gogh, *Van Gogh's Chair*, 1888. ©The National Gallery, London.

p. 73   Gerhard Richter, *Tante Marianne*, 1965. © Gerhard Richter 2017 (19092016).

p. 73   Gerhard Richter, *Abstract Painting (Grey)*, 2002 (CR 880–03). © Gerhard Richter 2017 (19092016) / Tate, London 2015.

p. 79   Friedlieb Ferdinand Runge (1794–1867). Lithophanie der Königlichen Porzellanmanufaktur Berlin, c. 1845. Courtesy of Kreismuseum Oberhavel, Oranienburg.

p. 79   Birthplace of F. Runge. From Max Rehberg, *Friedlieb Ferdinand Runge*, 1993, Kreismuseum Oranienburg. Courtesy of Kreismuseum Oberhavel, Oranienburg.

p. 81   Katsushika Hokusai, *Under the Wave off Kanagawa*, print, c. 1831. (Museum number: 2008, 3008.1.JA). © The Trustees of the British Museum.

Chapter 5

p. 106   Dante Gabriel Rossetti (1828–82), *Found*, begun 1859. Oil on canvas, 35 x 30 5/8 inches. Delaware Art Museum, Samuel and Mary R. Bancroft Memorial, 1935.

p. 109   William Holman Hunt, *The Awakening Conscience*, 1853. Photograph © Tate, London 2015.

Chapter 6

p. 112   Photograph of Eleanor Rathbone. © Hulton Archive/Getty Images. Stamp design © Royal Mail Group Limited 2008.

p. 123   Death certificate of Sigmund Kahn, 1 December 1940, Gurs. Courtesy of Département des Pyrénées-Atlantiques – Archives départementales. Reference 72 W 211.

p. 125   Internment record for Leonie Kahn, 3 December 1941, Gurs. Courtesy of Département des Pyrénées-Atlantiques – Archives départementales. Reference 72 W 62.

p. 131   Page from transport list, convoy no. 33 from Drancy. Courtesy of Mémorial de la Shoah/ Paris (France).

p.140   Sir James Gunn, *Eleanor Florence Rathbone*, 1933. © National Portrait Gallery, London.

Chapter 7

p. 144 Photograph of Henry Simon and his family outside Lawnhurst, 1898. Courtesy of Margaret Simon.

p. 152 Clara von Rappard, *Portrait of Henry Simon*, 1885. Courtesy of Margaret Simon.

p. 153 Photographs of Polhøgda from website of Fridtjof Nansens Institutt (www.fni.no/polhogda-tour.html). Photos of interior by Maryanne Rygg. Photo of exterior by Jan Dalsgaard Sørensen.

p. 158 Kurt Schwitters (1887–1948), *Portrait of Fred Uhlman*, 1940 (oil on canvas). © DACS 2016 / Hatton Gallery, University of Newcastle Upon Tyne, UK / Bridgeman Images.

p. 158 Isle of Man stamp, based on Kurt Schwitters, *Portrait of Klaus Hinrichsen*, 1941. © DACS 2016 / Isle of Man Post Office.

p. 160 Kurt Schwitters (1887–1948), *'Merzbarn' Wall Relief*, 1947–48 (mixed media). © DACS 2016 / Hatton Gallery, University of Newcastle Upon Tyne, UK / Bridgeman Images.

Chapter 8

p. 162 Isle of Man stamp from 2010, based on Ernst Eisenmayer drawing of a violinist. © Ernst Eisenmayer / Isle of Man Post Office.

p. 167 Cover of Charmian Brinson and William Kaczynksi, *Fleeing from the Führer: A Postal History of Refugees from the Nazis*, 2011. Courtesy of the History Press.

p. 168 Map of Saarland. Courtesy of Geoatlas.

p. 182 Photograph showing ORACEFA (Oranienburger Chemische Fabrik), 1930. From *Oranienburg. Bilder einer Stadt*, Kreismuseum Oranienburg, 1996. Courtesy of Kreismuseum Oberhavel, Oranienburg.

p. 186 Sachsenhausen Tower A. Courtesy of Brandenburg Memorials Foundation. Photographer: Friedhelm Hoffmann.

p. 186 Sachsenhausen monument. Courtesy of Brandenburg Memorials Foundation. Photographer: Lars Wendt.

Chapter 9

p. 192 George Romney, *The Spinstress: Lady Emma Hamilton at the Spinning Wheel*, 1782–86, The Iveagh Bequest, Kenwood, English Heritage. © Historic England.

p. 206 Leonora Carrington, *Old Maids*, 1947, oil paint on board, 582 x 738 mm. Sainsbury Centre for Visual Arts, University of East Anglia. © Estate of Leonora Carrington / ARS, NY and DACS, London 2016.

p. 210 Kathleen McEnery, *Portrait of Margaret Holahan*, Memorial Art Gallery, Rochester, New York. Gift of Rochester Area Community Foundation from the Collection of Elizabeth Gibson Holahan. 2011.4.

p. 211 Kathleen McEnery, *Portrait of Elizabeth Holahan*, Memorial Art Gallery, Rochester, New York. Gift of Rochester Area Community Foundation from the Collection of Elizabeth Gibson Holahan. 2011.5.

p. 214 Photograph of Sara Burstall, 1890s. Manchester High School for Girls Archive.

p. 215 Photograph of Agnes Bozman, 1950s. Manchester High School for Girls Archive.

Chapter 10

p. 227 Giovanni Bellini, *Angel of the Annunciation and Virgin Annunciate*, c. 1500, Gallerie dell'Accademia, Venice. Reproduced by permission of the Italian Ministry of Cultural Heritage, Activities and Tourism.

p. 228 Artist unknown (Bruges), *Annunciation*, c. 1520, Tempera and oil on panel, 1955.935. © Sterling and Francine Clark Art Institute, Williamstown, Massachusetts (photo by Michael Agee).

p. 228 Francesco Pesellino (Francesco di Stefano), *Diptych – Annunciation* (detail), c. 1450–55, tempera on panel. ©The Samuel Courtauld Trust, The Courtauld Gallery, London.

p. 229 Petrus Christus, *Die Verkündigung an Maria*, 1452, bpk / Gemäldegalerie, Staatliche Museen zu Berlin / Jörg P. Anders.

p. 229 Rogier van der Weyden, *The Annunciation*, c. 1455, bpk / Bayerische Staatsgemäldesammlungen.

p. 231 Paolo Veronese, *The Annunciation*, 1578, Gallerie dell'Accademia, Venice. Reproduced by permission of the Italian Ministry of Cultural Heritage, Activities and Tourism.

p. 231 Dante Gabriel Rossetti, *Ecce Ancilla Domini! (The Annunciation)*, 1849–50. Photograph © Tate, London 2015.

p. 231 Dante Gabriel Rossetti (1828–82), *Found*, begun 1859. Oil on canvas, 35 x 30 5/8 inches. Delaware Art Museum, Samuel and Mary R. Bancroft Memorial, 1935

p. 237 Gino Severini, *Blue Dancer*, 1912. Collection Mattioli, Italy.

Postscript

p. 241 Images of Claude Levy. Film stills from Peter Blystone's film *The Jewish Cemetery –The Last Jews of the Wasgau*. Courtesy of Peter Blystone.

Bibliography

Chapter 1

Arnold, Lorna, *Windscale 1957: Anatomy of a Nuclear Accident* (Basingstoke: Palgrave Macmillan, 2007 [1992]).

Cappello, Mary, *Night Bloom: A Memoir* (Boston: Beacon Press, 1998).

Cesarani, David, *Justice Delayed: How Britain Became a Refuge for Nazi War Criminals* (London: Heinemann, 1992).

Davies, Hunter, ed., *Sellafield Stories: Life with Britain's First Nuclear Plant* (London: Constable & Robinson Ltd, 2012).

Feldman, David, 'The importance of being English: Jewish immigration and the decay of liberal England', in David Feldman and Gareth S. Jones, eds, *Metropolis-London: Histories and Representations since 1800* (London: Routledge, 1989).

Garland, J.A. and R. Wakeford, 'Atmospheric emissions from the Windscale accident of October 1957', *Atmospheric Environment* Vol. 41, Issue 18, June 2007, 3904–20. Accessed online 9 October 2007.

Hirsch, Marianne, 'Mourning and postmemory', in *Family Frames: Photography Narrative and Postmemory* (Cambridge, Massachusetts: Harvard University Press, 1997).

Hoggart, Richard, *The Uses of Literacy* (London: Chatto & Windus, 1957).

Hoggart, Richard, *A Sort of Clowning: Life and Times: 1940–59* (London: Chatto & Windus, 1990).

Karpf, Anne, *The War After: Living with the Holocaust* (London: Heinemann, 1996).

McKie, Robin, 'Windscale radiation "doubly dangerous"', *Observer*, 7 October 2007. Accessed online 26 November 2009.

Osborne, John, *Damn You England: Collected Prose* (London: Faber and Faber, 1999).

Perutz, M.F., 'Is Britain "befouled"?', *The New York Review of Books*, 23 November 1989. See also exchange between Marilynne Robinson and M.F. Perutz, *The New York Review of Books*, 12 April 1990.

Robinson, Marilynne, *Mother Country: Britain, the Welfare State and Nuclear Pollution* (New York: Farrar, Straus & Giroux, 1980).

Runyon, Damon, 'The lemon drop kid' [1934], in *Guys and Dolls: The Stories of Damon Runyon* (London: Penguin, 1956).

Shields, David, *Reality Hunger: A Manifesto* (London: Hamish Hamilton, 2010).

Wakeford, Richard, 'Editorial: The Windscale reactor accident – 50 years on', *Journal of Radiological Protection*, Vol. 27, 2007, 211–15.

Wolff, Janet, *Resident Alien: Feminist Cultural Criticism* (Cambridge: Polity Press, 1995).

Wolff, Janet, 'The failure of a hard sponge: class, ethnicity and the art of Mark Gertler', *New Formations*, No. 28, May 1996, 46–64. Reprinted in *AngloModern: Painting and Modernity in Britain and the United States* (Ithaca, New York: Cornell University Press, 2003).

Chapter 2

Comini, Alessandra, *In Passionate Pursuit: A Memoir* (New York: George Braziller, 2004).

Fraser, Ronald, *In Search of a Past: The Manor House, Amnersfield, 1933–1945* (London: Verso, 1984).

Horgan, Paul, *The Fault of Angels* (New York and London: Harper & Brothers Publishers, 1933).

Horgan, Paul, 'Rouben Mamoulian in the Rochester Renaissance', in *A Certain Climate: Essays in History, Arts, and Letters* (Middletown, Connecticut: Wesleyan University Press, 1988), 195–220.

Ireland, Corydon, 'Elizabeth Holahan, a lifelong friend to city, dies', *Democrat and Chronicle*, 29 December 2002), 3B–4B.

Kellner, Bruce, 'Nina Balaban', in *Kiss Me Again: An Invitation to a Group of Noble Dames* (New York: Turtle Point Press, 2002), 209–28.

Slonimsky, Nicolas, *Perfect Pitch: An Autobiography* (New York: Schirmer Trade Books, 2002 [1988]).

Steedman, Carolyn, *Landscape for a Good Woman: A Story of Two Lives* (London: Virago, 1986).

Stern, Herbert: 'Some retrospective views (II)', in 'The films of J.S. Watson, Jr., and Melville Webber', *The University of Rochester Library Bulletin*, Vol. XXVIII, No. 2, winter 1975, 77–8.

Tall, Deborah, *From Where We Stand: Recovering a Sense of Place* (New York: Alfred Knopf, 1993).

Tufts, Eleanor, Catalogue entry on Kathleen McEnery Cunningham, in Tufts, ed., *American Women Artists 1830–1930* (Washington, DC: The National Museum of Women in the Arts, 1987).

Wilder, Alec, 'Some retrospective views (III)', in 'The films of J.S. Watson, Jr., and Melville Webber', *The University of Rochester Library Bulletin*, Vol. XXVIII, No. 2, winter 1975, 79–85.

Wolff, Janet, 'Questions of discovery: the art of Kathleen McEnery', in *AngloModern: Painting and Modernity in Britain and the United States* (Ithaca and London: Cornell University Press, 2003).

Chapter 3

Cesarani, David, *Justice Delayed: How Britain became a Refuge for Nazi War Criminals* (London: Heinemann, 1992).

Cesarani, David, and Tony Kushner, eds, *The Internment of Aliens in Twentieth Century Britain* (London: Frank Cass and Co. Ltd, 1993).

Chappell, Connery, *Island of Barbed Wire: The Remarkable Story of World War Two Internment on the Isle of Man* (London: Robert Hale, 1984).

Cresswell, Yvonne M., ed., *Living with the Wire: Civilian Internment in the Isle of Man during the Two World Wars* (Douglas: Manx National Heritage, 1994).

Feather, Jessica, *Art Behind Barbed Wire* (National Museums Liverpool, 2004).

Gillman, Peter and Leni, *'Collar the Lot!' How Britain Interned and Expelled Its Wartime Refugees* (London: Quartet Books Ltd, 1980).

Klauck, Hans Peter, *Jüdisches Leben in der Stadt und im Landkreis Saarlouis 1680–1940* (Landkreis Saarlouis: Vereinigung für die Heimatkunde im Landkreis Saarlouis e. V., 2016).

Kushner, Tony, *The Persistence of Prejudice: Antisemitism in British Society during the Second World War* (Manchester: Manchester University Press, 1989).

Lafitte, François, *The Internment of Aliens* (London: Libris, 1988 [1940]).

Rowlands, Alan, *Trautmann: The Biography* (Derby: Breedon Books Publishing, 1990).

Stent, Ronald, *A Bespattered Page? The Internment of His Majesty's 'Most Loyal Enemy Aliens'* (London: André Deutsch, 1980).

Uhlman, Fred, *The Making of an Englishman* (London: Victor Gollancz Ltd, 1960).

Chapter 4

Ball, Philip, *Bright Earth: The Invention of Colour* (London: Penguin, 2002 [2001]).

Baxandall, Michael, *Painting and Experience in Fifteenth Century Italy* (Oxford: Oxford University Press, 1974 [1972]).

Bomford, David, and Ashok Roy, *Colour* (London: National Gallery Company London, 2000).

Brightman, R., 'Manchester and the origin of the dyestuffs industry', *Chemistry & Industry*, Vol. 4, 1957, 86–91.

Day, Elizabeth, 'Till death do us part: the short and extraordinary life of author Tim Guest', *Observer* New Review, 28 March 2010.

Delamare, Françoise and Bernard Guineau, *Colors: The Story of Dyes and Pigments* (New York: Harry N. Abrams, 2000).

Fox, M.R., *Dye-makers of Great Britain 1856–1976: A History of Chemists, Companies, Products and Changes* (Manchester: ICI, 1987).

Gage, John, *Colour in Art* (London: Thames and Hudson, 2006).

Gage, John, *Colour and Culture* (London: Thames and Hudson, 1993).

Garfield, Simon, *Mauve* (London: Faber and Faber, 2000).

Geraghty, Ann, *In the Dark and Still Moving* (Whitehaven, Cumbria: The Tenth Bull, 2007).

Guest, Tim, *My Life in Orange* (London: Granta Books, 2004).

Guest, Tim, *Second Lives: A Journey through Virtual Worlds* (London: Arrow Books, 2008 [2007]).

Kargon, Robert H., *Science in Victorian Manchester* (Manchester: Manchester University Press, 1977).

Kristeva, Julia, 'Giotto's joy', in *Desire in Language* (Oxford: Blackwell, 1981).

Leslie, Esther, *Synthetic Worlds: Nature, Art and the Chemical Industry* (London: Reaktion Books, 2005).

Levi, Primo, 'The gray zone' and 'Shame', in *The Drowned and the Saved* (New York: Vintage, 1989).

Neale, Steve, 'Technicolor', in Angela Dalle Vacche and Brian Price, eds, *Color: The Film Reader* (London: Routledge, 2006).

Pastoureau, Michel, *Blue: The History of a Color* (Princeton, New Jersey: Princeton University Press, 2001).

Tóibín, Colm, 'In lovely blueness: adventures in troubled light', catalogue to *Blue* exhibition at Chester Beatty Library, Dublin, 2004.

Wolff, Janet, *The Aesthetics of Uncertainty* (New York: Columbia University Press, 2008).

Chapter 5

Cappello, Mary, *Night Bloom: A Memoir* (Boston: Beacon Press, 1998).

Dobkin, Monty, *Broughton and Cheetham Hill in Regency and Victorian Times* (Manchester: Neil Richardson, 1984).

Hardy, Clive, *Manchester at War* (Altrincham, Cheshire: First Edition Limited, 2005 [1986]).

Jacobson, Howard, *Coming from Behind* (London: Chatto & Windus / The Hogarth Press, 1983).

Karpf, Anne, *The War After: Living with the Holocaust* (London: Heinemann, 1996).

Miller, Alice, *The Drama of the Gifted Child* (New York: Basic Books, Inc., 1981).

Mosco, Maisie, *Almonds and Raisins* (London: New English Library, 1979).

Mosco, Maisie, *Scattered Seed* (London: New English Library, 1980).

Nicholson, Virginia, *Millions Like Us: Women's Lives in War and Peace 1939–1949* (London: Viking, 2011).

Nochlin, Linda, 'Lost and Found: once more the fallen woman', in Norma Broude and Mary D. Garrard, eds, *Feminism and Art History: Questioning the Litany* (New York: Harper & Row, 1982).

Phythian, Graham, *Blitz Britain: Manchester and Salford* (Stroud, Gloucestershire: The History Press, 2015).

Scott, Sir Walter, 'Rosabelle', in Palgrave's *Golden Treasury*, Sixth Edition (Oxford: Oxford University Press, 1994).

Scott, William Bell, 'Rosabell. Recitative with songs', in W. Minto, ed., *Autobiographical Notes of the Life of William Bell Scott* (New York: Harper & Brothers, 1892).

Smith, Peter J.C., *Luftwaffe over Manchester. The Blitz Years 1940–1944* (Manchester: Neil Richardson, 2003).

Spring, Howard, *Shabby Tiger* (London: Fontana Books, 1954 [1934]).

Spring, Howard, *Rachel Rosing* (London: Fontana Books, 1955 [1935]).

Surtees, Virginia, *The Paintings and Drawings of Dante Gabriel Rossetti (1828–1882)* (Oxford: The Clarendon Press, 1971).

Williams, Bill, *The Making of Manchester Jewry 1740–1875* (Manchester: Manchester University Press, 1976).

www.victorianweb.org/painting/dgr/paintings/11.html (accessed 6 October 2012).

www.victorianweb.org/authors/dgr/3.html (accessed 24 January 2006).

www.manchester2002-uk.com/districts/cheetham.html (accessed 16 October 2012).

Chapter 6

Alberti, Johanna, *Eleanor Rathbone* (London: Sage, 1996).

Benjamin, Walter, 'Marseilles' (1929) and 'Hashish in Marseilles' (1932), in Michael W. Jennings, ed., *Walter Benjamin: Selected Writings*, Vol. 2: 1927–34 (Cambridge, Massachusetts: Harvard University Press, 1999).

Cohen, Susan, *Rescue the Perishing: Eleanor Rathbone and the Refugees* (London: Vallentine Mitchell, 2010).

Fittko, Lisa, *Escape through the Pyrenees* (Evanston, Illinois: Northwestern University Press, 2000).

Gilloch, Graeme, 'Fragments, cityscapes, modernity. Kracauer on the Cannebière', *Journal of Classical Sociology*, Vol. 13, No. 1, February 2013, 20–9.

Koestler, Arthur, *Scum of the Earth* (London: Hutchinson, 1968 [1941]).

Laharie, Claude, *Le Camp de Gurs 1939–1943: un aspect méconnu de l'histoire de Vichy* (Biarritz: J & D Editions, 1993).

Laharie, Claude, *Gurs: 1939–1945: un camp d'internement en Béarn* (Biarritz: Atlantica, 2005).

Laharie, Claude, *Gurs: L'art derrière les barbelés: 1939–1944* (Biarritz: Atlantica, 2007).

Mitchell, Juliet, *Siblings: Sex and Violence* (Cambridge: Polity Press, 2003).

Pedersen, Susan, *Eleanor Rathbone and the Politics of Conscience* (New Haven and London: Yale University Press, 2004).

Ryan, Donna F., *The Holocaust and the Jews of Marseille: The Enforcement of Anti-Semitic Policies in Vichy France* (Urbana and Chicago: University of Illinois Press, 1996).

Schwertfeger, Ruth, *In Transit: Narratives of German Jews in Exile, Flight, and Internment during 'The Dark Years' of France* (Berlin: Frank & Timme GmBH, 2012).

Seghers, Anna, *Transit* (New York: New York Review Books, 2013 [1951]).

Wardi, Dina, *Memorial Candles: Children of the Holocaust* (London: Routledge, 1992).

Zuccotti, Susan, *The Holocaust, the French, and the Jews* (New York: BasicBooks, 1993).

Chapter 7

Chambers, Emma, and Karin Orchard, eds, *Schwitters in Britain* (London: Tate Publishing, 2013).

Crossley, Barbara, *The Triumph of Kurt Schwitters* (Ambleside: Armitt Trust, 2005).

France, E., and T.F. Woodall, *A New History of Didsbury* (Didsbury, Manchester: E.J. Morten, 1976).

Huntford, Roland, *Nansen: The Explorer as Hero* (London: Abacus, 2001 [1997]).

Nansen, Odd, *From Day to Day: The Concentration Camp Diary of Odd Nansen* (New York: G. P. Putnam's Sons, 1949).

Shapley, Olive, *Broadcasting a Life: The Autobiography of Olive Shapley* (London: Scarlet Press, 1996).

Simon, Anthony, *The Simon Engineering Group* (Stockport: Simon Engineering Group, 1953).

Simon, Brian, *Henry Simon of Manchester 1835–1899: In Search of a Grandfather* (Leicester: The Pendene Press, 1997).

Simon, Brian, *Henry Simon's Children* (Leicester: The Pendene Press, 1999).

Stocks, Mary, *Ernest Simon of Manchester* (Manchester: Manchester University Press, 1963).

Uhlman, Fred, *The Making of an Englishman* (London: Victor Gollancz Ltd, 1960).

Webster, Gwendolyn, *Kurt Merz Schwitters: A Biographical Study* (Cardiff: University of Wales Press, 1997).

http://en.wikipedia.org/wiki/Fridtjof_Nansen (accessed 1 February 2014).

Chapter 8

Brinson, Charmian, and William Kaczynski, *Fleeing from the Führer: A Postal History of Refugees from the Nazis* (Stroud, Gloucestershire: The History Press, 2011).

Crome, Len, 'Sachsenhausen' and 'Jonny Hüttner in Sachsenhausen' in *Unbroken: Resistance and Survival in the Concentration Camps* (New York: Schocken Books, 1988).

Eisenmayer, Ernst, *A Strange Haircut* (Eisenmayer, 2008).

Hager, Thomas, *The Alchemy of Air: A Jewish Genius, a Doomed Tycoon, and the Scientific Discovery that Fed the World but Fuelled the Rise of Hitler* (New York: Broadway Books, 2008).

Keilson, Hans, *The Death of the Adversary* (New York: Farrar, Straus and Giroux, 2010 [1959]).

Leslie, Esther, *Synthetic Worlds: Nature, Art and the Chemical Industry* (London: Reaktion Books, 2005).

Levi, Primo, *The Periodic Table* (London: Penguin Books, 2000 [1975]).

Levi, Primo, *Survival in Auschwitz* (New York: Simon & Schuster, 1996 [1958]). Also published under the title *If This Is a Man* in 1993.

Levi, Primo, *The Mirror Maker* (London: Abacus, 1997 [1986]).

Lloyd, Fran, 'Ernst Eisenmayer: a modern Babel', in Sarah MacDougall and Rachel Dickson, eds, *Forced Journeys: Artists in Exile in Britain, c. 1933–45* (London: The London Jewish Museum of Art, 2009).

Nansen, Odd, *From Day to Day: The Concentration Camp Diary of Odd Nansen* (New York: G.P. Putnam's Sons, 1949).

Pindera, Jerzy, *Liebe Mutti: One Man's Struggle to Survive in KZ Sachsenhausen, 1939–1945* (Lanham, Maryland: University Press of America, 2004).

Rürup, Miriam, *Ehrensache: Jüdische Studentenverbindungen an Deutschen Universitäten 1886–1937* (Göttingen: Wallstein Verlag, 2008).

Wiborny, Willi, *Oranienburg: Bilder einer Stadt* (Oranienburg: Kreismuseum Oranienburg, 1996).

Wiedmer, Caroline, 'Sachsenhausen', in *The Claims of Memory: Representations of the Holocaust in Contemporary Germany and France* (Ithaca and London: Cornell University Press, 1999).

Wolff, Janet, 'Calico connections: science, manufacture and culture in mid-nineteenth-century Manchester', in Janet Wolff and Mike Savage, eds, *Culture in Manchester. Institutions and Urban Change since 1850* (Manchester: Manchester University Press, 2013).

Young, James E., *The Texture of Memory: Holocaust Memorials and Meaning* (New Haven and London: Yale University Press, 1993).

Young, James E., ed., *The Art of Memory: Holocaust Memorials in History* (New York: The Jewish Museum / Prestel-Verlag, 1994).

http://en.wikipedia.org/wiki/Sachsenhausen_concentration_camp (accessed 12 June 2014).

http://www.encyclopedia.com/topic/Saarland.aspx (accessed 31 May 2014).

Chapter 9

Burstall, Sara Annie, *The Story of Manchester High School for Girls, 1871–1911* (Memphis: General Books LLC, 2012).

Burstall, Sara A., *Retrospect and Prospect: Sixty Years of Women's Education* (London: Longmans, Green and Co., 1933).

Chambers-Schiller, Lee Virginia, *Liberty, A Better Husband. Single Women in America: The Generations of 1780–1840* (New Haven and London: Yale University Press, 1984).

Doan, Laura L., ed., *Old Maids to Radical Spinsters: Unmarried Women in the Twentieth-Century Novel* (Urbana and Chicago: University of Illinois Press 1991).

Gaskell, Elizabeth, *Cranford* (London: Penguin Books, 2005 [1853]).

Gissing, George, *The Odd Women* (London: Virago 1980 [1893]).

Harman, Claire, ed., *The Diaries of Sylvia Townsend Warner* (London: Chatto & Windus, 1994).

Holden, Katherine, *The Shadow of Marriage: Singleness in England 1914–60* (Manchester: Manchester University Press, 2007).

Jeffreys, Sheila, *The Spinster and Her Enemies: Feminism and Sexuality 1880–1930* (London: Pandora Press 1985).

Judd, Peter Haring, *The Akeing Heart: Passionate Attachments and Their Aftermath* (New York; Peter Haring Judd, 2013).

Little, Judy, '"Endless different ways": Muriel Spark's re-visions of the spinster', in Doan, ed. *Old Maids to Radical Spinsters*.

Nicholson, Virginia, *Singled Out: How Two Million Women Survived Without Men after the First World War* (London: Penguin Books, 2008).

Oram, Alison, 'Repressed and thwarted, or bearer of the new world? The spinster in inter-war feminist discourses', *Women's History Review*, Vol. 1, No. 3, 1992, 413–33.

Warner, Sylvia Townsend, *Lolly Willowes* (London: Virago, 2012 [1926]).

Chapter 10

Battersby, Christine, *Gender and Genius: Towards a Feminist Aesthetics* (London: The Women's Press, 1989).

Baxandall, Michael, *Painting and Experience in Fifteenth Century Italy* (Oxford: Oxford University Press, 1972).

Butler, Sandra, and Barbara Rosenblum, *Cancer in Two Voices* (San Francisco: Spinsters Book Company, 1991)

Friedman, Susan Stanford, 'Creativity and the childbirth metaphor: gender difference in literary discourse', *Feminist Studies*, Vol. 13, No. 1, spring 1987, 49–82.

Gunthorp, Dale, 'Catherine Rae Arthur: another way of seeing', and Debbie Dickinson, 'Many voices', in Patricia Duncker and Vicky Wilson, eds, *Cancer: Through the Eyes of Ten Women* (London: Pandora, 1996).

Hoffman, Eva, *Lost in Translation: A Life in a New Language* (London: Penguin, 1990)

Kaplan, Alice, *French Lessons: A Memoir* (Chicago and London: The University of Chicago Press, 1993).

LaVerdiere, Eugene, *The Annunciation to Mary: A Story of Faith. Luke 1:26–38* (Chicago: Liturgy Training Publications, 2004).

Nochlin, Linda, 'Lost and *Found*: once more the fallen woman', in Norma Broude and Mary D. Garrard, eds, *Feminism and Art History: Questioning the Litany* (New York: Harper & Row, 1982).

Parker, Roszika, and Griselda Pollock, *Old Mistresses: Women, Art and Ideology* (London: Routledge & Kegan Paul, 1981).

Potok, Chaim, *My Name Is Asher Lev* (New York: Anchor Books, 2003 [1972]).

Smith, Raffaele Fazio, 'Iconography of the Annunciation', 'Symbolism in the Annunciation' and 'Interpreting the Annunciation', *The Global Dispatches*, 10 February, 4 August, 1 December, 2010 (www.theglobaldispatches.com/articles/iconography-of-the-annunciation: accessed 1 December 2014).

Sontag, Susan, *Illness as Metaphor and AIDS and Its Metaphors* (New York: Picador, 1990).

Stacey, Jackie, *Teratologies: A Cultural Study of Cancer* (London and New York: Routledge, 1997).

Wolff, Janet, 'Max Ferber and the persistence of pre-memory in Mancunian exile', in Jean-Marc Dreyfus and Janet Wolff, eds, *Traces, Memory and the Holocaust in the Writings of W.G. Sebald* (Piscataway, New Jersey: Gorgias Press, 2012). Also online at: www.melilahjournal.org/p/2012-supplement-2.html.

Wolff, Janet, 'Manchester, capital of the nineteenth century', *Journal of Classical Sociology*, Vol. 13, Issue 1, February 2013, 69–86.

Janet Wolff is the author of several books on aesthetics and the sociology of art. She has taught at the University of Leeds, the University of Rochester and Columbia University, and is currently Professor Emerita at the University of Manchester.

AFTER ~~✈~~ RETURN TO

William Chien

~~eral~~ P. O. Box 137

York City U. S. A.

TRANS ATLANTIC AIR MAIL

Madame Lebrie

Clof I Baraque

~~St Préfecture~~

~~Campfuden Stane~~

Basses- Pyrénées

l'avenue Olivia...

timbre, PV dessi.

Hôtel du devant
Marseille
VIA
PLEAS
AIR MAIL

Kahn

2 Unoccupied

REGISTERED Paris

Nº 383060

REGISTER